BREXIT TIME

Leaving the EU – Why, How and When?

result of the UK referendum in June 2016 on membership of the
ɔpean Union had immediate repercussions across the UK, the
and internationally. As the dust begins to settle, attention is now
ɪrally drawn to understanding why this momentous decision
ɪe about and how and when the UK will leave the EU. What are
options for the new legal settlements between the UK and the
? What will happen to our current political landscape within
ɘ UK in the time up to and including its exit from the EU? What
out legal and political life after Brexit? Within a series of short
ɪays, *Brexit Time* explores and contextualises each stage of Brexit
turn: pre-referendum; the result; the process of withdrawal;
hinking EU relations; and post-Brexit. During a time of intense
ɘculation and commentary, this book offers an indispensable
ide to the key issues surrounding a historic event and its uncertain
ɘrmath.

NNETH A. ARMSTRONG is Professor of European Law and
Director of the Centre for European Legal Studies at the University
of Cambridge. He is a Fellow of Sidney Sussex College and Editor-
in-Chief of the *Cambridge Yearbook of European Legal Studies*.
Before joining the Faculty of Law, Kenneth was Professor of EU Law
at Queen Mary University of London. His accompanying blog on
Brexit can be found at brexittime.com.

BREXIT TIME

Leaving the EU – Why, How and When?

KENNETH A. ARMSTRONG

University of Cambridge

CAMBRIDGE
UNIVERSITY PRESS

CAMBRIDGE
UNIVERSITY PRESS

University Printing House, Cambridge CB2 8BS, United Kingdom

One Liberty Plaza, 20th Floor, New York, NY 10006, USA

477 Williamstown Road, Port Melbourne, VIC 3207, Australia

4843/24, 2nd Floor, Ansari Road, Daryaganj, Delhi – 110002, India

79 Anson Road, #06–04/06, Singapore 079906

Cambridge University Press is part of the University of Cambridge.

It furthers the University's mission by disseminating knowledge in the pursuit of education, learning, and research at the highest international levels of excellence.

www.cambridge.org
Information on this title: www.cambridge.org/9781108415378
DOI: 10.1017/9781108233385

© Kenneth A. Armstrong 2017

First published 2017

Printed in the United Kingdom by TJ International Ltd, Padstow, Cornwall

A catalogue record for this publication is available from the British Library.

ISBN 978-1-108-41537-8 Hardback
ISBN 978-1-108-40127-2 Paperback

For Ian

CONTENTS

vii

CONTENTS

ACKNOWLEDGEMENTS

It is the irony of a book called Brexit Time that its writing, production and publication have all been achieved in a startlingly small amount of time. I am enormously grateful to Cambridge University Press and to Finola O'Sullivan for taking on this project. I am also thankful to Chris Burrows, Morten Jensen, Jeremy Langworthy, Andrew Sykes and Lorenza Toffolon for all their support throughout the process.

There is a risk of being thought of, or holding oneself out as, a Brexit 'expert'. The subject matter of this book, and indeed any analysis of Brexit is, in reality, extremely exposing of the gaps in our knowledge. As someone who thought he knew a reasonable amount about the EU and how it works, the period since the referendum has been humbling and I am all too happy to acknowledge that in the process of writing this book I have learned a great deal. That said, it is only right to acknowledge and thank all my friends and colleagues who read drafts, answered queries and generally helped me to make sense of what I thought I was doing. In particular I want to thank: Simon Bulmer, Iain Begg, Lorand Bartels, Gráinne de Búrca, Marise Cremona, Mark Elliott, Tamara Hervey, Christophe Hillion, Mario Mendez, Jo Murkens, Andrew Scott, Joanne Scott and Jo Shaw. As ever, any errors are mine alone.

The book was begun during a period of sabbatical leave from the Faculty of Law and I am grateful to colleagues for giving me the time to get the project up and running. I am particularly indebted to Albertina Albors-Llorens who not only took on the role of acting Director of the Centre for European Legal Studies but also supervised some of my students while I was on leave. Thanks are due to Alicia Hinarejos and Felicity Eves-Rey for all their assistance in running the Centre while I was on leave. I am also extremely thankful to Sidney Sussex College, Cambridge not just for allowing me to be on leave, but also for providing me with a congenial working environment from which to embark on this book. The stimulating and difficult questions posed by my Sidney colleagues played no small part in helping me understand what people might want to know about Brexit.

As ever, family and friends have been hugely supportive. Above and beyond all, my husband Ian has lived with this book since I first, tentatively, suggested I might write it. I cannot begin to thank him for all the support during the writing process and for his unfailing belief that I would get it done. This book is dedicated to him, with all my love.

Kenneth A. Armstrong
Cambridge
March 2017

Introducing Brexit Time

In a referendum held on 23 June 2016, voters in the United Kingdom (UK) agreed with the proposition that the UK should leave the European Union (EU). The UK government has acted on that referendum result by beginning the process by which the UK will withdraw from the EU. So begins a process known as 'Brexit'.

The argument advanced in this book is that Brexit was not the UK's 'manifest destiny'. It was a choice. Like all choices it was a product of a variety of forces and the structures that mediate those forces. One of those structures is time.[1]

The word 'Brexit' has its own place in time. It derived from the use of the term 'Grexit' to describe the potential withdrawal of Greece from the eurozone during its sovereign debt crisis. Its transformation into 'Brexit' is attributed to the founder and director of the think-tank *British Influence*, Peter Wilding. By December 2016, the word had entered the *Oxford English Dictionary*. Over time, the language of Brexit has been adapted and supplemented as a means of characterising responses to the referendum result. When used as a way of describing pro-withdrawal supporters – especially in the form

---

[1] SJ Bulmer, 'Politics in time meets the politics of time: historical institutionalism and the EU timescape' (2009) 16(2) *Journal of European Public Policy* 307.

of 'Brexiteer' – it conjures up imagery of individuals battling to restore control to British institutions, to be contrasted with the 'Remoaners' unwilling and apparently unable to accept the outcome of the referendum.[2]

The aim of *Brexit Time* is to explore why, how and when is the UK leaving the EU. These questions are organised by reference to: a 'Time before Brexit', a 'Time of Brexit', a 'Time for Brexit' and a 'Time to Brexit'.

As to 'why' the UK is leaving the EU, as one of the leading protagonists of the 2016 referendum campaign captures, it is tempting when confronted by decisions that produce big outcomes to try and locate a big cause rather than drilling down into the 'branching histories' which create the possibilities and potentials for certain choices to be made.[3]

In the 'Time before Brexit' the choice of the UK to become a Member State of the then European Economic Community and the reasons behind that choice are explored. The background to the 2016 referendum is revealed focusing on the ambition of the then Prime Minister, David Cameron, to seek reform and renegotiation prior to the referendum. In a 'Time of Brexit' the explanations turn to how a balance

---

[2] I Katz, 'Victory of the swashbucklers. Did the word "Brexiteer" help the Leave campaign win?', *The Spectator* [print version] (24 September 2016). The three key ministers – and Leave campaigners – whose portfolios are inextricably linked to Brexit were, unsurprisingly, termed 'The Three Brexiteers': S Heffer, 'Meet the Three Brexiteers: the men who could change how we exit the EU', *New Statesman* (13 September 2016).

[3] D Cummings, 'On the referendum #21 Branching histories of the 2016 referendum and the "frogs before the storm"', www.dominiccummings .wordpresss.com (9 January 2017).

between the forces of nationalism and internationalism changed and a new nationalism and new internationalism surfaced. More specifically, the success of the campaign for the UK to leave the EU was its capacity to persuade voters to 'take back control' from the EU. Through an exploration of the key campaign themes of 'control over borders', 'control over money', 'democratic control', 'control over laws' and 'control over trade', the chapters in a 'Time of Brexit' reflect on how the sorts of concerns which had been around throughout the UK's membership of the EU came together during the referendum campaign.

The 'how' of exiting the EU reveals the economic, political, legal and institutional complexity of untangling the UK from over forty years of EU membership. In a 'Time for Brexit' the chapters look to how the result of the referendum has been translated by a new Prime Minister, Theresa May, and her government into a manifesto for change that is not just about defining a new relationship between the UK and the EU but is also about redefining Britain both at home and globally. At the same time, this process of extracting the UK from the EU poses fundamental questions about the capacity of the UK as a multinational state to not just work together but hold together, not least given the strong preference amongst voters in Scotland for the UK to remain in the UK and the desire of the Scottish National Party to keep the dream of an independent Scotland in the EU alive.

The 'how' and 'when' of leaving the EU are brought together in the chapters that form a 'Time to Brexit'. In 2009, the Treaty of Lisbon introduced a new Article 50 into the

Treaty on European Union (TEU). For the first time, the EU had a specific mechanism to allow a Member State to withdraw from the EU. Yet the process of triggering that mechanism was a matter of controversy and of litigation, with UK courts becoming a focal point for contestation of who had the authority to pull the Article 50 trigger. Much of the problem lay with legislation enacted in 2015 that had made provision for a referendum but not for its consequences in 2016. As Thaler argues, the 'choice architecture' created in 2009 at EU level, and in 2015 at UK level, shaped and moulded post-referendum legal and political choices.[4]

The conclusion of the Supreme Court that legislation was needed before Article 50 could be triggered brought Parliament back in as a participant in the Brexit process. However, the principal institutional changes were those within the UK government as Whitehall geared up for Brexit. Meanwhile, an expectant European Union awaited the UK's notification of its intention to withdraw while also pondering what the future of the EU might be.

In different times and in different locations, choices are made that shape Brexit. These choices have causes and they have consequences. These are choices in time, and of time. This book tracks those choices up to the point of the UK's notification of its intention to withdraw from the EU.

It is not a book about whether withdrawal from the EU is a good or a bad thing. It is objective in its presentation of

---

[4] R Thaler, 'Britain pays the price for a badly designed Brexit choice', *Financial Times* (17 August 2016).

data and arguments, but necessarily subjective in its interpretation of their significance.

Brexit Time is ongoing. Further reflections on the UK's withdrawal from the EU will be offered on a companion blog brexittime.com.

This is Brexit Time.

Part I

Time before Brexit

1

Before and After Membership

The UK arrived late to membership of the European Economic Community (EEC). Created by the Treaty of Rome in 1957 by six founding 'Member States', the EEC set itself the goal of establishing a 'Common Market'.[1] The foundations of that Common Market would be built on the free movement of goods, as well as the free movement of people, of services and of capital. Its construction would be facilitated by a set of political institutions with tasks to apply and to develop the basic legal principles set out in the EEC Treaty. A Court of Justice would ensure that the Community's Member States held true to the commitments they had entered into under the treaties. This was the EEC that the UK joined in 1973. More than forty years of participation later, in 2017 the UK served notice of its intention to cancel its membership of what had become the EU.

The decision to end the UK's membership was a choice. It was a choice given to the electorate through a referendum held on 23 June 2016. The decision to hold the referendum was also a choice: a product of both long-term and more immediate domestic party politics over the UK's relationship with the EU.[2] It followed a renegotiation of aspects of the UK's membership by

---

[1] The original Member States were France, Germany, Italy, Belgium, Netherlands and Luxembourg.

[2] T Bale, '"Banging on about Europe": how the Eurosceptics got their referendum', http://blogs.lse.ac.uk (23 June 2016).

the then Prime Minister David Cameron, and a short, polarising referendum campaign. These and other choices – together with the critical junctures that shaped how those choices came about and were exercised – will be explored in subsequent chapters. Of more immediate interest is what can be learned by turning the clock back to explore why the UK chose to join the EEC in 1973 and why it had not chosen to do so earlier. Those choices can be seen to entail a calculation as to how best to reconcile the desire for, and demands of, of 'nationalism' and 'internationalism'. It is the relationship between a new nationalism and a new internationalism which also underlies Britain's withdrawal from the EU (Brexit).

Stephen George identifies nationalism with ideas of parliamentary sovereignty and national pride: the idea of Britain as a model of parliamentary democracy with a particular, historic place in the world. Internationalism, meanwhile, stands for economic liberalism and an outward-looking globalism: the UK as a promoter of free trade and an actor on the international stage.[3] At specific points in time and at different points in time, these aspects have combined and been interpreted in varying ways.

For the Conservative Winston Churchill, the post-war project of European integration – even a federal project – made a certain sense. But it did not necessarily need UK participation. Instead, the UK's alternative approach was, in 1956, to propose the establishment of a European Free Trade Association (EFTA). A Free Trade Area that allowed tariff-free movement

---

[3] S George, 'British Policy in the European Community: the Commitment to Globalism' (1991) unpublished paper.

of goods between participating states, but which also allowed participating states to retain control over their trade policies with non-participating states, provided a degree of international economic liberalism without the sorts of limitations on national sovereignty which membership of the EEC might have entailed. The UK was not alone in favouring this approach to European co-operation. Six other states joined with the UK in establishing EFTA in 1960. European states could, therefore, choose between two models of membership: membership of EFTA promoting tariff-free trade in industrial goods with a loose 'intergovernmental' form of co-operation versus membership of an EEC with a more extensive economic integration in a Common Market under the supervision of political and judicial institutions exercising 'supranational' oversight.

With the ability to still conduct its own external trade policy, the UK chose EFTA membership. After all, the 1947 General Agreement on Tariffs and Trade (GATT) had been signed by the UK together with twenty-two countries including the United States, Canada, Australia and South Africa. The US Trade Expansion Act of 1962 had opened the way for the Kennedy administration to open a new round of GATT talks that were eventually concluded in 1967. There was even the possibility of a multilateral North Atlantic Free Trade Association that could see the UK, EFTA, the United States, Canada and other industrialised countries advancing free trade above the levels of the GATT.[4] By comparison with

---

[4] HG Johnson, 'Some aspects of the Multilateral Free Trade Association proposal' (1969) 37(3) *The Manchester School of Economic and Social Studies* 189.

the bigger rewards that might be reaped from more international trade liberalisation, EEC membership could be viewed as a less-valued prize given its small regional focus.

Nonetheless, the EEC was a political and economic reality. The EEC was establishing its customs union and endeavouring to create a Common Market in goods, services, workers and capital by the end of 1969. Meanwhile, during the 1960s, the UK economy lagged substantially behind its European neighbours and, in economic terms, nationalistic pride was in short supply. The currency was even devalued in 1967. By the end of the 1960s and with a new Republican administration in office in the United States, the plan of pursuing a North Atlantic Free Trade Area was shelved, leaving the British government to rethink its relative trading ambitions with the United States and the EEC.[5] Indeed, for Cold War geopolitical reasons, it was the preference of the United States that the UK joined the EEC.[6]

It was in light of these changing national, European and international political and economic considerations that Harold Macmillan's Conservative government, and later the Labour government of Harold Wilson, calculated that EEC membership was in the UK's best interests.[7] The formal application to join the EEC made by Macmillan in 1961 encountered French opposition and was rejected by President de

[5] NH Rossbach, *Heath, Nixon and the Rebirth of the Special Relationship: Britain, the US and the EC 1969–1974* (Palgrave Macmillan, 2009).
[6] G Rosen, 'A British free trade deal outside the EU? History shows that's easier said than done', *The Telegraph* (3 March 2016).
[7] P Ludlow, 'When Britain first applied to join the EU? What can Macmillan's predicament teach us?', http://blogs.lse.ac.uk (15 April 2016).

Gaulle. The second application made by Wilson in 1967 was also rebuffed.[8] France was concerned that enlargement of the EEC – not just the UK, but also Ireland, Denmark and Norway were expected to make applications – would not only complicate decision-making within the EEC, but also risked diverting its focus from achieving greater 'internal' political integration and solidarity towards a more expansive internationalist 'external' free trade agenda.

However, if anything, the second rejection of membership helped facilitate the UK's eventual membership. Apart from France, the other five EEC Member States were in favour of UK membership. Indeed, France had further isolated itself within the EEC in the form of the 1966 'empty chair' crisis during which French representation within the EEC Council of Ministers was withdrawn over a dispute over the funding of the Common Agricultural Policy (CAP) and the move away from unanimous voting in certain areas. Viewed from outside the EEC, British Foreign Office officials feared that the EEC itself might stumble and with it, the political and economic framework that held France and Germany together.[9] Membership of the EEC could turn out

---

[8] Ludlow highlights that Macmillan's 1961 application was conditional – the UK would only proceed with its application once it was satisfied with the terms on offer – whereas Wilson's 1967 application was without conditions: NP Ludlow, 'A short-term defeat: the Community institutions and the second British application to join the EEC' in OJ Daddow (ed), *Harold Wilson and European Integration* (Frank Cass, 2003; Routledge, 2016). That said, Wilson would later contest the conditions of membership actually agreed by Edward Heath.

[9] See Rossbach, *Heath, Nixon and the Rebirth of the Special Relationship*, p 14.

to be an opportunity for the UK to exercise international leadership within and through the EEC and act as an additional political counterweight to Germany.

In September 1967, the European Commission recommended the immediate opening of membership negotiations with the UK, Ireland, Denmark and Norway. But General de Gaulle remained opposed. At a press conference on 29 November 1967 – days after the second French veto – Harold Wilson gave a point-by-point refutation of French objections to the UK joining the Common Market, thereby confirming the UK's desire to be part of the EEC and to be a leading participant in a single European market. However, it would be Wilson's successor, Edward Heath that would begin negotiations in June 1970 that would lead to the signature on 22 January 1972 of the Treaty of Accession by which the UK, Ireland and Denmark formally agreed to join the EEC.[10] The European Communities Act 1972 which gave consequential domestic legal effect to the UK's membership of the EEC was given Royal Assent on 17 October 1972. On 1 January 1973, the UK became a Member State of the EEC.

So the calculation made in the 1960s and early 1970s involved a willingness by UK governments to accept certain restrictions on national sovereignty provided EEC membership helped the UK to pursue goals of trade liberalisation and external influence, albeit in a more restricted regional

[10] Norway completed negotiations for EEC membership in 1972 and despite parliamentary support for membership, a referendum resulted in a popular rejection of it. Instead Norway retained its status as an EFTA state and has access to the European Single Market through the European Economic Area agreement between the EU and EFTA.

form: constrained nationalism and modest internationalism. A different way of looking at this is expressed in Alan Milward's idea of the 'European rescue of the nation-state'.[11] Instead of viewing the nation state and European integration as necessarily entailing a relationship in which the latter replaced the former (a 'zero-sum' game), it was possible to argue that the latter sustained and facilitated the former (a 'positive-sum' game). In other words, through the processes and structures of co-operation at European level, nation states in Europe were actually able to preserve their relevance and protect themselves from forces that might otherwise have undermined the capacity of national governments to govern. In these terms it is not necessarily the case that nationalism and internationalism are both compromised to achieve some sort of second-best outcome, rather that international co-operation helps preserve the nation state and in turn, the continuing relevance and significance of nation states makes international co-operation possible.

Be that as it may, the assertion is sometimes made – somewhat nostalgically – that the UK joined a Common Market and not a European Union. Certainly, from its creation in the European Communities of the 1950s, the EEC continued to evolve and to enlarge. As EFTA shrank to an association of four states, the EEC grew into a European Union of twenty-eight Member States by the time of the 2016 referendum. There are two things that are particularly striking about this interpretation of the nature of the UK's membership. First, it suggests a kind of foundationalism and

[11] A Milward, *The European Rescue of the Nation-State* (Routledge, 1992).

15

originalism to the form and type of UK membership: 'market membership'. Thus, it is said that while the UK was willing to join up to the economic side of the European integration project, its commitment to the EU beyond free trade was more ambivalent. This links to claims that the UK was never committed to the concept of 'ever closer union' inasmuch as it suggested a direction of travel from economic co-operation to political integration. Of course, the reference to 'ever closer union' was already in the Preamble not just to the EEC Treaty but also the 1972 Treaty of Accession which formalised the UK's EEC membership. Nonetheless, it suggests perhaps a more complex understanding of the relationship between nationalism and internationalism as one that varies and differentiates across not just time but also policy areas.

The second thing that is worth noting – and which is linked to the idea that the UK was only committed to market membership and not closer integration – is that the UK's consent was required for every new treaty that entrusted the EU with new policy competences and for every treaty of accession that enlarged the number of EU Member States. If the character of the EU, and the quality of its membership did change, it did so with the UK's consent. Insofar as those changes had to be reflected in domestic law, the consent was not just of consecutive Labour and Conservative governments, but also the UK Parliament. To the extent that the UK's calculation of its interests departed from other EU states – on joining the Single Currency, on participating in the Schengen system of border-free movement, on co-operation on police and criminal matters – the UK negotiated opt-outs. And the UK was not alone. If anything, the EU exhibit more 'differentiated integration' with different constituencies of states managing their membership in a rather more flexible manner, not least outside the core of the Single Market.[12]

Examples of UK exceptionalism during its years of membership meant that the UK acquired the reputation of being an 'awkward partner' of the other Member States.[13] However, it would be wrong to view awkwardness as inherently an impediment to European integration. Famously, Prime Minister Thatcher made demands for a rebate on the UK's budgetary contributions. While perhaps an indicator of awkwardness, the resolution of this issue following the 1984 Fontainbleu Summit allowed a new impetus to be given to the unfinished task of building a Single Market. Indeed, to the extent that the UK did see its membership through the lens of market-making, it was the UK government – as well as British EU Commissioners and British Commission officials – that helped propel the Single Market programme and European integration forward.[14]

Nor is awkwardness a uniquely British characteristic. It may in fact be a signifier of a more general awkwardness in how European governments square the demands of domestic and European politics. While John Major's government may have had to battle to get the ratification of the Maastricht Treaty through the House of Commons in 1992–3, it was

[12] D Leuffen, R Rittberger and F Schimmelfennig, *Differentiated Integration: Explaining Variation in the European Union* (Palgrave, 2012).

[13] S George, *An Awkward Partner: Britain in the European Community* (Oxford University Press, 1990).

[14] KA Armstrong and S Bulmer, *The Governance of the Single European Market* (Manchester University Press, 1998).

a referendum in Denmark that initially rejected ratification. And while the Nice Treaty was again initially rejected in a referendum in Ireland, as indeed was the later Lisbon Treaty,[15] there was little obstacle to its approval in the UK in 2001 with a Labour government then enjoying a substantial majority in the Commons and with a party then united in support of European integration and European enlargement. Indeed, up until 2016, the strongest body blows to the EU project came from two of its founding members when the electorates in France and the Netherlands in 2005 both rejected ratification of the Treaty establishing a Constitution for Europe.

National governments stand at the interface of the national and the international. They navigate a path between pursuing national interests externally while trying to remain responsive to their domestic constituencies. At times, governments can be successful in exploiting their EU membership–escaping domestic constraints while also shifting blame to EU institutions – but at other times, the conflicts between European and national policy contexts become all too apparent. National governments find themselves playing 'two-level' games.[16] But it is not just national governments that mediate this relationship between the domestic and international spheres. Indeed, what might be as important is the way in which the expected pros and cons, opportunities and constraints of EU membership are understood, promoted

[15] In both instances, later referendums secured Irish ratification of the two treaties.
[16] RD Putnam, 'Diplomacy and domestic politics: the logic of two-level games' (1988) 42(3) *International Organization* 427.

and contested by domestic constitutional structures (parliament, courts, elections and referendums), domestic political actors (governments, oppositions, national and sub-national parties, social movements and campaigns) and media outlets (including the newer forms of social media that provide a steady stream of news, facts and 'alternative facts').

So if we are to make sense of EU membership – the forces that give rise to membership; the choices made by members to participate or not to participate in different aspects of EU policy co-operation; and ultimately the decision to relinquish membership – we must continually pay attention to the relationship between nationalism and internationalism and the domestic structures and actors that interpret what that relationship means in the context of membership of an entity like the EU. It requires the maintenance of a kind of social, economic, political and legal equilibrium.

Fast forward to 2016. The relationship between nationalism and internationalism has been cast in very different terms from those that gave rise to UK membership of the Common Market. The political and economic gains and losses have been recalibrated. Politically, the rhetoric generated by the decision of the UK to leave the European Union suggests an alternative positive-sum game to that which inspires the idea of a European rescue of the nation state. The benefits of Brexit are to be reaped through a new nationalism – 'taking back control' – together with a new internationalism – the UK as a global free trade champion. Economically, whereas in the 1960s it was the UK economy that was the laggard, GDP growth in the eurozone has been sluggish and uneven. The financial and economic crisis of

2008 also exposed structural weaknesses in European economic governance.

However, the context in which the UK will once again stand apart from the structures of European cooperation is very different now to that of post-war Europe. Brexit exposes whether the contemporary challenges facing modern European governments are better addressed inside or outside of membership of an organisation like the EU. Brexit will be as much a test for the EU as it will for the UK.

2

Reform and Renegotiation

In November 2015, David Cameron sent a letter to the President of the European Council, Donald Tusk setting out the central themes of the so-called 'new settlement' that the UK wanted to negotiate with its EU partners. The Prime Minister's mantra was 'reform, renegotiation, referendum'. It was on the basis of a renegotiated membership that David Cameron intended to argue the case for the UK's continuing EU membership in a referendum to be held before the end of 2017.

The idea of holding a referendum following a renegotiation of membership terms was not a new one. After all, some forty years earlier, Harold Wilson had defeated Edward Heath in a general election, with Wilson promising to renegotiate the terms of UK membership to which Heath had agreed and then to hold a referendum on whether the UK should remain in the European Economic Community (EEC). The 1975 and 2016 referendums were similarly exercises in the management of internal party political divisions. While the roots of the 2016 referendum lie in the problems the Conservative Party has faced over Europe – and the threat from the United Kingdom Independence Party (UKIP) on the Right – it is important to recall that the UK's membership of the EEC also divided the Labour Party.[1] Wilson's referendum

[1] T Nairn, 'The Left against Europe?' (1972) I/75 *New Left Review* 1.

was equally a device to manage divisions within his party, between those who had sided with Heath in pushing through accession to the EEC and those for whom a Common Market and European institutions risked the capacity of a Labour government to exercise parliamentary sovereignty and to intervene in the economy. Nonetheless, the 1975 referendum did not settle divisions and in the 1980s, it was the Labour Party's policy of getting out of the EEC that led senior Labour figures to quit the party and to found the Social Democratic Party (later merging with the Liberals to form the pro-European Liberal Democratic Party).[2]

Substantively, Wilson wanted to see changes to the CAP together with reforms to the EEC Budget, and a retention of sovereignty over regional, economic and industrial policies. Harmonisation of Value Added Tax was also opposed. In the wake of the turbulence generated by the collapse of the Bretton Woods system of fixed exchange rates, proposals tabled at the Paris Summit of 1972 to inject new energy into plans for European Economic and Monetary Union were also a significant cause for concern.[3]

Negotiations began with EU partners and institutions following Wilson's election victory.[4] There is one particularly

[2] J Smith, 'The European dividing line in party politics' (2012) 88(6) *International Affairs* 1277.

[3] V Miller, 'The 1974–75 UK renegotiation of EEC membership and referendum', *House of Commons Library Briefing Paper*, No. 7253 (13 July 2015).

[4] For a detailed account see S Wall, *The Official History of Britain in the European Community*, II: *From Rejection to Referendum 1963–1975* (Routledge, 2012).

important aspect of timing that was relevant to this renegotiation and later to David Cameron's renegotiation. The experiences of the late 1960s and 1970s had shown the difficulties in exercising leadership through the EEC's bureaucratic executive institutions. Periodic 'summits' of Presidents and Prime Ministers had developed outside of the formal EEC institutional framework. The election of Giscard d'Estaing to the French presidency in 1974 and Helmut Schmidt to the Germany Chancellor's position gave impetus to more institutionalised – albeit still largely informal – summits in a configuration that became known as the 'European Council'.[5] It held its first meeting in Dublin in March 1975. This meeting was crucial to finalising Wilson's renegotiation, including agreeing a 'correction mechanism' to deal with UK demands about its budget contributions – the UK had been set to have a share of contributions to the EEC budget that was greater than its share of EEC Gross National Product – and to enable a review of the arrangements under Protocol 18 of the Accession Treaty dealing with imports of dairy products from New Zealand. The aim had been to resolve issues with the UK without the need to reopen negotiations over the EEC Treaty itself.[6] The institutional focal point of the European Council and the desire to avoid immediate treaty change would be key characteristics of David Cameron's 2016 renegotiation.

In a statement to the House of Commons following the Dublin European Council meeting, Wilson stated that

---

[5] S Bulmer, 'The European Council's first decade: between interdependence and domestic politics' (1985) 22(4) *Journal of Common Market Studies* 89.
[6] See Wall, *The Official History of Britain in the European Community*, II.

renegotiations 'had now gone as far as they could usefully go' and that the government would recommend to the British people that the UK should remain in the EEC.[7] In the leaflet sent to voters to urge them to vote for the UK to remain in the Common Market,[8] the Prime Minister stated that the UK's 'renegotiation objectives have been substantially though not completely achieved'. But, the leaflet did highlight a claim that £125 million a year would be returned to the UK under the Dublin agreement.

Forty years later, it was David Cameron's time to seek to negotiate the UK's membership of the EU in advance of a referendum. His decision to hold an in/out referendum on the UK's membership was an exercise of political choice, albeit a choice that had perhaps become inevitable. In the mid 1990s Sir James Goldsmith had founded the Referendum Party, funding candidates across the country to contest the 1997 General Election which ultimately swept the Labour Party into government and Tony Blair into Downing Street. It is important to recall that the Labour government of Prime Minister Tony Blair had planned to hold a referendum to approve the EU Constitutional Treaty. But that didn't take place once voters in the Netherlands and France had rejected the treaty in their referendums. Indeed, it was the failure to hold a referendum on the Constitutional Treaty that gave momentum to calls to hold a referendum on its replacement, the Lisbon Treaty. As Opposition leader, in September 2007,

[7] House of Commons Debate, Hansard, Vol 888, Cols 509–22 (12 March 1975).
[8] A copy of the leaflet can be found at www.harvard-digital.co.uk/euro/pa mphlet.htm#8.

David Cameron had given a 'cast-iron guarantee' that any treaty that followed from the negotiations in the wake of the failure of the Constitutional Treaty would be put to a referendum. But with the Lisbon Treaty ratified and in force before David Cameron became Prime Minister in 2010, the promise of a referendum on a specific treaty change could not be delivered.

The Coalition government which took office under David Cameron's premiership legislated for referendums to be triggered where any new treaty transferred powers and competences from the UK to the EU: the European Union Act 2011. But this did not quell the pressure within his own party for a commitment to an in/out referendum and, in October 2011, more than eighty of his own Conservative MPs rebelled in a Commons vote on a motion proposing such a referendum. Despite the advice of his own Chancellor against holding a referendum, in his Bloomberg speech in January 2013, David Cameron bowed to pressure and conceded that following a renegotiation, an in/out referendum on EU membership would be held.[9]

It was a political calculation designed to manage internal party divisions; to deal with the external threat from UKIP; and to create clear water between a Labour Party that opposed a referendum and the Conservative Party, in the 2015 general election. The risks were obvious too. The referendum campaign would expose rifts in the Prime Minister's own party; it would give UKIP a focal point and a platform; and

---

[9] T Bale, '"Banging on about Europe": how the Eurosceptics got their referendum', http://blogs.lse.ac.uk (23 June 2016).

in order for the Prime Minister to achieve his goal of keeping the UK in a reformed EU, he would need an active and campaigning Labour Party to help forge a centre-ground consensus.

But if Wilson had a clear idea of what he would and could negotiate, it was much less obvious what Cameron would or could attain.[10] Like Wilson, the work on reforms began shortly after the general election. In the five months that led to the formal letter being sent to the European Council, the UK's position was developed. That position was based on the Prime Minister's 2013 Bloomberg speech in which David Cameron set out his vision for the UK in the EU. In that speech, the Prime Minister identified three key challenges: the future integration of the eurozone and the need for safeguards for non-eurozone countries like the UK; confronting the EU's competitiveness problem; and the enduring problem of democratic accountability in the EU.

The UK's reform priorities were set out at the June 2015 European Council meeting. In his statement to the House of Commons following the summit, David Cameron outlined the key themes of the reform package:[11]

- sovereignty – no UK commitment to 'ever closer union'
- fairness – integration of the eurozone not to be to detriment of non-eurozone countries
- immigration – address the effect of welfare incentives
- competitiveness – enhancing growth, jobs and innovation.

[10] R Saunders, 'A tale of two referendums: 1976 and 2016' (2016) 87(3) *The Political Quarterly* 318.

[11] House of Commons Debate, Hansard, Vol 597, Cols 1176–7 (29 June 2015).

Until the UK addressed its letter to the European Council in November, there was no formal position and informal discussions at EU level and with national capitals revolved around the content of the Bloomberg speech, the Conservative election manifesto and the themes outlined at the June 2015 European Council. The unwillingness of the British to commit anything to paper – afraid of leaks and desperately trying to placate the British media – was difficult for EU bureaucratic structures more used to developing responses to written proposals.

It is not enough to have an objective for negotiations; there also needs to be a process. Within the UK government, at ministerial level, the process of developing the UK's position was led by the Prime Minister together with the Chancellor and Treasury, the Foreign Office and the Cabinet Office. A new Europe Cabinet Committee was established chaired by the Prime Minister to consider issues related to the referendum. In evidence given to the House of Lords European Committee, the then Minister for Europe, David Lidington was pressed on whether the large number of government departments involved made it difficult to answer the 'Kissinger' question of who to call to get the UK's position.[12] He responded that government 'works by network rather than by hierarchy' but noted that a group of senior officials in Downing Street, the Treasury, the Foreign Office and Cabinet Office were 'intimately involved'. Indeed, as the negotiations developed, it was the then UK ambassador to the EU – the

---

[12] House of Lords European Select Committee, 'The referendum on UK membership of the EU: assessing the reform process', HL Paper 30, Session 2015–16 (28 July 2015).

Permanent Representative – Sir Ivan Rogers and the head of the European and Global Issues Secretariat within the Cabinet Office – in effect, the Prime Minister's Europe adviser – Tom Scholar who lead the process.

At EU level, and following the June European Council, 'technical discussions' began under the supervision of the European Council President. If Wilson encountered the embryonic form of the European Council in 1975, by 2015 it had not only become a formal EU institution, it had a President and a pivotal role in managing the EU's political and economic problems.[13] David Cameron had, on previous occasions, misjudged the workings of the European Council: first, he was isolated on the Franco-German plan for a 'fiscal compact' treaty amendment – his veto simply meant that EU Member States adopted a treaty outside of the EU treaty framework – and, secondly, Angela Merkel's support for British opposition to the appointment of Jean-Claude Juncker as European Commission President, failed to materialise. Although the European Council would be the focal point for the 'end-game' of negotiations, and despite a tour of capitals in which the Prime Minister sought to build support among fellow EU leaders, the EU position was being developed in a range of institutional settings.

In the summer of 2015, the President of the European Commission established a Task Force for Strategic Issues related to the UK referendum headed by a senior

---

[13] U Puetter, *The European Council and the Council: New Intergovernmentalism and Institutional Change* (Oxford University Press, 2014).

Commission official – Jonathan Faull – who also happened to be British. To complete the institutional triangle, the European Parliament appointed 'sherpas' from the main political grouping to give the Parliament's input into the process. The national permanent representatives were regularly briefed and bilateral 'confessionals' were held with each Member State to determine their views.

The technical discussions focused specifically on the legal framework of any future deal, and lawyers from the Commission and Council legal services were ever-present in discussions. It was decided early on that any deal had to be based on what could be done without treaty revision. Opening a treaty revision process would mean that the UK deal could end up linked to other issues, widening the scope, and prolonging the process, of negotiation. The need for unanimity among the Member States, as well as domestic ratification, risked vetoes and failure. So, the focus was on being able to do a deal that was legally binding even if consequential treaty and legislative changes would have to follow.

In his November letter to the European Council President, David Cameron expanded on the four areas he had identified in June 2015. The four 'baskets' of negotiations concerned sovereignty, competitiveness, the eurozone and immigration. Even before the negotiations started, the proposals were roundly criticised by Eurosceptics within the Prime Ministers own party. But equally on the EU side, it was clear that Central and Eastern European countries would find proposals on limiting immigration difficult, while other states like Belgium with a stronger commitment to the idea of 'ever closer union' clearly found the whole renegotiation process challenging. The December European Council failed to reach an agreement and a final 'new settlement' had to wait until the European Council met again in February 2016. This could have been an act of political theatre intended to help David Cameron show his negotiating muscle but the December meeting was probably too early to allow European capitals and EU institutions to finalise their positions.

Over the course of 18 and 19 February 2016, the terms and legal framework of the UK's 'new settlement' were finally agreed. In creating the legal framework there were two obvious precedents: the renegotiations that followed the referendums in Denmark and Ireland rejecting the Maastricht and Lisbon Treaties, respectively. The legal responses to these political problems created a template that could be followed. Without opening a treaty renegotiation, it was possible for the Prime Ministers and Presidents as Heads of State and Governments to adopt a 'Decision' – in effect a simplified treaty – that would be binding in international law. Such a Decision could not change the EU treaties or be incompatible with them, but would constitute an agreement as to the meaning and interpretation of the treaties which, even as a matter of international law, could create legal effects within the EU legal order.[14] A future treaty revision could then amend the treaties or add a Protocol to the EU treaties to incorporate the decision within primary EU law.

[14] Sir Alan Dashwood QC, 'The UK's "New Settlement" within the EU – a reform package for the whole of the EU', www.hendersonchambers.co .uk (19 May 2016).

The Decision contained separate sections each deal-ing with the distinct 'baskets' that had formed the substance of negotiations together with any necessary draft instruments for their implementation.

On 'economic governance', the Decision laid down certain principles designed to reconcile a Single Market of all Member States with a Eurozone and Banking Union applic-able to a subset of EU states. Non-eurozone states committed not to impede further integration of the eurozone, while eurozone states committed to respect the rights and compe-tences of non-eurozone states. Earlier in 2015 the UK had won an important legal challenge to a European Central Bank (ECB) plan that would oblige euro-denominated payment and clearing operations to be relocated in the eurozone, directly impacting on activities carried out in the UK.[15] The new settlement expressly prohibited currency discrimi-nation and the single rulebook for credit institutions would apply across the Single Market to create a level playing field. Supervisory responsibilities of the ECB would be limited to institutions in eurozone states. Financial stability measures to support the eurozone would be paid for by eurozone states and any support from the EU general budget had to entail reimbursement mechanisms for non-eurozone countries.

To ensure adherence to these principles of mutual respect, and to avoid the risk of eurozone states acting as a bloc in disregard of these principles, a Council Decision was proposed to supplement an existing Council Decision

---

[15] *United Kingdom v European Central Bank*, Case T-496/11, EU: T:2015:133.

governing voting rules in the Council.[16] The new Decision created a mechanism by which any Member State not participating in the Banking Union could stop the Council from adopting a measure that it considered breached the agreed principles. The Council would then need to seek to resolve the issue and if necessary refer the matter to the European Council.

The section on 'competitiveness' was brief and declaratory: the idea of making the EU competitive was hardly objectionable. It urged EU institutions and Member States to further the Single Market and improve its regulatory framework. On 'sovereignty' the Decision focused on two issues: the concept of 'ever closer union' and the role of 'national parliaments'. The groundwork had already been well-prepared on 'ever closer union', with the text highlighting the wide range of areas where the UK had special arrangements – including on the euro, Schengen and its Protocol on the application of the EU Charter of Fundamental Rights – to emphasise that 'ever closer union' was compatible with 'differentiated integration', allowing some states to choose to deepen integration while others do not. But more specifically, the Decision offered interpretative clarification that 'ever closer union' did not provide a legal basis for extending the scope of provisions of EU treaties or legislation, nor for an extensive interpretation of the competences of the Union.

The Decision also sought to enhance the capacity of national parliaments to signal their concerns where new EU legislative proposals conflicted with the subsidiarity

---

[16] Council Decision 2009/857/EC [2009] OJ L314/73.

principle – the principle that says that the EU should not legislate on matters that can better be regulated at national level. The EU already has an 'early warning system' by which national parliaments can raise objections to EU proposals on subsidiarity grounds.[17] The new settlement stopped short of giving individual national parliaments a veto. Rather if 55 per cent of voting chambers of national parliaments signalled their concerns within twelve weeks of a draft EU proposal then the Council would have to discuss the issue and discontinue consideration of the proposal unless the draft was amended to accommodate the concerns. The key difficulty, however, is that even under the existing warning system it has often proved difficult to obtain the requisite threshold of 'opinions' from national parliaments to trigger EU-level rethinks on draft proposals. The proposal would have increased rather than decreased the threshold.

The primary area of contention was inevitably going to be in respect of immigration. The UK wanted to find a mechanism to cap numbers as it had repeatedly made pledges to cap net migration to the UK. But in an EU where free movement, residence and access to the labour market are protected rights, a numerical cap would directly contradict treaty principles and so could not be achieved without a treaty revision to which other Member States would not agree. The negotiation focused instead on welfare incentives. A series of rulings from the Court of Justice had already clarified that

---

[17] P Kiiver, 'The early warning system for the principle of subsidiarity: the national parliament as a *conseil d'etat* for Europe' (2011) 36 *European Law Review* 98.

Member States could restrict access to certain social assistance benefits,[18] and much of the Decision repeated what was already accepted as a matter of EU law.

The focus switched to EU social security regulations and entitlements to in-work benefits. The UK wanted to prohibit new EU migrants from claiming in-work benefits for the first four years of residence in the UK. Instead what was agreed was an amendment to Regulation 492/2011 to create a safeguard mechanism by which – due to 'exceptional' in-flows of migrants affecting 'essential aspects' of the social security system or which placed 'excessive pressure' on public services – any Member State could request that the Council authorise that state to restrict in-work benefits for up to four years. The Council would act on a recommendation by the Commission. In a Declaration attached to the Decision, the Commission stated that on the basis of information provided by the UK, the sort of exceptional situation envisaged by the safeguard mechanism 'exists in the United Kingdom today' and that the UK would be 'justified in triggering the mechanism in the full expectation of obtaining approval'. Recall, however that it would be for the Council to authorise and not the Commission. Moreover, any authorising decision might be vulnerable to legal challenge, not least on whether there was the evidence to support the claimed impact on social security and public services.

---

[18] D Kramer, 'Earning social citizenship in the European Union: free movement and access to social assistance benefits reconstructed' (2016) 18 *Cambridge Yearbook of European Legal Studies* 270.

Lastly, the Decision dealt with the exportability of child benefits. The UK had sought to end the right of migrant EU workers to claim child benefits for a child not resident in the UK. What was offered instead was an amendment to Regulation 883/2004 that would give states an option to index benefits to the conditions of the Member State where the child resided. But this would only apply to new claimants up to 2020 and then to all claimants thereafter.

Although derided in the press and by his own MPs, the Prime Minister's 'new settlement' was more wide-reaching and substantive than what Harold Wilson had achieved. Despite its legal status and legal effects, domestic critics of the government felt that it fell short of a 'binding and irrevocable' agreement and did not constitute a wholesale reform of the EU. The latter expectation was wholly unrealistic: only a full-scale treaty change could bring about substantial reform. But whether or not expectations were realistic, the result did not satisfy expectations. It failed to define the terms of the political conversation over the UK's position in the EU. Nor was it part of a wider strategy that might have identified key UK priorities for the EU under the UK's presidency of the EU which was scheduled for the second half of 2017. There was no big ticket item on immigration or the budget or any of the other issues that ended up dominating political debate.

Hardly had the renegotiation been concluded and it was forgotten. Reform and renegotiation gave way to the referendum and the referendum campaign.

3

Referendums and European Integration

Referendums are not uncommon across Europe. The one exception is the European Union itself which has never conducted an EU-wide referendum. While the day-to-day work of the EU relies on democratic legitimacy flowing through elected national governments and a directly elected European Parliament, the key moments of change – accession of new states, amendments to the treaties, or significant policy developments like the introduction of the euro – have been approved by Member States according to their own constitutional traditions and domestic political needs.

Whether or not a country holds a referendum on a European issue is, therefore, a domestic matter. The events that trigger a referendum, the status of a referendum – advisory or binding – and, its consequences are typically the interaction of political forces and constitutional arrangements. In this way, referendums on 'Europe' are actually rather national affairs. But these national decisions have effects upwards – they can approve or limit events at EU level – and sideways – a referendum decision can have consequences for other Member States as well as for the EU.

Given the increased frequency of referendums relating to European integration, there is now a body of comparative research that can shed light on their features. It is possible to categorise referendums according to the different reasons why they are held and their subject matter. In some Member

States referendums are constitutionally mandated; particular events necessarily mean that a referendum must be held. Otherwise, referendums are discretionary. In some instances, political and historical factors mean that in practice the discretion is limited and the appropriateness of a referendum is simply accepted. In other cases, the decision is overtly politically motivated.[1]

As to their subject matter, scholars typically distinguish between three categories of European integration referendums: (1) membership referendums, (2) policy issue referendums and (3) treaty amendment referendums.[2] Referendums on EU membership have been common with twenty-two held since 1972. While typically referendums have confirmed EU accession, membership of the EU was rejected twice in Norway, while voters in Switzerland decided not to pursue EU candidacy. Three membership referendums – two in the UK and one in a territory of a Member State, Greenland – have been on withdrawal. Referendums have also been held on specific policy issues such as whether or not to join the EU single currency (Denmark and Sweden both voted not to become part of the eurozone). But perhaps the best known contentious referendums are those relating to EU treaty changes.

Beginning with the Danish rejection of the Maastricht Treaty in 1992, securing a referendum result in

---

[1] F Mendez and M Mendez, *Referendums on EU Matters: Study for the Committee on Constitutional Affairs* (European Parliament, 2017).

[2] F Mendez, M Mendez and V Triga, *Referendums and the European Union* (Cambridge University Press, 2014).

favour of new EU treaties has become more difficult. Ireland, where referendums on significant treaty changes are constitutionally mandated, initially rejected both the Nice and Lisbon treaties. French and Dutch popular rejection of the Treaty establishing a Constitution for Europe in 2005 was the death knell for that project of European integration. However, with the exception of the demise of the Constitutional Treaty, referendum defeats on new or amending EU treaties have not proved fatal to these texts. This is surprising given that Article 48 of the Treaty on European Union requires all Member States to ratify a treaty modification before it can enter force. However, referendum defeats on treaty revision have been followed by intense negotiations at EU level to find ways of responding to referendum failures.

The desire to find a negotiated solution to a referendum veto is understandable given that the effect is felt by all the other EU states. However, this capacity for referendums to produce externalities for the EU and other EU states poses something of a democracy dilemma. On the one hand, an electorate is surely entitled to have its say on whether or not it agrees with a particular development in European integration that requires treaty changes. On the other hand, voters in other Member States are affected by referendum decisions without a vote and often without a voice. Indeed, there is a risk that negotiations that respond to a referendum veto end up offering special deals or arrangements that create differentiated and fragmented arrangements which risk undermining European integration. It is noteworthy that while elements of the 'new settlement' deal agreed by the European Council in February 2016 were framed as responses to UK concerns, the instruments and mechanisms relating to economic governance, subsidiarity and migration were open to other EU states to apply.

Second referendums to accept treaty revisions have overturned earlier defeats. If the initial veto was an attempt to bring negotiators back to the table, the second referendum can be framed in terms of what is new and specific to the particular Member State – acceptance or rejection of whatever new guarantees have been offered – with the risks of failure becoming starker second time round.[3] But the tension between the EU's constitutional need to secure ratification under conditions of unanimity and the concern that voters are being asked to keep voting until they give the right answer is self-evident.[4]

The 2016 referendum was clearly of a different nature to other EU-related referendums. First, it was a membership referendum not a referendum on accepting treaty changes. Whereas the worst that happens if a new treaty or treaty amendment is rejected is that the status quo is maintained – after all, that was the consequence of the Dutch and French rejection of the Constitutional Treaty – a popular decision to reject membership – if followed through – is necessarily going to result in radical changes. Secondly, unlike the Danish and Irish referendums which triggered further EU-level negotiations, David Cameron sought to pre-emptively negotiate

---

[3] EO Atikcan, 'The puzzle of double referendums in the European Union' (2015) 53(5) *Journal of Common Market Studies* 937.

[4] G de Búrca, 'If at first you don't succeed: vote, vote again. Analyzing the second referendum phenomenon in EU treaty change' (2010) 33(5) *Fordham International Law Journal* 1472.

a 'new settlement' for the UK in advance of the referendum. In that sense, the 2016 referendum had more in common with the 1975 UK membership referendum.

Thirdly, if the experience of second referendums tends to show that the campaigns focused more directly on what was new and the heightened risks from failure, it is not at all clear that the 'new settlement' deal was all that relevant to how British voters decided in 2016 and nor were voters unduly concerned by the risks of withdrawal. If anything, the sense that the new settlement did not go far enough crystallised views that the UK had already ceded too much sovereignty and that far-reaching reforms simply were unobtainable.

Fourthly, even if voters had been minded to vote in favour of the UK retaining its EU membership on the basis of the new settlement deal, there would equally be uncertainty as to how it might be implemented. The legal structure of the deal was inspired directly by the solutions found for Irish and Danish rejections of treaty amendments. These entailed adoption of decisions binding as a matter of international law but with future consequential changes to EU practices requiring a future EU treaty change. That device may have been enough to persuade Danish and Irish voters that the proposed changes were incrementally preferable to the status quo, where the status quo meant retaining EU membership and operating under prevailing rules and procedures. But in the context of a membership referendum, UK voters may simply have worried about a temporal lag between the conclusion of the deal and its ultimate implementation, especially if they had not been persuaded that the deal was 'binding and irreversible' in the first place.

But what if the Prime Minister had changed the sequencing of his mantra of 'reform, renegotiation and referendum' to 'referendum, renegotiation and reform'? If the experiences of Ireland and Denmark suggested that the threat of veto had brought negotiators to the table, then perhaps the weakness of a pre-emptive new settlement deal was that it was simply not backed by a credible threat of withdrawal. After all, the Prime Minister was intending to back continuing UK membership based on his renegotiation. And the prospect of the UK leaving the EU may have seemed remote to EU partners.

The idea of a referendum as a pretext for a renegotiation was floated by, amongst others, the then London Mayor, Boris Johnson. A second referendum might then follow finally to determine membership based on any reforms agreed. The Johnson idea was scorned by the Prime Minister. Yet one advantage of the proposal was that the 'advisory' status of the first referendum would be clearer than was perhaps the case with the June 2016 referendum. It would simply be intended to offer the government a provisional view of the mood of the country with a view to the opening of future negotiations. Only once those negotiations had concluded would the voters then be presented with a determinative vote on leaving or remaining in the EU based on any reforms agreed or envisaged.

As a tactic to bring negotiators to the table the Johnson plan has an obvious difficulty: what if the electorate simply voted to remain in the EU? One response might be that this indicated more support for the EU than was perhaps apparent and accordingly, reforms to address voter concerns were simply unnecessary or at least not a deal-breaker for voters. The scenario on which Johnson's proposal is premised is more one where voters clearly decide (provisionally) to leave the EU and so strengthen a Prime Minister's hand in negotiating the conditions of continuing EU membership. But having voted to leave what would it take to then persuade those voters to remain following a renegotiation? In any event, if the ultimate vote was in favour of leaving the EU, the government would still be faced with the same problems of negotiating the UK's departure. It would only postpone and not resolve a determination of the issues of the UK's future relationship with the EU. Moreover, if the core issue was the credibility of the threat to withdraw, perhaps the way of addressing that would not be an advisory referendum but a stronger political intention to recommend a vote to leave unless EU leaders were prepared to begin a process of fundamental reforms.

Given the political pressure on the British Prime Minister to hold a referendum, the alternative to an in/out referendum following a renegotiation was either to wait for other EU states to propose a treaty renegotiation or for the UK to seek to initiate that process itself. In a sense this would then combine a membership referendum with a treaty amendment referendum. This would pose some difficulties. The first problem would be domestic. The Conservative election manifesto had promised a straightforward in/out referendum by the end of 2017. Making a referendum conditional on a wider treaty negotiation would more likely push that date back. A later referendum would mean that the issue of 'Europe' would dominate domestic politics just at the point that the

Conservatives had formed a majority government. Given that David Cameron had already announced that he would not seek a further term as Prime Minister, there would also be the possibility of a leadership election taking place at the same time as reform negotiations were developing.

The second problem would be the linkage of a UK membership referendum with an EU treaty amendment referendum. As the phenomenon of second referendums in Denmark and Ireland highlight, it is not enough for EU leaders to reach a deal. Treaty amendments must be approved domestically in accordance with the domestic ratification requirements of EU states. That creates the risk of veto and failure. Even before British voters got the chance to put their crosses on the ballot paper, politicians or voters in other European states might scupper the process. But these antecedents also highlighted that linking a membership referendum to a treaty amendment referendum risked delays, vetoes and failures that would mean that the process could end up out of the hands of the UK government. However valuable might have been the long-term prize of more fundamental reforms of the EU, short-term political pressures were demanding a simple membership referendum.

The experience of the adoption of the Lisbon Treaty had a more direct impact on UK constitutional law. When the Coalition government took office in 2010, David Cameron wanted to ensure there was a mechanism by which the government's hands would be tied by legislation that would trigger a referendum on certain EU-related issues. The European Union Act 2011 established the sorts of things that would require a referendum in the UK, from treaty revisions that would transfer powers from the UK to the EU, to more specific policy issues such as joining the single currency, removing border controls or participating in the European Public Prosecutor's Office. The Prime Minister wanted to emulate the referendum 'locks' that other EU countries like Germany placed on future European integration.[5] Rather than referendums on EU issues being a matter of political discretion, they would be legally obligated. The 2016 EU membership referendum was not, however, triggered by the provisions of the 2011 Act. It was an exercise of discretion and choice, structured not by the demands of law but of politics, and a politics framed by time.

[5] P Craig, 'The European Union Act 2011: locks, limits and legality' (2011) 48 *Common Market Law Review* 1915.

4

The 2016 Referendum

The apparent popularity of referendums in modern democracies may be borne of competing dynamics.[1] On the one hand, the attractiveness of a referendum is the appeal of direct democracy. Referendums in the modern media age create new channels and mechanisms for popular debate and political discourse outside of the regular institutions and circuits of political authority. Without replacing traditional institutions, on this view, referendums may help galvanise and mobilise an electorate, making voters interested in politics. Certainly, one of the claims often made about the Scottish independence referendum in 2014 is that it reinvigorated Scottish politics. On the other hand, the popularity of referendums may be a signifier of the failures of representative democracy, regular politics and political parties. A referendum can be a symptom of an estrangement of a political class from voters.

Critiques of referendums typically work at two main levels. The first criticism relates to 'voter competence' and raises question both as to the sort of issues that can realistically be decided by referendum and whether voters actually decide on the issues. Although these questions arise in any referendum – indeed, they are not immaterial to any

---

[1] T Donovan and JA Karp, 'Popular support for direct democracy' (2006) 12(5) *Party Politics* 671.

election – they have been particularly relevant to European referendums. An EU-related referendum may be considered undesirable given the low levels of understanding of the complexities of EU decision-making among the public. A referendum on EU membership is not exactly a single-issue subject given the kinds of trade-offs and uncertainties involved in deciding one way or another. But while voters may be confronted with significant gaps in their knowledge, what becomes key is the campaign process and its capacity to generate information. Referendum campaigns provide direct information as well as 'heuristics' or shortcuts including the positions taken by the main political parties.[2] But even if a referendum campaign addresses information deficits, whether voters decide on the issues or 'second-order' questions such as the performance of the government of the day is particularly relevant to referendums on European issues.[3]

The second point of concern is institutional and procedural and asks who is accountable for a decision made in a referendum. Representative democracy is a mechanism that allows for deliberation, contestation and decision-making, with scrutiny and accountability as decisions are being formed, and once made, the electorate has the ultimate means of holding decision-makers to account. Dissatisfaction

[2] S Hobolt, 'Taking cues on Europe? Voter competence and party endorsements in referendums on European integration' (2007) 46(2) *European Journal of Political Research* 151.

[3] J Garry, M Marsh and R Sinnott, '"Second-order" versus "issue-voting" effects in EU referendums: evidence from the Irish Nice Treaty referendums' (2005) 6(2) *European Union Politics* 201.

with the outcome of an earlier election can be corrected at the next election. With a referendum, the accountability dimension is more complex. If a referendum result is not the one preferred by a political leader – especially a leader that has put the issue to the electorate in a referendum as a matter of political choice – the political damage is likely to be significant and may even lead to resignation. Such was the case for David Cameron and also for Matteo Renzi, the Italian Prime Minister, whose constitutional reform plans were rejected in a referendum in December 2016. There is a personal accountability. Nonetheless, if the popular rejection of a proposal maintains the *status quo*, then whoever is in office simply remains accountable for the conduct of government in the normal way.

Conversely if a government's proposal is backed then it will be accountable for delivering its preferred policy. The problem is what happens when – as in 2016 – a government is defeated in a referendum but the defeat does not result in maintenance of the status quo, but rather, very significant political, economic and legal upheaval. It will be left to the normal process of representative democracy to seek to bring accountability for the implementation of the referendum result.

Faced with these sorts of issues, a constitutional system may try and put in place rules about the conduct of referendums to deal both with the process of the referendum as well as its consequences. Whatever one's view on whether a referendum is the correct way to decide complex issues, it matters that the outcome of a referendum is regarded as fair and legitimate. This is especially important where the resort to a referendum in the first place – to decide a matter that is contentious, with deeply held views on either side – suggests that whoever is on the losing side will feel aggrieved. As Tierney suggests, for instrumental reasons – to avoid post-decision conflicts – and for good constitutional reasons – to ensure that voters have 'meaningful participation' in the political process – it is important that referendums are conducted according to certain rules and norms.[4] Which begs the question as to how such referendums are conducted in a constitutional system that has historically placed Parliament at the centre of its decision-making.

Referendums are not quite the constitutional novelty that they once were in the UK. Yet their use has been relatively limited. The process of devolution of powers to the constituent nations of the UK and subsequently the transfer of powers to elected mayors has increased their frequency. Referendums on independence for Scotland were conducted in 1979 and again in 2014. Aside from these 'territorial' referendums, the 2016 EU referendum was only the third UK-wide referendum. The first such referendum was the 1975 referendum which confirmed the UK's membership of the European Economic Community (EEC). The second referendum, held in 2011 at the insistence of the Liberal Democrat Party – then in a coalition government with the Conservative Party – considered whether there should be a change to the voting

---

[4] S Tierney, 'The Scottish independence referendum: a model of good practice in direct democracy?' in A McHarg, T Mullen, A Page and N Walker (eds), *The Scottish Independence Referendum: Constitutional and Political Implications* (Oxford University Press, 2016).

system for general elections. However, the proposal to switch to the Alternative Vote (AV) electoral system was rejected and the traditional first-past-the-post system was retained.

It is worth reflecting for a moment on whether a change in the voting system would have produced a different outcome in the general election in 2015, and whether any change would have made a referendum on EU membership more or less likely. The AV system is a majoritarian rather than a proportional system. If a candidate does not secure more than 50 per cent of first-preference votes then the candidate with the lowest votes is eliminated and the second, third etc preferences of these voters are reallocated to the remaining candidates until one obtains a majority. The projections of the Electoral Reform Society indicate that such a system would have actually enhanced the Conservative majority.[5] It needs to be recalled that the UK Independence Party (UKIP) secured 12.6 per cent of the popular vote but achieved the election of only one MP. Under an AV system of voting, this would not have increased the UKIP parliamentary representation, but the likely allocation of second-preference votes to the Conservatives would have enhanced the Conservative majority. Indeed, any more proportional system of voting would have probably produced a Conservative–UKIP coalition. So regardless of the outcome of the 2011 referendum and regardless of any other potential voting system, the distribution of votes for the political parties in 2015 meant

---

[5] J Garland and C Terry, *The 2015 General Election: A Voting System in Crisis* (The Electoral Reform Society, 2015), www.electoral-reform.org.uk.

that, all things being equal, the choice to hold a referendum became a political inevitability.

With referendums becoming a constitutionally accepted device for decision-making, in 2000, the Political Parties, Elections and Referendums Act was passed to lay down some basic legal principles and default rules that could be applied to the conduct of future referendums. That included the creation of an Electoral Commission with over-sight responsibilities, including giving advice on referendum questions. The Commission tests questions to determine their intelligibility to voters and on their neutrality.

The European Union Referendum Bill was introduced into the House of Commons on 28 May 2015. As published, the bill proposed a Yes/No referendum question: 'Should the United Kingdom remain a member of the European Union?' The Electoral Commission tested the EU referendum question posed in the European Referendum Bill. It did so in light of a previous exercise that arose when James Wharton MP introduced a Private Member's Bill into Parliament in June 2013 to make provision for a referendum on EU membership.[6] The Electoral Commission had then tested the proposed question 'Do you think that the United

---

[6] The bill arose when James Wharton MP came top of the ballot to introduce a Private Member's Bill. Such bills are often a means of getting public attention for an issue as the capacity of these bills to enter into law is dependent upon parliamentary time being available and their ability to generate support, which typically requires assistance from the government of the day. Wharton's bill made good progress and got through its report and committee stages in the House of Commons but was blocked in the Lords when it voted not to give more parliamentary time to its consideration.

Kingdom should be a member of the European Union?' and found that this raised the issue of whether or not voters knew that the UK was already an EU Member State. But more significantly, the Commission highlighted concerns with the use of questions that elicited simple Yes/No answers and called on Parliament to consider whether this type of formulation should be used in future referendums. If this approach was to be adopted it recommended reformulating the question as 'Should the United Kingdom remain a member of the European Union? Yes/No'. This was the formula subsequently proposed by the government in its original European Referendum Bill.

However, the Electoral Commission had also tested a range of other questions that focused on the use of the word 'Leave' as well as 'Remain'. While its research found that when used in isolation, voters felt that the word 'Leave' was a strong term that might dissuade voters, when presented with the options of both 'Remain' or 'Leave' this was considered to offer the required neutrality. In light of this, the Commission offered an alternative proposal namely, 'Should the United Kingdom remain a member of the European Union or leave the European Union?'.

With the publication of the European Referendum Bill, the Electoral Commission again considered the intelligibility of the wording of the referendum question. In relying not just on its earlier testing but new analysis, it recommended a 'Remain' or 'Leave' formulation of the question and the government accepted that recommendation in amending the bill. It was a change supported by UKIP who felt that the government's original proposal was biased in favour of the status quo. And so the lexicon of 'Remain' and 'Leave' entered political discourse.

The European Referendum Bill also dealt with the issue of the franchise for the referendum. Two key issues immediately arose. The first was whether 16- and 17-year-old voters would be given the right to vote as they had been in the Scottish independence referendum. The second controversy related to whether UK citizens resident abroad would be eligible to vote.

The inclusion of younger voters in the franchise for the Scottish independence referendum is considered by some to be a significant achievement in ensuring that those affected by the referendum outcome were allowed to participate in the decision-making process. More cynical observers might have thought that the unprecedented inclusion of 16 and 17 year olds was a tactic intended to swell the numbers of people likely to vote for independence. However, in the EU referendum, the government did not intend to repeat the experiment.

In the House of Commons, Labour amendments to the bill to extend the franchise to 16- and 17-year-olds were defeated. But, in November 2015, the House of Lords did amend the bill to give these teenagers a right to vote in the referendum. This amendment could have had two important effects on the timing of the referendum. First, Electoral Commission best practice suggested that there be at least six months between the finalisation of the legislative framework and the date of the referendum.[7] If the political debate over

---

[7] Electoral Commission, 'European Union Referendum Bill 2015 House of Commons Second Reading Briefing' (9 June 2015).

the extension of the franchise had delayed the passage of the bill, then the referendum date would itself be pushed back. Secondly, including a new group of voters would have required a process of getting teenagers registered to vote, as well as amendments to guidance and information campaigns targeting this group. This could have added a nine-month delay. However, the Lords amendment was overturned in the Commons in December 2015. Importantly, the Commons claimed 'financial privilege' in respect of the amendment – on the basis that it would incur costs said by the government to be around £6 million – with convention dictating that the Lords ought not to insist on their amendment.[8] A revised Lords amendment was tabled but defeated and so 16- and 17-year-olds were denied the opportunity to vote.

But would the inclusion of this group have made any difference to the result? There are around 1.5 million 16- and 17-year-olds in the UK.[9] The first task would have been to get these people onto the electoral register to ensure their eligibility to vote. Then there would be the issue of turnout. Figures from the Scottish independence referendum suggest upwards of 85 per cent of those in this age group eligible to vote did in fact vote. That would be around 1.275 million voters in the UK. Yet that figure might have been hard to replicate across the whole of the UK in a June poll. Finally, we would need to make an evaluation of voter intention. One

---

[8] M Russell and D Gover, 'The Lords, financial privilege and the EU referendum franchise', UK Constitutional Law Blog (16 December 2015), https://ukconstitutionallaw.org/.

[9] A Renwick and B McCay, 'Votes at 16: what effect would it have?', www.ukandeu.ac.uk.

quite small sample of under-18s indicated a likely Remain vote of around 69 per cent in this cohort.[10] All in all, it seems safer to conclude that the Leave margin of victory would have narrowed very considerably had under 18s been allowed to vote, but it may not have changed the result in June 2016. But perhaps the more intriguing point is that if combined with demographic changes, if a referendum were held in the same terms in 2021, the UK might vote to remain in the EU.[11]

As to the franchise more generally, this was based on eligibility to vote in a general election and so excluded EU citizens except Irish citizens. UK citizens who had been resident abroad for more than fifteen years were also excluded from the franchise: the legality of this was upheld in legal proceedings before the Divisional Court (*Shindler* and *Maclennan* [2016] EWHC 957).

What becomes clear is that the focus of constitutional attention, understandably, has been towards the process of the referendum rather than the implementation of the substance of the decision. As the result of the referendum has exposed, voters may have had very different understandings of what 'Leave' might entail. Indeed, the debate following the referendum has highlighted whether 'Leave' could mean leaving the EU without also requiring the UK to leave the EU single market. Yet, the political mechanism for implementing the referendum outcome is simply the normal operation of parliamentary democracy. A government which supported

[10] Source: the British Election Study, britishelectionstudy.com.
[11] J Burn-Murdoch, 'Brexit: everything you wanted to know about turnout by age at the EU referendum', *Financial Times* (1 July 2016), http://blogs.ft.com/ftdata/.

the UK remaining in the EU is now having to manage the process by which it will leave. There has been a change of personnel at the heart of government but without the normal mechanism by which such changes occur – a general election. The European Referendum Act was also completely silent on the procedural steps that might follow from a vote to leave the EU.

There are important lessons to be learned from the UK's recent experimentation with referendums. It is, perhaps, time to look again at the Political Parties, Elections and Referendum Act of 2010 in light of a wide-ranging analysis of the core constitutional questions of who gets to vote, on what, by what means, and with what consequences.

5

Campaign Times

For those agitating for a referendum on the UK's relationship with the EU, the 2016 referendum had been a long-time coming. A combination of forces and events had brought the UK to this moment in time. Yet this 'moment' was equally a series of more specific campaign times, structured by law – the combined effects of the Political Parties, Elections and Referendums Act 2000 and the European Referendum Act 2015 – and by politics. The flow of campaign time would, however, disrupt the usual conduct of government in two specific ways.

First, the Prime Minister agreed to relax the normal rules on collective Cabinet responsibility – requiring ministers to adhere to official government policy while holding ministerial office – to allow ministers who opposed the government's position on the UK remaining in the EU to speak freely without having to tender their resignations. A minister could, of course, choose to resign but none did so.[1] Harold Wilson had been faced with the same issue in 1975 and had also relaxed the rules on collective Cabinet responsibility. A key issue, however, would be one of timing.

Ministers who opposed EU membership were particularly keen to lend their voices – and their political profile – to

---

[1] The Secretary of State for Work and Pensions and high-profile Eurosceptic Ian Duncan-Smith did resign in March 2016 but ostensibly in opposition to Treasury cuts to disability benefits.

the Leave campaigns. However, as the position of the government was to renegotiate the UK's relationship with the EU, the Prime Minister had written to Cabinet colleagues to make clear that there would be no change to the rule on collective responsibility until the 'new settlement' negotiations had ended.[2] It was only after the Prime Minister had briefed his Cabinet colleagues following the February European Council summit that the rules were relaxed. In the end, four members of the Cabinet and one minister of state attending Cabinet did not back the government's policy of the UK remaining in the EU.[3] The Cabinet Secretary, Sir Jeremy Heywood issued guidance to civil servants noting that it would not be appropriate or permissible for civil servants to provide briefings or speech material for use by ministers campaigning against the policy of the government. This lead to accusations of bias and politicisation of the civil service.[4]

The second restriction on the conduct of government arose from section 125 of the 2000 Act which prevents the government and other bodies whose expenses are paid out of public funds from publishing material relevant to the referendum or to issues relevant to the referendum question. This period of purdah applies for the four weeks leading up to the

---

[2] C Oliver, *Unleashing Demons: The Inside Story of Brexit* (Hodder and Stoughton, 2016).

[3] Chris Grayling (Leader of the House), Michael Gove (Justice Secretary), John Whittingdale (Culture Secretary), Theresa Villiers (Norther Ireland Secretary) and Priti Patel (Minister of State for Employment).

[4] The Cabinet Secretary defended the guidance issued to civil servants in oral evidence to the House of Commons Public Administration and Constitutional Affairs Committee: HC 792 (2 March 2016).

date of the referendum. However, when introduced to Parliament, the European Referendum Bill had proposed disapplying section 125. But as a sign of the divisions with the Conservative Party and as an effect of the slim majority obtained by the Conservatives in the 2015 election, an Opposition amendment reinstating the purdah rules attracted the support of a sufficient number of rebel Conservative MPs to amend the bill.

The date of the referendum had not been resolved by the European Referendum Act. It simply provided for a referendum to be held by 31 December 2017, leaving it up to ministers to decide by regulations the precise date for the referendum. For several reasons, it was more likely that the referendum would take place in 2016 than 2017. First, it was clear that the Prime Minister wanted to get on with the referendum following the general election. Secondly, in the second half of 2017, the UK was due to hold the rotating presidency of the EU Council of Ministers. It would have been extremely difficult for the UK to be engaging in a renegotiation of its membership and then running a referendum campaign while at the same time taking charge of the meetings of the EU Council.

In terms of 2016, the government's preference might have been for a May ballot. That would have given it just enough time to complete its renegotiation and have a ten-week campaign. However, the Electoral Commission's advice was the referendum should not coincide with other elections. On 5 May 2016, numerous elections were being held including elections to the Scottish Parliament, Welsh and Northern Ireland Assemblies as well as the London Mayoral election.

The government had accepted this, and the European Referendum Act made clear that the referendum could not take place on either 5 May 2016 or 4 May 2017 when English local authority elections are held.

In many ways, it would have made sense to hold the referendum in September 2016. Indeed, there would be a considerable advantage in having the campaign run through August when Parliament would be in recess and normal government business would be quieter making it easier to apply the rules on purdah.[5] A September plebiscite would also give the Prime Minister more time, if necessary, to undertake the reforms and renegotiation that would precede the referendum. But aside from the potential delay that a September referendum might entail, the main reason for avoiding September was the fear that newspaper and television headlines could be dominated by a summer refugee crisis.

The summer months of 2015 had already produced harrowing scenes of hundreds of thousands of refugees from conflicts in Syria, Afghanistan, Somalia and elsewhere making their way into Europe through Italy and Greece, destined for Germany and other EU countries. The refugee crisis had dominated political attention in Europe and overshadowed the meetings of the European Council at a time when the UK was seeking to press its case for reform and renegotiation. The refugee crisis also fuelled the intensifying political attention being paid to issues of migration and controlling borders. The consequence was that opinion crystallised around a June

---

[5] S Payne, 'When will the EU Referendum be held? Here are three possible dates', http://blogs.spectator.co.uk (2 September 2015).

referendum. Even if the deal on the UK's 'new settlement' had to wait until the February 2016 European Council, there would be enough time for the referendum campaign.

On 3 March 2016, the European Union Referendum (Date of referendum etc) Regulations 2016 designated 23 June 2016 as the date of the referendum. That meant that the ten-week 'referendum period' – significant in triggering the campaign rules of the 2000 Act – would commence on 15 April 2016. At the institutional heart of the regulation of the campaign stood the Electoral Commission. Not only was it responsible for reviewing the referendum question and providing guidance on the timing of the referendum, it served a more overt regulatory function in registering campaign groups and ensuring that 'permitted participants' acted within the financial and other constraints imposed upon them.

Under the legislative framework, the Electoral Commission could designate lead campaign group status on a body campaigning for the outcome on either side of the referendum, or a body on one side only or not to designate any body at all. In designating a lead campaign group, the Electoral Commission must decide whether an organisation has the capacity to represent adequately those campaigning for an outcome and, if more than one organisation applies for the designation, which of them represents to the greatest extent those campaigning for an outcome. The core benefit of being a designated lead campaign organisation would be the ability to spend up to £7 million; to have access to the electoral role and to be able to make one free distribution of information to voters; and the right to make referendum campaign broadcasts. While this would not exclude other groups from registering as campaigners, their spending limits would be capped for expenditure incurred during the ten-week referendum period. Self-evidently, designation as a lead campaigner would give an organisation a high level of control over the tone and content of the debate as well as the flow of information towards voters. On 13 April 2016 – two days before the start of the referendum period – the Electoral Commission designated two lead campaigners.

For the Remain outcome, only one group applied for, and was designated as the lead campaigner – 'Britain Stronger in Europe'. However, three organisations sought lead campaigner designation for the Leave outcome – 'Vote Leave', 'GO Movement' and the 'Trade Union and Socialist Coalition' with the real choice being between Vote Leave and GO Movement. The competition for lead campaigner status highlighted the different splits and factions on the Leave side, especially between, on the one hand, those with a more direct association to the United Kingdom Independence Party (UKIP) and the campaigning group Leave.EU (supported financially by Arron Banks), and on the other hand, a more mainstream political group of mainly Eurosceptic Conservative politicians (including Michael Gove and, later, Boris Johnson) backing Vote Leave. The Electoral Commission's evaluation didn't find much to choose between the two submissions but concluded that Vote Leave should be the designated lead campaigner for the Leave outcome; none of which prevented those organisations associated with the GO Movement – like Grassroots Out backed by Nigel Farage (UKIP) and Kate Hoey (Labour) – from registering as permitted participants.

Apart from political parties, permitted participants were entitled to incur expenditure during the referendum period of up to £700,000. For political parties, the ceilings were formulated depending on performance at the 2015 General Election. Accordingly, both Labour and Conservatives were free to spend up to £7 million each, UKIP up to £4 million, the Liberal Democrats up to £3 million and the nationalist parties up to £700,000. To monitor compliance, permitted participants submitted expenditure reports by 23 September 2016 for expenditure of less than £250,000, and by 23 December 2016 for expenditure of more than £250,000 (to be independently audited).

On 24 February 2017, the Electoral Commission published figures showing just how much had been spent by the different registered parties and participants.[6] Overall £27 million was spent with the Remain side spending just over £16 million and the Leave side £11.5 million. The designated lead campaigners each spent £6.7 million. In terms of the UK political parties, on the Remain side, the Labour Party spent £4.8 million, while the Liberal Democrats spent £2.25 million. On the Leave side, UKIP spent £1.3 million of their £4 million limit. As for sub-national political parties, the SNP spent just £90,000 of the £700,000 they could have spent on the Remain side, compared with the £425,000 spent by the Democratic Unionist Party in backing Leave. The Electoral Commission also announced that it was carrying out further investigations into missing information from the lead

---

[6] Electoral Commission, 'Details of major campaign spending during EU referendum', www.electoralcommission.org.uk (24 February 2017).

campaign groups as well as some of the other registered participants.

It is one thing to control campaign finances and another to seek to regulate the content of referendum campaigns. The production and distribution of information, analysis, beliefs, claims and counterclaims is central to any referendum. The campaign context organises and directs these resources towards voters in the formation of their opinions, and then linking those opinions to the subject matter to be decided.[7] A key issue for any country is what role, if any, to give to government or publicly funded bodies in the provision of information.

Under sections 6 and 7 of the European Referendum Act 2015, the government was required to present certain reports to Parliament.[8] It is not obvious that these documents had any real prominence in the campaign beyond their repetition of the sorts of arguments that the government was making generally about its case for the UK remaining in the EU. More visible, and more controversial, was the decision by the government to spend £9.3 million publishing and distributing to all

---

[7] SB Hobolt, 'When Europe matters: the impact of political information on voting behaviour in EU referendums' (2005) 15(1) *Journal of Elections, Public Opinion and Parties* 85.

[8] A report on the outcome of the renegotiation – published as *The Best of Both Worlds: The United Kingdom's Special Status in a Reformed European Union* – a report on alternatives to EU membership – published as *Alternatives to Membership: Possible Models for the United Kingdom Outside of the European Union* – and a report on rights and obligations – published as *Rights and Obligations of European Union Membership*. The government also published a report on the Article 50 process for withdrawal from the EU.

households a leaflet recommending that the UK should remain in the EU. The leaflet drew criticism that both sides of the argument were not being presented in an even-handed way and an e-petition critical of the leaflet attracted more than 200,000 signatures, prompting an official government response. Unsurprisingly, the government rejected the criticism and pointed to the precedent of the Labour government's decision to produce a leaflet backing membership of the EEC in 1975.

It is useful to compare the UK's approach with that of Ireland and the Referendum Commissions established in advance of its EU-related referendums. For the second Lisbon Treaty referendum, the Irish Referendum Commission produced a guide to the Lisbon Treaty that was distributed to all households. It also established a dedicated website and ran television and information campaigns about the main issues. The Referendum Commission did not replace the campaigns on either side and nor did it adjudicate between the claims made on either side. For the UK's EU referendum, the UK's Electoral Commission distributed a leaflet to voters focusing on issues of eligibility to vote, voter registration and the formalities of voting. However, the two designated lead campaigns were each afforded two pages in the leaflet to set out their arguments. Otherwise, the different sides were free – within their spending limits – to conduct their own campaigns.

The Leave campaign had a difficult start to its campaign not least because it was not clear until days before the referendum period began who would be entitled to be the lead campaigner. Before the purdah period kicked in on 27 May 2016, there would also be six weeks of the referendum campaign during which time government could actively pursue its policy of remaining in the EU, and contest the claims and assertions of Leave campaigners. This also gave the government a clear deadline by which to publish reports in support of its position. Particularly noteworthy in that regard was an analysis released by the Treasury days before the purdah deadline in which it was predicted that Brexit would create a recession, loss of jobs and a currency devaluation. The report was heavily criticised by Leave campaigners, who challenged the economic assumptions behind the report and indeed, the role of 'experts' in public decision-making. At a more institutional level, it was even suggested that a traditionally sceptical Treasury had been overtly politicised towards supporting a Remain vote.[9] For other observers, while the Treasury analysis itself was consistent with the analytical standards of departmental reports, the presentation of the findings on the Treasury website in ways that echoed the political spin placed on the report by the then Chancellor had drawn the civil service more directly into the political arena.[10] The negative reactions to the work of the Treasury would later be criticised as a 'consequence of departmental cultural hubris' in a report prepared by Lord Kerslake, the former head of the Civil Service.[11]

The Vote Leave slogan of 'take back control' became the unifying feature of its campaign. The central message was

[9] C Giles, 'How a Eurosceptic Treasury became Remain's anti-Brexit champion', *Financial Times* (31 May 2016).
[10] UK in a Changing Europe, written evidence to the House of Commons Public Administration and Constitutional Affairs Committee inquiry 'Lessons learned from the EU referendum' (September 2016).
[11] Lord Kerslake, 'Rethinking the Treasury' (February 2017).

a nationalistic one of the recovery of control over democracy, law, trade, money, people and borders. It was a simple slogan that the Remain campaign neither matched nor displaced. Taking control was also a narrative that cut across the Left and Right of politics, creating its own new political centre-ground. Meanwhile, the traditional centre-ground political consensus on EU membership had fractured not just on the Right, but also on the Left as the Labour Party leadership appeared to prefer to watch the Right split than make a conscious attempt either to make a Left-wing case for EU membership,[12] or to provide effective and visible leadership support for the Stronger In campaign. Despite the money spent by Labour during the campaign, voters often did not know that the position of the party was to back EU membership. With Vote Leave forging a new anti-EU centre-ground around a range of themes and with UKIP cultivating its own voter base around its traditional themes like controlling immigration, the momentum building behind a vote to leave the EU was clear. Oddly, the combination of an official Vote Leave campaign and an unofficial UKIP campaign seemed to work, despite the obvious tensions between the various parties and personalities.[13]

For the Remain campaign, the focal point was the risks to the economy, jobs and investment that might result from a decision to leave the EU. Deploying language that had

---

[12] A half-hearted effort can be seen in P Mason, 'The Left-wing case for Brexit (one day)', *The Guardian* (16 May 2016).

[13] HD Clarke, M Goodwin and P Whitely, *Brexit: Why Britain Voted to Leave the European Union* (Cambridge University Press, 2017).

been used in the context of the Scottish independence referendum, campaigners on the Leave side challenged these accounts as being examples of 'Project Fear'. Of course, there was equally a 'Project Fear' being stoked by those elements on the Leave side closest to UKIP, and in the tabloid media of the *Daily Mail* and *Express* newspapers, that preyed on fears about immigration. The low-point came when Nigel Farage unveiled UKIP's 'Breaking Point' poster: an image not of EU migrant workers but of refugees, prompting the official Vote Leave campaign to distance itself from the poster, while others suggested it incited racial hatred.

Overall, the campaigns were believed by many to have done little to provide useful information to voters and to have resulted in statements and assertions that were either completely untrue or exaggerated.[14] In policing the referendum, the Electoral Commission made its position clear that it is not, and cannot act as, a 'Truth Commission'.[15] Organisations like Full Fact and Channel 4's Fact Check did, however, seek to test claims. The British Broadcasting Corporation (BBC), however, came under attack for its apparent unwillingness to challenge or correct assertions. Provided the claims on either side were portrayed equally, then the BBC could legitimately say that it was acting impartially.[16]

---

[14] Perhaps the clearest example of controversy was the repeated assertion that the UK paid £350 million a week to the EU.

[15] The 2016 EU Referendum, www.electoralcommission.org.uk (Electoral Commission, September 2016).

[16] James Harding, the BBC's Director of News and Current Affairs wrote this defence of the BBC's referendum coverage: 'A truly balanced view from the BBC: don't blame us for Brexit', *The Guardian* (25 September 2016).

As with elections, different newspapers took different sides. Broadsheets like *The Times, The Guardian* and the *Financial Times* backed retention of EU membership, while *The Sun, Daily Mail, Daily Telegraph, Sunday Times* and *Daily Express* all supported the UK leaving the EU. Media analysis of their coverage when weighted to take into consideration their respective circulation showed that around 80 per cent of the coverage backed withdrawal.[17] But this was also a campaign fought on social media which had its highs – the availability of analysis from a wide range of organisations – and its lows – the further perpetuation of myths and falsehoods, the creation of 'echo chamber' politics that confirmed rather than contested opinions,[18] as well as trolling. As if to sum up the quality of the EU referendum campaign, the Oxford English Dictionary's word of the year for 2016 was 'post-truth'.

As the date of the referendum drew nearer and as the campaigns intensified, it was important to both sides to ensure that its supporters were registered to vote. The deadline for voters to register for the referendum was midnight on 7 June 2016. However, amidst the campaign urging people to register – and with people already registered interpreting repeated warnings about not losing out on the right to vote as a basis for making multiple attempts to register – the government website handling registrations crashed. Secondary legislation was passed to enable registrations to be extended to 23.59

---

[17] Loughborough University Centre for Research in Communication and Culture, 'Media coverage of the EU referendum' (5th Report), http://blog .lboro.ac.uk/crcc/eu-referendum (27 June 2016).

[18] J Chater, 'What the EU referendum result tells us about the dangers of the echo chamber', *New Statesman* (6 July 2016).

on 9 June. However, the move was criticised by UKIP who considered it to be an attempt to swell the pool of likely Remain voters.

For three days, campaign time stopped. On 16 June – a week before the referendum vote – the Labour MP Jo Cox was murdered in her constituency. Her killer, Thomas Mair, repeatedly stabbed and shot the MP. At his trial, the jury was told that Mair was a white supremacist who, during the attack, had shouted slogans about putting 'Britain first' and 'keep Britain independent'. Campaigning resumed on the 19 June.

The campaigns ended when voters went to the polls on 23 June. At 7.01 on 24 June 2016, Jenny Watson the Chief Counting Officer for the referendum and Chair of the Electoral Commission announced the referendum result: 17,410,742 votes were in favour of Leave; 16,141,241 were in favour of Remain. The UK had voted to leave the EU.

Part II

Time of Brexit

6

Control over Borders

The issue of migration was a primary focal point for the referendum campaign. In his renegotiation with the EU, David Cameron had attempted to find a mechanism that would reduce incentives on EU nationals to come to the UK. The mechanism that was agreed stopped short of the sort of cap on numbers or 'emergency brake' which had been discussed. This was important given that David Cameron's Conservative Party had been elected to government in 2015 with its election manifesto continuing to pledge to reduce net migration to the UK to the 'tens of thousands' as set out in its 2010 manifesto. Yet it was clear that the government was significantly adrift from its target. Despite having control over non-EU migration, overall net migration was increasing and immigration from the EU was playing a role in the overall figures. Meanwhile, the refugee crisis had also added to anxieties about movements of people across borders, including border-free movement within the EU's Schengen area.

Both Vote Leave and the United Kingdom Independence Party (UKIP) argued that outside of the EU, the UK would be able to exert greater control over its borders. Anxieties about migration were fuelled by sections of the print media that displayed a daily obsession with 'migrants'. These anxieties were exploited by UKIP during the campaign with its controversial 'Breaking Point' poster. It was also claimed by Leave campaigners that European courts made it difficult or impossible to deport criminals, though it was unclear whether this was principally an EU law or European Convention issue. The concerns were often contradictory: were migrants in the UK to take jobs or take welfare benefits? Migrant labour was also blamed for placing pressures on public services, and yet economically active migrants contribute to the tax revenues that pay for public services as well as providing a source of labour for valued public services like the National Health Service.

The Remain campaign claimed that leaving the EU would not in fact increase control over net migration especially if the 'points-based' immigration system proposed by UKIP and supported by prominent Vote Leave campaigners including Boris Johnson, Michael Gove, Priti Patel and Gisela Stuart[1] was put in place. There was also an attempt to shift the focus of debate around free movement onto the benefits that arose from EU-facilitated free movement: low-cost air travel, reduced mobile phone roaming charges and access to emergency healthcare as a tourist. Nonetheless, these arguments gained little traction. They tended to emphasise episodic, even optional, benefits that were, moreover, experienced by travelling outside the UK to EU countries. They didn't speak to the experience of life in the UK itself.

By the time of the June 2016 referendum, estimated annual net migration to the UK – the number of people moving to the UK minus those leaving the UK – stood at

---

[1] Vote Leave, 'Restoring trust in immigration policy – a points-based non-discriminatory immigration system', www.voteleavetakecontrol.org (1 June 2016).

335,000 people. The estimated total number of EU nationals moving annually to the UK was at its highest at 284,000 people. Net migration of EU nationals was estimated at 189,000 or just less than the net estimate of non-EU nationals.[2] If we differentiate between migrants from states that were Member States prior to the 2004 EU enlargement – the EU15 – and those from the post-2004 enlargement of the EU – the EU8 – and subsequent enlargement to include Bulgaria and Romania – the EU2 – we can identify some trends. Of these, perhaps the most important is the very significant spike in migration from Bulgaria and Romania following the lifting of transitional restrictions in 2014.

Up until the early 2000s there was a broadly equitable balance between people leaving the UK and EU15 nationals moving to the UK. Migration from the EU15 began to grow from this period and accelerated following the financial and economic crisis with estimated EU15 migration to the UK reaching 138,000 or 49 per cent of the total EU migration to the UK by the end of 2015. In net terms in the year preceding the referendum, 84,000 EU15 nationals were estimated to have moved to the UK. Immigration from the EU8 to the UK peaked in 2007 at 112,000 falling to an estimated 73,000 in the year preceding the referendum (or 42,000 in net terms). However, this fall was offset by the sharp spike in immigration

---

[2] 196,000 non-EU nationals (net) were estimated to have move to the UK. To arrive at the overall net migration figure one needs to deduct the number of UK citizens moving back to the UK. Figures from Office for National Statistics, *Migration Statistics Quarterly Report: Dec 2016*, www.ons.gsi.gov.uk (1 December 2016); and ONS interactive online tool, https://visual.ons.gov.uk/explore-50-years-of-international-migration/.

from the EU2 once transitional restrictions on Bulgarian and Romanian nationals ended. By the time of the referendum, estimated annual net migration from the EU2 was 61,000; some 25 per cent of the total EU migration to the UK. Taken together, long-term immigration from the EU was rising from 2012 so that by the time of the referendum, just less than half of immigrants to the UK came from within the EU.[3]

Tim Shipman's detailed and insightful analysis of the background to the EU referendum suggests that had David Cameron's new settlement negotiations sought and obtained an 'emergency brake' on the numbers of EU migrants coming to the UK, this might have tipped the balance in favour of the UK remaining in the EU.[4] At least one EU academic lawyer suggested that perhaps more could have been done to emphasise the power of states to derogate from free movement principles on treaty-derived grounds of public policy,[5] although it does need to be acknowledged how limited this derogation is in the context of direct discrimination against nationals from other EU states. The decision to focus instead on restricting access to in-work benefits became regarded as an illustration of civil servants and lawyers restricting the Prime Minister's room for manoeuvre. This narrative subsequently gained further ground with the resignation of Sir Ivan Rogers, the UK ambassador to the EU on 3 January 2017. Sir Ivan and others' advice as

---

[3] See n 2.
[4] T Shipman, *All Out War: The Full Story of How Brexit Sank Britain's Political Class* (Harper Collins, 2016).
[5] G Davies, 'Could it all have been avoided? Brexit and Treaty-permitted restrictions on movement of workers', www.europeanlawblog.eu (18 August 2016).

to what was politically and legally feasible was important to David Cameron's approach to the negotiations. Following the referendum, Sir Ivan's attitude of speaking 'truth to power' was regarded by some Brexit supporters as mere 'pessimism'. But it wasn't a lack of optimism or a failure of negotiating strategy that meant that Prime Minister Cameron opted for controls on access to benefits. A push for treaty change would have significantly altered the timeframe for the referendum.

However, the appeal of the UK as a destination for EU nationals has largely been its labour market rather than its welfare system. By the time of the referendum, 57 per cent of EU migrants had a definite job. The percentage of EU15 and EU8 migrants with a definite job had, however, declined from the previous year.[6] Yet this migrant entry to the labour market was not at the expense of UK nationals looking for work. Looking at the data, although UK employment rates fell following the financial and economic crisis, in the period from 2012 (during which time EU migration rose), employment rates increased from 70.3 to 74.5 per cent.[7] Migrant labour was accessing new jobs, not least as chains of coffee and sandwich shops expanded their networks across the UK. In other words, there is no fixed reservoir of jobs but rather a constantly shifting labour market. Losses of employment are associated with changes in technology and global competition rather than a burgeoning number of EU-national baristas.

---

[6] See *Migration Statistics Quarterly Report: Dec 2016*, see n 2 in this chapter.

[7] Office for National Statistics, *UK Labour Market: Dec 2016*, www.ons.gsi .gov.uk (14 December 2016).

For those EU nationals without a job but seeking employment, EU law itself does not require Member States to provide financial support to job-seekers within the first three months of residence and, thereafter, the right to invoke the principle of equal treatment to access social assistance has been qualified and limited by the Court of Justice in several rulings. In the week before the EU referendum, the Court rejected a European Commission complaint that the UK's habitual residence test – when applied to in-work child benefits and tax credits – violated EU rules. Even without changing the resources of EU law available to the UK government through the 'new settlement', a combination of domestic rules and the exploitation of existing capacities within EU law afforded the UK government opportunities to exercise certain types of control over access to benefits for migrant EU nationals.[8]

However, two other assertions were often made about the effects of increased immigration to the UK: it depressed wages and put public services under strain. During the referendum campaign, former Work and Pensions Secretary and leading Leave campaigner Iain Duncan-Smith suggested that UK wages were 10 per cent lower because of rising EU immigration. But as the Centre for Economic Performance reported, this dramatic fall in wages during this period was a consequence of the post-2008 recession and not increasing immigration: coincidence is

---

[8] J Shaw, 'Between law and political truth? Member States preferences, EU free movement rules and national immigration law' (2015) 17 *Cambridge Yearbook of European Legal Studies* 247.

not causation.[9] Indeed, right across the EU, reductions in wages was a common response to the crisis as a means of averting more significant job losses.

As for public services like education, transport, health and social care, these are typically delivered at a local level. Any impact of immigration on such services is difficult to evidence let alone to break it down as between EU and non-EU migration. Under the last Labour government, a Migration Impacts Fund had been established in 2009 with £35 million available annually, funded by a £50 levy on immigration applications from non-European Economic Area (EEA) nationals. The distribution of funds between local authorities saw some areas receiving hundreds of thousands of pounds while others received substantially less. In any event, in 2010, the Coalition government withdrew the fund as a cost-saving measure.[10] Indeed, in the crucial time period leading up to the referendum, very significant pressure on public services was coming not from the effects of immigration but from government policies connected to deficit reduction and fiscal discipline. This more local dimension of immigration – explored further below – also draws attention to potential North–South and other disparities in terms of the geographic distribution of wealth, employment opportunities and pressures on public services.

---

[9] J Wadsworth, S Dhingra, G Ottaviano and J Van Reenen, 'Brexit and the impact of immigration on the UK', *CEP Brexit Analysis No. 5*, www.cep.lse.ac.uk (May 2016)

[10] M Gower, 'A new "Controlling Migration Fund" for the UK?', *House of Commons Library Briefing Paper*, Number 7673 (1 August 2016).

In thinking about the locality of immigration, statistically it can be difficult to tell the composition of local populations. Census data is helpful but the last UK census was in 2011 and it is difficult to find sources of data post-2011 that distinguish between EU and non-EU migration flows. This time period is particularly sensitive. From 2004 to 2011, migrant workers from EU8 states had to register under the UK's Worker Registration Scheme. For workers from Romania and Bulgaria, tougher restrictions applied for seven years up until the end of December 2013. From January 2014 onwards, nationals of Romania and Bulgaria also enjoyed unrestricted rights of free movement. So the period from 2011 onwards is particularly interesting but poses an issue in terms of data at a local level. One useful proxy indicator is National Insurance registrations (NINos) where not only is it possible to identify EU nationals, it is also possible to distinguish between nationals of the 'old' and 'new' EU states as well as the post-2004 EU8 and post-2007 EU2 states.[11]

Looking at individual counting areas with the strongest Leave votes – of more than 68 per cent – these were typically grouped in the West and East Midlands and the East and North-East of England. Local counting areas in the Tees Valley in the North-East all showed significant Leave votes with Middlesbrough, Hartlepool and Redcar and Cleveland each returning Leave results in excess of 65 per cent of the

---

[11] However, as the Office for National Statistics cautions: 'NINo registrations data are not a good measure of [long-term immigration], but they do provide a valuable source of information to highlight emerging changes in patterns of migration': Information Note, www.ons .gov.uk (12 May 2016).

votes cast. In an area like Middlesbrough, while the 2011 census actually indicated a decline in the overall number of inhabitants – with the Tees Valley showing a net population outflow – its Black, Asian and Minority Ethnic (BAME) population proportion doubled and unemployment rose (with an employment rate well below the national average).

If we look at nationals from post-2004 EU states registering to work under the Worker Registration Scheme, the numbers in the Tees Valley were lower than elsewhere in the region and declined significantly from 2007 to the scheme's closure in 2011. Indeed, in the post-2011 period the number of EU8 migrants resident in Middlesbrough, Hartlepool, Redcar and Cleveland and making National Insurance registrations were comparatively small and relatively stable. But following the removal of restrictions on nationals from Romania and Bulgaria from 2014, Middlesbrough showed a distinct increase in NI registrations from 25 in 2013 to 145 in 2014 and 434 in 2015.

While London voters overall voted for Remain – indeed seven of the top ten Remain constituencies were in London – the adjacent constituencies of Barking and Dagenham, and Havering returned Leave votes. Based on the 2011 census, Havering was the least diverse London borough with over 80 per cent of residents being of White British ethnicity compared to a London average of 45 per cent. Yet, as between the 2001 and 2011 census, Havering's BAME population doubled, largely drawn from Africa, the Caribbean and Pakistan.[12] While BAME voters might have been expected to

---

[12] London Borough of Havering, 'Demographic, diversity and socio-economic profile of Havering's population', www.havering.gov.uk (January 2013).

have a preference to vote Remain, post-referendum data does suggest that in some London wards with high numbers of residents of Asian origin, a distinctive pattern of voting Leave can be detected.[13]

Looking again at the 2011 census data, in Havering, only 2.3 per cent of residents reported holding an EU passport compared to 82.1 per cent holding UK passports. The highest percentage of worker registrations from the EU8 between 2004 and 2011 was 0.19 per cent of the working age population compared to a range of 0.39–0.54 per cent for London and 0.3–0.57 per cent for England as a whole.[14] From 2011 onwards, the number of migrants from EU8 states making National Insurance registrations in Havering continued to be relatively stable each year and the total of less than 2,000 registrations across that period was significantly lower than in a 'Remain' area like Ealing with almost 19,000 registrations. But in 2014 – following the end of restrictions on their nationals – the number of registrations from Romanian and Bulgarian nationals shot up to over 1,000 per year, with the total number of registrations for these nationals being almost double that of the EU8 across the same period. What also appeared to change in Havering between 2001 and 2014 was unemployment. Beginning towards the end of 2008 and lasting until early 2014, unemployment – and particularly male unemployment – doubled. But, by the time of the referendum campaign in

---

[13] M Rosenbaum, 'Local voting figures shed new light on EU referendum', www.bbc.co.uk/news (6 February 2017).
[14] See www.haveringdata.net.

spring 2016 unemployment rates had fallen back to their 2008 levels.

These examples are simply a snapshot. We find a mix of experiences of increasing or decreasing local populations; increased non-EU immigration; fluctuations in local employment opportunities; and a spike in immigration from Bulgaria and Romania. This tends to confirm that, rather than there being an 'immigration paradox' – in which cities like London with high levels of immigration were more likely to vote for the UK to stay in the EU – it is a more localised experience of population change combined with other factors, including levels of educational attainment[15] – that may go some way towards explaining voter behaviour.[16]

The issue of immigration is difficult for mainstream political parties. The political saliency of the issue has increased over time, cutting across both Right and Left and exposing tensions not just between political parties but within them. It clearly divided those Conservatives for whom a cap on numbers was a political red line and those perhaps more inclined to the idea that increased immigration signalled a growing economy with numbers adjusting as labour market forces played out. Meanwhile, the Labour Party had its own troubles with immigration. While out on the General Election campaign trail in Rochdale in April 2010, the then Labour Prime Minister Gordon Brown encountered Gillian Duffy. Following a conversation in which the Labour-supporting woman expressed her concerns about levels of immigration,

---

[15] Rosenbaum, 'Local voting figures shed new light on EU referendum'.
[16] 'Britain's immigration paradox', *The Economist* (8 July 2016).

Brown was recorded as referring to Duffy as a 'bigoted woman'. A political firestorm ensued. Labour lost the General Election. Some six years later, and interviewed by a British tabloid newspaper, Duffy stated she was voting for the UK to leave the EU.

If the control of immigration was important to referendum politics, then post-referendum, UKIP expected to be a major beneficiary of Labour's apparent difficulties in connecting with its traditional voter base, including over its position on immigration. However, as two by-elections held on 23 February 2017 demonstrated – one in Stoke-on-Trent (which voted overwhelmingly for Brexit) and one in Copeland – it may be that it is the Conservatives that have squeezed Labour more than UKIP.[17]

Brexit will have its own effect on immigration but as with the wider economy, it is difficult to predict precisely what the effects will be and when they will manifest themselves. Figures reported in February 2017 showed a fall of 49,000 people in the overall estimated net migration figures, with the numbers of migrants equally split between EU and non-EU nationals. Migration from the EU8 decreased but, consistent with the trend since 2014, the number of migrants from the EU2 was at its highest levels.[18] As Portes has noted, employment growth in the UK prior to the referendum was showing signs of easing and is likely to reduce economic

---

[17] UKIP's new leader Paul Nuttall failed to beat Labour in contesting the Stoke seat, while the Conservatives took Copeland from Labour, a seat Labour had held for eighty years.

[18] Office for National Statistics, *Migration Statistics Quarterly Report: February 2017*, www.ons.gsi.gov.uk (23 February 2017).

migration. Negotiations on the rights of EU nationals currently legally resident in the UK, the legal uncertainty, mixed with emotional disquiet may also lead European nationals to decide to quit the UK.[19] In the end, the effects of the referendum on immigration may lie less in the power of governments to exert direct control over migration and more in economic and wider social factors, including the control which migrant EU nationals and their families will take into their own hands in deciding where they wish to live.

[19] J Portes 'Brexit, migration and the labour market', www.niesr.ac.uk
    (17 August 2016).

7

Control over Money

Emblazoned across posters, leaflets and big red buses, the Vote Leave campaign stated in stark terms that membership of the EU cost UK taxpayers £350 million per week. It was a figure repeatedly challenged by the Remain campaign and by fact-checking organisations who pointed out that it ignored the automatic deduction of a rebate before any contributions are made to the EU budget. This was, after all, the rebate that Margaret Thatcher had secured in 1984 and which helped create the political conditions for a new impetus to complete the European Single Market.[1] It wasn't even the case that money was 'sent' and then a proportion 'returned': it was never sent in the first place.

Actual contributions vary between years depending on changes in Gross National Income, but with the application of the rebate, in 2014 the weekly contribution was more like £282 million or £14.7 billion for the year. The £350 million figure also failed to account for the money transferred back to the UK public sector under a range of EU programmes. Once these are taken into account the Office for National Statistics calculated the UK's net contribution in 2014 at £190 million a week or £9.9 billion for the year.[2]

---

[1] R Whitman, 'On Europe: Margaret Thatcher's lasting legacy', www.chathamhouse.org (9 April 2013).

[2] Source: Office for National Statistics, *UK Perspectives 2016: The UK Contribution to the EU Budget*, http://visual.ons.gov.uk/uk-perspectives-2016-the-uk-contribution-to-the-eu-budget/ (25 May 2016).

But whether the figure was £350 million or some other figure probably wasn't relevant. The point was that voters either couldn't see or didn't value what they got for their money, underlying what has sometimes been seen as a 'transactionalist' approach to EU membership rather than a more value-driven concept of membership. Voters were, however, clearer that the UK had experienced a post-financial crisis period of austerity and budget cuts. EU contributions were being made as domestic spending was being squeezed. If we are to understand what taking back control over money might mean, answers lie in the different features of EU and domestic public spending and the relationship between the two.

For the EU 2016 budget, annual spending commitments on all EU policies amounted to €155 billion.[3] By comparison, UK government spending in 2016–17 was expected to be £772 billion, with spending on health alone (£145 billion) amounting to more than the total annual EU budget.[4] These figures tell us something important about the differences between EU and domestic public spending. The main items of domestic expenditure reflect the primary role of the nation state in redistributive policies and the provision of public goods. It is precisely in the areas of welfare, health and education that the EU plays a limited role, principally by ensuring non-discriminatory access to these services for certain beneficiaries under EU law and in creating a framework

---

[3] The annual budget for the EU contains figures for 'commitments' and for 'payments'. Commitments are legal undertakings to spend money whereas payments refer to what is paid out. If a decision is made to cut the actual payments this simply postpones the date when spending occurs.

[4] Source: HM Treasury, *Budget 2016–17*, HC 901 (March 2016).

for co-ordination to ensure continuity of access when people move across borders. The EU itself does not provide these public goods and services.

Instead, EU spending focuses on a set of policy initiatives that reflect the specific tasks and competences of the EU as well as priorities set by EU leaders. To give consistency over time and to set spending ceilings, each annual EU budget is subject to the revenue and expenditure provisions set out in the relevant Multiannual Financial Framework (MFF). Under Article 312(2) of the Treaty on the Functioning of the European Union (TFEU), acting unanimously on a proposal from the Commission, the Council adopts the regulation setting out the MFF, with the consent of the European Parliament. However, national leaders acting through the European Council took overall political control over the 2014–20 MFF,[5] with the then UK Prime Minister David Cameron leading the call for an overall cut in EU spending. The deal finally agreed in February 2013 saw a €34 billion cut compared with the previous MFF period. This was, after all, a time when the EU itself was demanding that Member States – and particularly eurozone states – exercise fiscal discipline and budgetary restraint.

For 2016, the EU annual budget set out principal headings for expenditure: €19 billion allocated to supporting growth, jobs and competitiveness, including €9.5 billion for Horizon 2020, the EU's strategy to support research and innovation; €50 billion for territorial cohesion (tackling

---

[5] R Crowe, 'The European Council and the multiannual financial framework' (2016) 17 *Cambridge Yearbook of European Legal Studies* 69.

economic disparities between different parts of the EU); and
€42 billion supporting farmers under the CAP. The EU budget is, of course, partly spent in the UK.[6] From the EU budget,
the UK is allocated funding through its 'European Structural
and Investment Funds' (ESIF) and the 'European Agricultural
Guarantee Fund' (EAGF). ESIF is a key instrument of EU
cohesion policy and is composed of a number of separate
funds. The most significant funds for UK purposes are the
'European Regional Development Fund' (ERDF) which sup-
ports disadvantaged regions and the 'European Social Fund'
(ESF) which promotes skills and training to support labour
market participation. In terms of the MFF for 2014–20, the UK
is allocated €17.2 billion in funding under the ESIF.

Particularly in its first decade of membership, the UK
was a major beneficiary of EU funding under the EU's cohesion policy, with numerous regions and localities qualifying
for support. The level of support gradually declined, and with
the post-2004 enlargement of the EU – which saw a large
number of less economically developed states join the EU –
funding to the UK reduced rapidly. Bachtler and Begg's analysis suggests that the UK's share of funds declined from
25 per cent in the 1970s to 2.5 per cent by the time of the
referendum.[7] The distribution of funds within the territories
of the UK is also different with Wales (particularly West
Wales and the Valleys), the South-West of England

---

[6] S Ayres, 'UK funding from the EU', House of Commons Library Research
Briefing No. 7847 (29 December 2016).

[7] J Bachtler and I Begg, 'Cohesion and cohesion policies in the UK: what
might Brexit entail?', www.ukandeu.ac.uk (21 March 2016).

(particularly Cornwall) and the North-West of England being the main recipients of ERDF and ESF funding.[8] Yet despite this asymmetric EU expenditure within the UK, the effect was not that constituencies in those regions receiving funding were more likely to vote for the UK to stay in the EU. Indeed, the opposite was clearly the case with 52.5 per cent of voters in Wales and 56.5 per cent of voters in Cornwall voting for the UK to leave the EU.

The EAGF is the principal source of direct payment to farmers under the Common Agricultural Policy (CAP). The MFF allocation to the UK for 2014–20 is €22.5 billion. The position of the National Farmers Union was that it supported the UK's continuing membership of the EU, while recognising that there were diverse views among its members. More broadly, the CAP has always been a source of controversy given the direct subsidies that are given to farmers. The Vote Leave campaign claimed that the CAP kept food prices artificially high (it remains to be seen whether the depreciation of sterling following the referendum will itself increase the price of food imported from the EU). Moreover, with large farming conglomerates receiving particularly significant slices of EU funding, the accusation could also be made that EU membership was simply working for the interests of big business.

Once it is recognised that sums of money flow back to the UK from the EU budget, it becomes even more apparent that there never could have been a £350 million a week Brexit

---

[8] Sheffield Political Economy Research Institute, *UK Regions and Structural and Investment Funds*, SPERI Political Economy Brief No. 24, www.speri.dept.shef.ac.uk (2016).

bonus for the UK to spend on the NHS. The only way of getting close even to the figure of £282 million that took the rebate into account would be to cut to zero all the expenditure on things like research, regional policy and support for farmers that currently comes back out of the EU budget. Certainly in the short term, that doesn't seem a likely prospect with the UK Chancellor committing to maintain current levels of direct payments to farmers under the CAP until 2020. Nonetheless, what does seem likely is that reforms to direct payments to farmers will occur, driven not just by Treasury demands but also the devolution of control over agricultural spending to the devolved administrations (and all subject to compliance with World Trade Organization (WTO) requirements on agricultural subsidies). Having control over money also entails having responsibility for the political choice to spend money on the NHS or on farmers. While that control may be important, the trade-offs it creates may not have been apparent to voters.

Moreover, depending on how the UK defined its future relationship with the EU, the UK could continue to make contributions to the EU budget post-Brexit: Norway contributes around £724 million annually.[9] Continuing contributions would reduce any potential Brexit dividend still further. None of which takes into account any of the potential costs should Brexit have a significant effect on the UK economy. There will simply be much less money to control than voters had in mind when they thought about how much the UK paid for its EU membership and what sort of Brexit bonus might be reaped to spend on valued public services.

[9] Source: www.eu-norway.org.

For the Remain side, one of the principal privileges of EU membership is the UK's participation in the Single Market and the benefits that it brings in terms of tariff- and barrier-free trade. Free trade is not free as in 'costless'. But the costs are principally those involved in supporting the negotiation, adoption, amendment, implementation and enforcement of EU rules. The EU is sometimes described as a form of 'regulatory state' in recognition of the primary role it plays in market liberalisation and market regulation rather that the provision of core state activities like public spending on health, education and welfare.[10] The EU's overall administrative costs are relatively low: 5.7 per cent of the budget or €8.9 billion was allocated for all its administrative costs.[11] Assuming a UK contribution of 8.5 per cent of EU budget commitments, the UK would contribute around €14.5 million a week as its share of the administrative costs of the EU: this compares with around £16 million a week for the administrative budget of the UK's Department for Work and Pensions.[12]

In terms, however, of who benefits from the Single Market, the suggestion could be made that the main beneficiaries of this EU regulatory activity are large corporations engaged in cross-border trade and not the thousands of small businesses for whom domestic markets remain important.

[10] G Majone, 'The regulatory state and its legitimacy problems' (1999) 22(1) *West European Politics* 1.
[11] Source: European Commission, http://ec.europa.eu/budget/annual/index_en.cfm.
[12] Source: HM Treasury, *Public Expenditure. Statistical Analysis* (July 2016). According to the Treasury, the administrative budget for the Department for Work and Pensions in 2015–16 was £835 million.

Of course, economic growth and supply chains mean that small businesses can be beneficiaries too, but perhaps in ways that are less obviously attributable to EU membership. However, when it came to compliance costs (or 'red tape'), the burden of compliance with EU legislative requirements may have felt greater for small and medium-sized enterprises than larger multinational corporations.

The same sorts of arguments about costs and benefits of EU membership have been made at various points in the UK's history of EU membership. What sharpened this concern about control over money at this particular moment in time was its linkage to the policies of austerity and anxieties about where the EU was heading in terms of the deepening of integration within the eurozone.

Following the financial and economic crisis, fiscal discipline and cuts in public spending became the key tenets of government policy in the UK and elsewhere in Europe. In the eurozone, the picture was worse with Greece, Cyprus, Portugal, Ireland and Spain receiving financial support through loans and loan guarantees from variously the EU budget, other EU states, the European Stability Mechanism or the International Monetary Fund. Attached to those loans were an extensive range of conditions from a variety of legal and para-legal sources, entailing significant cuts in public expenditure and increases in taxes for the citizens of indebted states[13] The EU also responded by revising and strengthening existing rules and

---

[13] C Kilpatrick, 'On the rule of law and economic emergency: the degredation of basic legal values in Europe's bailouts' (2015) 35(2) *Oxford Journal of European Legal Studies* 325.

sanctions on public deficits and debt, and put in place new rules to permit EU institutions to evaluate the national budgets of eurozone state and to check for emerging 'macroeconomic imbalances'. With the agreement of a 'fiscal compact', eurozone states also agreed to enshrine in domestic law balanced budget rules, including making domestic constitutional adjustments.[14]

Many of the EU's responses to the crisis simply did not apply to the UK because of the historic stance it has taken on not joining the single currency. Retention of the national currency has been a focal point for different degrees of Euroscepticism and not just the United Kingdom Independence Party (UKIP) variety, although not for nothing does UKIP have a large '£' symbol as the backdrop to its logo. William Hague's spell as leader of the Conservative Party saw him launch a 'Keep the Pound' campaign. At the time, while the then Prime Minister Tony Blair was open to the idea of the UK joining the euro, his then Chancellor Gordon Brown had made entry into the single currency conditional on five economic tests being met, making it difficult for the Prime Minister to make a purely political decision to take the UK into the euro.[15] In the context of David Cameron's renegotiation of the UK's relationship

---

[14] The fiscal compact arose when David Cameron refused to agree a revision to the EU treaties without the UK getting some safeguards for UK financial services in return, leading other EU states to agree the compact as an international treaty, thereby rendering futile the Prime Minister's veto.

[15] E Potton and A Mellows-Facer, 'The euro: background to the five economic tests', House of Commons Library Research Paper 03/53 (4 June 2003).

with the EU, the 'new settlement' deal underscored that financial support to secure the stability of the euro could not entail financial contributions from non-eurozone states like the UK.

Nonetheless, the difficulties experienced by eurozone countries contributed to a heightened voter anxiety about the UK's EU membership. The problems in the eurozone were frequently used to suggest that the euro and the European Union were failing projects and were a manifestation of what happens when nations lose control over their currency. That the EU might respond by deepening integration within the eurozone could constitute evidence of inherent federalist and state-building ambitions while exacerbating a problematic division in the status of EU Member States between eurozone insiders and outsiders. Moreover, the claim that economic 'experts' hadn't predicted the crisis and/or had supported the UK joining the euro became part of a narrative to undermine the forecasts of 'experts' that leaving the EU would itself entail significant economic costs.

But beyond the narrow narratives of the referendum campaign, the wider context for concerns about control over money were to be found in the post-crisis politics of austerity. For voters who had felt the effects of a shrinking public sector both in terms of employment and the provision of public services, rejection of EU membership was an opportunity to challenge ideas that the economy was either simply a product of market forces or the object of a type of post-political technocratic managerialism that seemed to characterise the European response to the crisis. That a Conservative government was backing EU membership while pursuing policies of austerity that were, in any event, consistent with the prevailing European preference for fiscal discipline created a focal point for political resistance, not least for traditional Labour voters. Viewed in this way, we can also see more clearly why the idea of diverting resources from the EU to public spending on the NHS might have resonated strongly with voters.

Of course, voters in Scotland had, in 2015, delivered to Westminster, fifty-six Scottish National Party MPs (out of fifty-nine seats in Scotland) on a policy platform to resist and reform national austerity policies. Some 62 per cent of voters in Scotland had also voted for the UK to remain in the EU. It was apparently possible to be anti-austerity and yet pro-EU membership. But this reflected the different character of Scottish politics not least following the independence referendum where continuing membership of the EU was largely accepted by those seeking independence and those wishing to remain part of the UK. Compared with voters in England, when it came to discussing control over money, Scottish voters had different concerns and alternative resources for political expression outside of the EU referendum. The same may not have been true for voters in Wales for whom the benefits of EU funding may simply not have compensated for the effects of economic change and for whom the institutions of devolution (and the EU preferences of the parties in Wales) were less relevant compared to the effects of UK government policies.

If the legacy of austerity gives us clues as to the reasons why the UK voted to leave the EU, then it also holds important lessons for the rest of the EU. The 'mission legitimacy' of the EU has traditionally rested upon a post-war project of preserving peace and promoting stable, democratic government and an enlarging union of European states.[16] Nonetheless, as de Búrca observes, the *raison d'être* of the EU has been increasingly questioned, not least following the economic crisis.[17] As she puts it: why should EU citizens 'suffer unemployment, economic hardship and austerity in order to "save" the euro and the European Union?' The disillusionment felt by voters in the UK about its experience of EU membership is not a uniquely British phenomenon. As one observer has described it, there is now a 'European union of disenchantment'.[18]

What will remain to be seen following Brexit, is how this disenchantment plays out in elections in the founding EU states of France, Germany and the Netherlands. But Brexit may also produce its own sense of disillusion within the UK once the relative costs and benefits of non-EU membership become apparent, not least if it turns out that there is little if any new money over which to exercise control.

---

[16] JHH Weiler, '60 years since the first European Community: reflections on messianism' (2011) 22 *European Journal of International Law* 303.

[17] G de Búrca, 'Europe's *raison d'être*' in D Kochenov and F Amtenbrink (eds), *The European Union's Shaping of the International Legal Order* (Cambridge University Press, 2014).

[18] C Bickerton, 'Brexit is not the property of the political right: the left is disenchanted too', *The Guardian* (22 June 2016).

8

Democratic Control

Making democracy work within nation states is never easy.
Making it work in the context of a Union of twenty-eight
states is a fundamental challenge. Perhaps one broad area of
agreement between Leave and Remain voters is a feeling that
many of the decisions which affect daily lives are taken in
ways that voters often don't comprehend. Decision-making in
the EU is one context – but one of many – where the exercise
of power by institutions appears to be beyond the control of
familiar national institutions and mechanisms of democratic
accountability.

Arguments about the nature and extent of the EU's
'democratic deficit' have long featured in European studies.[1]
At an abstract level, it is said that as there is no single
European people – or *demos* – democracy in the EU is simply
an impossibility at least in the way it is practiced within nation
states.[2] For others, the EU doesn't actually need much by way
of democracy inasmuch as it is conceptualised as a technocratic body fulfilling the mandate laid down by Member States

---

[1] See eg F Scharpf, *Governing in Europe: Effective and Democratic?*
(Oxford University Press 1999); A Føllesdal and S Hix, 'Why there is
a democratic deficit in the EU: a response to Majone and Moravcsik'
(2006) 44(3) *Journal of Common Market Studies* 533.
[2] For discussion see JHH Weiler, UR Haltern and FC Mayer,
'European democracy and its critique' (1995) 18(3) *West European
Politics* 4.

in the treaties.[3] But if we accept that the exercise of power by the EU is a problem for democracy, potential responses have tended to be cast in institutional terms.

At EU level, the question of democratic control is related to the particular EU inter-institutional style of decision-making and the relationships between key political institutions: the European Council, the European Commission, the Council of Ministers and the European Parliament (EP). This parade of institutions is baffling to most voters and even causes confusion among those with greater understanding of how the EU works. The idea that to understand these institutions is to require a type of specialised knowledge exacerbates the sense of the remoteness of these institutions – and the people who study them – from the everyday preoccupations of citizens. It is hardly surprising that perhaps voters conclude that the better strategy is to seek to restore democratic control to more familiar domestic institutions.

Certainly the referendum debate attempted to increase the level of information about the EU's decision-making processes. But time and again the focal point of discussion returned to what seemed like the nub of the matter: the complaint that decision were being taken by unelected elites. Concerns about democratic control found a specific target in the form of the European Commission.

In thinking about the role of the European Commission and concerns about democratic control, we can begin to unravel the issues across four dimensions. The

---

[3] A Moravcsik, 'Reassessing legitimacy in the European Union' (2002) 40(4) *Journal of Common Market Studies* 603.

first dimension highlights how the European Commission's powers have been controlled within the EU's own institutional apparatus. Attention is paid to the influences of the directly elected EP and the Council of Ministers (representing national governments). The second dimension evaluates the plausibility of national parliaments controlling the Commission. The third dimension suggests that perhaps the problem is not so much that the Commission is doing things that the national governments don't like but rather that national governments have often worked with the Commission in extending the range of executive power and dominance not just beyond the nation state but also beyond the normal cycles of domestic electoral politics. The fourth dimension highlights the implausibility of extending electoral politics to the selection of the European Commission's President. The willingness of Member States to cede control over this process to the EP demonstrated the kind of gaps in the system of political responsibility which could be exploited to urge voters to take back control over democracy.

The European Commission exercises a range of powers. It is the body that initiates the EU's legislative process by drafting the proposals which the EP and the Council of Ministers negotiate and adopt. The Commission is also responsible for drawing up more detailed rules that supplement, amend or help in the implementation of the legislation that the EP and Council adopts. The Commission acts on behalf of the EU in conducting international trade negotiations. It monitors the economic and fiscal policies of Member States to ensure their compliance with EU rules that impose budgetary and fiscal discipline, especially on the states that are

members of the eurozone. The Commission enforces competition and state aid rules that seek to prevent concentrations of
economic power – whether in the hands of big business or in
the hands of the state – from distorting competition in the
Single Market. More generally, the Commission is tasked with
ensuring that Member States abide by their obligations under
EU law.

In exercising these powers, the fact that the
European Commission is unelected is in many ways unre-
markable. The European Commission is an executive, composed of civil servants acting under the direction of a College
of Commissioners and the European Commission president.
Bodies exercising executive authority are often unelected.
But what matters is that executive power is under control.[4]
Those controls can be democratic or they can take other
forms including judicial oversight. The focus here is more
specifically on those exercises of the Commission's powers
that require political oversight.

Democratic control is expressed institutionally in the
EU directly through the EP and indirectly through the representative of national governments (domestically elected) in
the Council of Ministers and, at leader level, through the
European Council. In terms of the exercise of democratic
control through the EP, while it may be true that the EP has
been directly elected since 1979, these periodic elections have
struggled to assume significance in domestic political life. All
too often, EP elections are 'second order' affairs with voters

---

[4] D Curtin, 'Challenging executive dominance in European democracy'
(2014) 77(1) *Modern Law Review* 1.

using the elections not to pass judgment on EU matters but on the state of domestic politics.[5] Rather, it is through the representatives of national governments that we may need to look for expressions of democratic control.

Historically, it was the individual and collective control of national governments that could keep the European Commission in check. In the legislative process, during the 1960s and 1970s, it was the Council of Ministers that had to agree to the Commission's draft proposals. Voting in the Council was by unanimous consent of all the Member States. In effect, any state had a veto. Even when the treaties anticipated a transition to a system of qualified majority voting, the so-called 'Luxembourg Compromise' allowed a national government to claim that an issue was of national interest that could not be overridden by a majority vote. Decisions would be made by consensus. In this way, national governments – democratically elected at national level – had collective and also individual control over the adoption of European laws proposed by the European Commission.

The institutional balance began to change from the 1980s and not just as a result of the growing power of the EP. With successive treaty revisions, the reach of qualified majority voting in the Council was extended meaning that, in the end, a state could be outvoted. The claim was made during the referendum campaign that the UK was the 'most ignored country in the EU' when it came to voting in the Council.[6]

---

[5] On which see H Schmitt, 'The European Parliament elections of June 2004: still second order?' (2005) 28(3) *West European Politics* 650.

[6] *Daily Express* (20 April 2016).

The source of the claim was research by VoteWatch Europe that showed that while the UK's voting position was aligned with the consensus 97 per cent of the time, in the situations where the UK opposed a measure – a phenomenon that increased in the years immediately leading up to the referendum – it was outvoted by a majority.[7]

Looking beyond the adoption of legislation, the reach of the European Commission's rule-making powers is perhaps felt more directly by European firms and businesses when the Commission exercises its powers to adopt delegated rules and implementing measures. It is at this level that the banning or authorising of particular goods, foods, supplements and chemicals acquires greater visibility and increased significance. The original system of decision-making required the European Commission to consult committees composed of representatives of national administrations (and also committees of experts). This is known as 'comitology'. This involvement of the national administrations recognised that for the most part the application and implementation of EU rules on the ground is a matter for the Member States. But it also gave the Member States a capacity to exercise control over the European Commission.[8]

The system of comitology expanded from the 1960s and went through a variety of procedural and institutional changes. The creation of new EU agencies took on some of

---

[7] Votewatch.eu. For analysis see S Hix, 'Does the UK have influence in the EU legislative process?' (2016) 87(2) *The Political Quarterly* 200.

[8] J Blom-Hansen, *The Comitology System in Theory and Practice: Keeping an Eye on the Commission?* (Palgrave, 2011).

the heavy-lifting in carrying out technical and scientific risk assessments. And in certain areas, the power to grant or restrict EU-wide authorisations was given to agencies – particularly in areas like aviation safety, new medicines, certain types of chemicals – on a mandate direct from the EU's legislative institutions. But much of this type of administration still rests with the European Commission albeit in a revised system since the 2009 Treaty of Lisbon.[9]

The capacity for this type of Commission-initiated rule-making to spark wider social interest can be illustrated in a range of areas, from applications to put genetically modified food onto the European market through to banning certain pesticides because of the risk they pose to bees. It is in the areas where there are diverse national opinions on risks, with strongly held, but competing views, that the Commission has often ended up having to take decisions, precisely because the national governments cannot form a clear view one way or another to either ban or permit something. This is a function of the rule-making system which leaves decisions to the Commission where there is no clear qualified majority vote one way or another. Yet the irony of this is that this is a situation which the European Commission itself laments. It is an area where the national governments are neither exercising control nor taking responsibility. It is no accident that, following the referendum decision in the UK, this is an area where the European Commission wants to see reforms aimed at

---

[9] GJ Brandsma and J Blom-Hansen 'Controlling delegated powers in the post-Lisbon European Union' (2016) 23(4) *Journal of European Public Policy* 531.

making national governments take greater responsibility. As the Commission President Jean-Claude Juncker stated in his 'State of the Union' speech to the EP on 14 September 2016:[10]

> It is not right that when EU countries cannot decide among themselves whether or not to ban the use of glyphosate in herbicides, the Commission is forced by Parliament and Council to take a decision. So we will change those rules – because that is not democracy.

Under the presidency of Jean-Claude Juncker, the European Commission has also sought to tackle complaints about the exercises of its law-initiating powers by simply legislating less. In its annual work programme for 2015 only fourteen new legislative proposals were identified (this compares with twenty pieces of legislation identified in the 2015 Queen's Speech setting out the legislative agenda of the UK government). Nonetheless, much of the recent activity to control the Commission's power has been focused on empowering national parliaments to raise their concerns.

One of David Cameron's ambitions for his 'new settlement' deal was to enhance the power of national parliaments to control draft legislation proposed by the European Commission. Since the Treaty of Lisbon, a 'subsidiarity' early warning system has operated to allow the chambers of national parliaments to highlight draft proposals that they consider do not require legislative action at EU level.[11] It was this system

---

[10] J-C Juncker, 'State of the Union 2016: towards a better Europe', www.ec.europa.eu (14 September 2016).

[11] P Kiiver, *The Early Warning System for the Principle of Subsidiarity* (Routledge 2012).

which David Cameron sought to improve by extending the amount of time national parliaments would have to review draft EU proposals and to flag their concerns. From its inception, the number of 'reasoned opinions' from national parliaments raising objections to EU measures steadily increased but in most cases in insufficient numbers on any individual proposal to trigger the requirement on the European Commission to reconsider its proposal. Certainly this is an area where some have argued for reforms designed to enhance direct democratic parliamentary control over the European Commission.[12]

However, this is also an area where reform is difficult. If national parliaments were to be permitted an effective veto over Commission proposals it would risk returning the EU to the days of decision-making paralysis before qualified majority voting in the Council was introduced. National parliamentary vetoes could delay or derail EU decision-making; a risk that can already be seen when national parliamentary approval is required for the ratification of EU trade agreements. A single national parliamentary veto could undermine the will of a majority of the EU governments and their national parliaments. Simply escalating the power to veto does not manage democracy in a multinational union.

Trying to understand the referendum debate about democratic control by reference to the European Commission as a British political bogeyman may be to miss what is actually important about the exercise of executive power in the EU. A better way to begin to grasp what's at stake is to suggest that

---

[12] D Chalmers, 'Democratic self-government in Europe: domestic solutions to the EU legitimacy crisis', www.policy-network.net (May 2013).

the fundamental problem is not one of conflict but, paradoxi-cally, the success of co-operation. From specifying maximum working weeks, to the proper use of metric weights and measures; from determining applicable rates of VAT to the co-ordination of social security, EU rules impact on a myr-iad of aspects of national life. If these rules are a source of voter discontent it is not because they were imposed by an unelected European Commission against the wishes of an elected national government, but if anything, because national governments have been all too eager to exercise control collectively through, and in partnership with, the EU. The EU and its executive arms have facilitated national governments in their capacity to exercise executive power when confronted with transnational issues that might have eroded the capacity of any single national government to exert its preferences. Put simply, EU membership has been a means of preserving and expanding executive power across borders.[13]

National government's play two-level games in push-ing for more initiatives to be pursued at EU level to escape domestic political constraints and to shift responsibility away from national governments to the European institutions. So the issue of democratic control isn't simply one of how to control the Commission but perhaps more significantly in how to control what national governments do in, and through, their co-operation with other national governments through international organisations. The appropriate course

[13] D Curtin, *Executive Power in the European Union: Law, Practice and Constitutionalism* (Oxford University Press, 2009).

of action would seem to be for national parliaments to take control over their own national governments and what they do or do not commit to at EU level. In the UK, a significant amount of scrutiny is routinely undertaken by the select committees of both House of Parliament, as well as the devolved parliaments. But here, there are limits to what the EU can or should do. It is not for the EU to tell national parliaments how to scrutinise or control their governments: that would transgress constitutional boundaries. The German Constitutional Court has done much to seek to protect parliamentary oversight by the Bundestag.[14] The UK's European Union Act 2011 also sought to enhance parliamentary controls, but primarily in respect of future EU treaty revisions.

But, the connection back to electoral politics is missing. European politics – as opposed to domestic politics about EU membership – has been almost entirely absent from British electoral politics. Political parties have not contested elections or discussed their policy preferences in terms of what they would, or would not like to see pursued in co-operation with other EU governments. Indeed, it is striking that David Cameron focused all his energy on getting a 'new settlement' to safeguard UK interests rather than setting out a vision of how he and his government wanted to pursue British interests through the EU, including under its 'presidency of the EU' which was due to take place in 2017 but which was cancelled following the referendum.

---

[14] P Kiiver, 'The Lisbon judgment of the German Constitutional Court: a court-ordered strengthening of the national legislature in the EU' (2010) 16(3) *European Law Journal* 578.

Rather than mainstreaming European politics into domestic political debates and electoral politics, 'Europe' has been a policy silo focused almost exclusively either on the question of membership of the EU itself, or joining the Single Currency. In this way, the referendum on EU membership was a proxy for all the debates about EU policies and politics that simply never took place, or only took place between an elite of policymakers and academics who were in the know. The British debate over Europe came down to a simple binary choice of whether to stay or go.

For some, the solution to this problem of democratic control lies not just with domestic election cycles but also with the need to inject a degree of contestation into the selection of the European Commission President. The political power of the Commission has varied over time and under different Presidents. Former Commission President Jacques Delors was regarded as a particularly significant leader of the Commission and was famously rubbished by elements of the British press. Yet the experience of the nomination of Jean Claude-Juncker as President did more to show how national governments lost control over the process and how Brussels elites carved up jobs.

The office of Commission President is one traditionally occupied by former prime ministers of EU states, historically, nominated by consensus by European leaders. Together with the national nominees for the positions of Commissioners, the entire College requires the approval of the EP. Following the entry into force of the Lisbon Treaty, a new provision was added to the treaties. It provided that 'taking into account the elections to the European Parliament' and after appropriate consultations, the European Council, by qualified majority vote, shall propose a candidate for the Commission presidency to the EP. The new idea was that the Commission President should be politically responsive to voters, albeit indirectly via the medium of the elections to the EP.

It was possible to read the new provisions as only making one fundamental change: the move from a nomination process that gave each state a veto to one where – contrary to the normal style of decision-making in the European Council – a majority vote could be held. Institutionally, there was no reason to view the European Council's collective control over the nomination as being diminished. Of course, the EP could – as in the past – refuse to accept a nomination and any sensible institution would seek to ensure that a candidate could be accepted (hence the appropriate consultations). But that could not turn a downstream right of rejection unto an upstream power to demand that the European Council nominate a particular candidate. Yet this was precisely what happened when the major political groupings in the Parliament conspired to invent a nomination process known as the *Spitzenkandidat* or 'lead candidate'.

Members of the EP sit in different political groupings depending on their national political affiliations. The Group of the European People's Party (EPP) represents centre-Right parties while the Group of the Progressive Alliance of Socialists and Democrats (S&D) represents centre-Left parties. During the 2014 EP elections, the EPP and S&D each chose a candidate who they expected to see take over the Commission presidency if the result of the election gave their grouping the largest share of the seats in the Parliament. Former Luxembourg Prime Minister Jean-Claude Juncker was the candidate for the EPP and the German politician Martin Schulz was the candidate for S&D. In the 2014 election, parties affiliated to the EPP secured 29.4 per cent of the vote (with a turnout of 42.6 per cent of the electorate), while parties affiliated to the S&D attained 25.4 per cent of the vote. The EPP share of the vote had fallen from 35.7 per cent since 2009, with the share of votes of more Eurosceptic groupings rising.

The EPP insisted that Juncker be the nominee for the presidency. Yet it was perfectly plausible to argue that the one message that came from the election was that voters were increasingly unhappy with the state of EU politics and wanted to see change. Nominating yet another Brussels insider to a top post looked just like business-as-usual. That the 'defeated' Martin Schulz would become the President of the European Parliament smacked of a political stitch up between the pro-EU centre Right and centre Left. David Cameron sought to block Juncker's nomination and counted on Angela Merkel to halt his nomination. Her support proved elusive (her own CDU party is affiliated to the EPP) and despite knowing he was going to lose, Cameron insisted that the matter be put to a vote. He lost. It was a spectacle that reinforced rather than challenged a view of the institutions and its leaders as elite and remote. It certainly did not help David Cameron in his bid to persuade British voters that the UK had influence in the EU.

Although the European Commission has been the focal point for democratic discontents, the desire for control over democracy runs deeper than this. As Curtin makes clear, it is a discontent with the phenomenon of the growth and dispersion of executive power.[15] National parliaments have struggled to cope with this phenomenon. The spirit of a new nationalism is meant to be the solution that will ensure that decisions will be taken by governments responsible to parliaments at both UK and devolved levels. Yet it is not clear how easy it will be to put the executive genie back into the parliamentary bottle. Nor is it obvious how the new internationalism and the striking of deals outside of the structures of EU decision-making will be rendered responsive to domestic parliamentary processes.

[15] Curtin, 'Challenging executive dominance in European democracy'.

9

Control over Laws

Anxieties about a loss of control over democracy blend with concerns about a loss of control over national laws. But three specific strands of disquiet can be detected operating at instrumental, constitutional and institutional levels. The instrumental level points to the density and reach of EU legal instruments within national law. The constitutional level refers to the accommodation of the primacy of EU law within a system in which the sovereignty of Parliament is the cardinal constitutional principle. The institutional level draws the European Court of Justice directly to the fore of critical analysis. Indeed, following the 2016 referendum, the political litmus test of taking control over laws increasingly seems to rest on removing the UK from the jurisdiction of the Court of Justice.

During the referendum campaign, one of the striking claims made by Boris Johnson – Vote Leave campaigner and subsequently Foreign Secretary – was that 60 per cent of British laws emanated from the European Union. It was a claim said to be based on research conducted and reported in a House of Commons Library research paper. How much of UK law derived from EU sources depends on the question you ask and as the original 2010 research paper made clear, 'there is no totally accurate, rational or useful way of calculating the percentage of national laws based on or influenced by the EU'.[1] But in a campaign where impressions mattered more than hard realities, Johnson's assertion amounted to a claim that the UK had lost control over its laws.

In fact much of EU law does not need to be incorporated into domestic law at all: it is 'directly applicable'. Key provisions of the EU treaties from the rules on free movement, to equal pay for men and women, through to the rules requiring businesses not to engage in anti-competitive activities can all be enforced in national courts without national legislation. When it comes to EU legislation – the more specific rules created by the EU's legislative institution – only directives require the Member States to transpose the requirements laid down in EU legislation into domestic legal rules. By contrast, 'regulations' are also directly applicable.

The consequence of this distinction between those sources of EU law that are directly applicable and those that are not is that while both apply and influence UK law, only directives need to be put into domestic legal form. Which explains why – using figures updated from the original 2010 research – on average only 9.4 per cent of UK statutory instruments implemented EU directives.[2] As chapter 14 demonstrates, one of the ironies of Brexit is that it is likely to produce a legislative explosion as the UK seeks to bring

---

[1] V Miller, 'How much legislation comes from Europe?', House of Commons Library Research Paper 10/62 (13 October 2010).

[2] Statutory instruments are measure that Parliament allows governments to enact, subject to parliamentary oversight. In the context of EU membership, Parliament's authority to government to transpose EU directives into national law via statutory instruments flows from the European Communities Act 1972.

directly applicable law into UK law in order to keep UK law compliant with EU law until it is decided otherwise. The consequence will be a taming of control over laws rather than an immediate taking of control.

Yet, for all the complaints about British businesses getting bound up in Brussels 'red-tape', concerns about control over law probably have very little to do with the density of law as such. The effects of a single instrument unrelated to EU law – the European Convention on Human Rights, incorporated into UK law through the Human Rights Act 1998 – are enough to illustrate how anxieties and fears about European interference in domestic legal affairs can be generated. It is the idea of recognising an external source of law as a constraint on what nation states can do that seems to be at the heart of the problem. And in the context of the European Union, it is the 'primacy' of that law over domestic law that heightens the existential angst about sovereignty.[3]

The principle of primacy was established by the Court of Justice in the 1960s.[4] Having established that provisions of EU treaties could be directly applicable and so enforced in national law, it was obvious that courts would be faced with conflicts between domestic and EU law. The principle of primacy determines which rule applies when there is a conflict –a rule of national law or one of EU law. The Court of Justice reasoned that it flowed from the nature of the EU legal

---

[3] M Claes, 'The primacy of EU law in European and national law' in
    A Arnull and D Chalmers (eds), *The Oxford Handbook of European
    Union Law* (Oxford University Press, 2015) www.oxfordhandbooks.com.
[4] *Costa v ENEL*, Case 6/64, EU:C:1964:66.

order that if national rules could take priority over EU rules when they conflicted, then this would prevent the uniform application of EU rules across all Member States and, in the process, make EU rule-making less credible. Therefore, EU law would take primacy in the event of any conflicts and national measures would have to be disapplied to the extent that they conflicted. It is important to note that this primacy principle neither rendered national law invalid – it could be applied and enforced to the extent that there was no conflict with EU law – nor did it empower the Court of Justice to 'strike down' national law.

While the principle of primacy made sense from the perspective of the Court of Justice, nonetheless, it would be the national courts that would have to be persuaded to accept the practical implications of the primacy doctrine. This was not without its difficulties, not least in those states with written constitutions, domestic guarantees of fundamental rights and specialised courts with jurisdictions to protect their constitutions or otherwise to control the exercise of domestic public authority. Perhaps most famously, the German Constitutional Court laid out the domestic constitutional conditions under which it will accept the primacy of EU law. Less visibly, in 2016 it was the Danish Supreme Court that found itself unable to disapply a provision of national law alleged to conflict with unwritten general principles of EU law.[5]

---

[5] S Klinge, 'Dialogue or disobedience between the European Court of Justice and the Danish Constitutional Court?', www.eulawanalysis .blogspot.co.uk (13 December 2016).

Despite the principle of the sovereignty of Parliament, it proved relatively easy for EU law to be given primacy and effect in the UK. In its ruling in *Factortame*, Lord Bridge identified that the principle of the primacy of EU law was well-established in the case law of the Court of Justice by the time that the UK joined the European Economic Community (EEC) in 1973.[6] Any limitation on the sovereignty of Parliament was, in his view, voluntarily undertaken by Parliament in enacting the European Communities Act 1972. If this implied that English courts simply went along with what the Court of Justice had said, for Lord Justice Laws, British courts were simply upholding the will of Parliament.[7] In the 'Metric Martyrs' case – concerning the prosecution of a trader in Sunderland for selling goods weighed in Imperial measure only – Lord Justice Laws concluded that Parliament, through the 1972 Act, had established that UK courts were to give priority to EU law over inconsistent domestic enactments. If Parliament used express language to legislate contrary to its EU law obligations, then UK courts would feel obliged to uphold the express will of Parliament. In more recent times in the *HS2* case, the Supreme Court suggested that the primacy principle may also reach its limit if it conflicts with other important domestic constitutional principles.[8] If there was doubt about the conceptual foundation upon

[6] *Secretary of State for Transport v Factortame* [1991] AC 603.

[7] *Thoburn v Sunderland City Council* [2003] QB 151.

[8] *R (HS2 Alliance) v Secretary of State for Transport* [2014] UKSC 3. M Elliott, 'Reflections on the HS2 case: a hierarchy of domestic constitutional norms and the qualified primacy of EU law', www.ukconstitutionallaw.org (23 January 2014).

which the primacy principle was accepted in UK law, then the European Union Act 2011 was meant to put it beyond doubt. Yet the 'sovereignty' clause in section 18 does no more than restate that EU law has effect in the UK by virtue of section 2(1) of the 1972 Act: it deals with the direct applicability side of EU law and not the primacy side. The 'new settlement' deal between the UK and EU agreed by David Cameron contained a 'sovereignty' heading but it did nothing to elaborate on the conditions under which primacy of EU law was either accepted or limited. Rumours of domestic legislation to make clear the continuing sovereignty of Parliament came to nothing. Intriguingly, the UK government's post-referendum Brexit White Paper stated that the principle of the sovereignty of Parliament had never actually gone away:[9]

> Whilst Parliament has remained sovereign throughout our membership of the EU, it has not always felt like that.

If correct, the taking of control over laws is largely about changing voter sentiment about how it feels to be governed. That said, the primacy issue will be resolved once and for all by the UK's withdrawal from the European Union and the repeal of the European Communities Act 1972.

Control over law is also about having control over who interprets the law. The role of the Court of Justice as the authoritative interpreter of EU law was at the fore of criticisms about a loss of control over law. The Court's interpretation of the primary law of the treaties is crucial because the

---

[9] HM Government, 'The United Kingdom's exit from and new partnership with the European Union', Cm 9417 (2 February 2017).

treaties contains fundamental rules on *inter alia* the reach of EU free movement rules, citizenship, aspects of equality law and competition law, together with the fundamental rights protected by the EU Charter of Fundamental Rights. Given that primary law can only be changed by national governments through a treaty revision process requiring the unanimous consent of national governments as well as ratification by all Member States, it is clearly extremely difficult for an individual state to try and reverse a Court of Justice ruling with which it disagrees.

The Court's extension of gender equality protection in respect of pay to include occupational pensions schemes can be cited as an example where the preferences of the Court and national governments diverged. It is also a rare example of a situation where Member States sought to regain control by agreeing the *Barber* Protocol to the treaties in order to limit the temporal effects of the Court's judgment in the occupational pension sphere and thereby minimise its financial repercussions.[10]

The Court of Justice's interpretation of EU legislation is also significant. As with the interpretation of the primary law of the treaties, there are examples where the Court gives binding interpretations that are out of step with the preferences of governments, employers and sometimes also employees. The example of the Working Time Directive is

---

[10] *Barber v Guardian Royal Exchange*, Case C-262/88, C:1990:209. The case and its aftermath are discussed in D Curtin, 'Scalping the Community legislator: occupational pensions and "Barber"' (1990) 27(3) *Common Market Law Review* 475. See also A Stone Sweet, *The Judicial Construction of Europe* (Oxford University Press, 2004), ch 4.

again a case in point. Clarifications given by the Court on what constitutes working time – to include the time that a person is required to be available for work (even if the person may rest while 'on call') – have been criticised for their impact on the organisation of emergency and health services. Legislative acts are not burdened by the same constitutional impediments to their alteration but it may, nonetheless, be difficult to find majority support for legislative change. Indeed, following controversial interpretations of the Posted Workers Directive by the Court of Justice,[11] the Commission found it extremely difficult to come up with substantive legislative proposals that would meet the very different interests of workers from 'old' and 'new' Member States. The Member States are also not free to amend EU legislation in a way that would conflict with the primary law of the treaty as interpreted by the Court of Justice.[12]

In an earlier time when the sorts of cases coming before the Court concerned prosaic issues such as the imposition of customs duties on the import of urea formaldehyde or the requirement that imports of Scotch whisky be accompanied by a certificate of origin, it was possible for the Court to cloak its institutional role in the guise of terse, abstract legalism. With national courts also willing to supply the Court of Justice with a steady stream of new cases, the domain of legal integration could continue to expand.[13] But in more modern

[11] *Laval*, Case C-341/05, EU:C:2007:809.
[12] G Davies, 'The European Union legislator as the agent of the European Court of Justice' (2016) 54(4) *Journal of Common Market Studies* 846.
[13] RD Kelemen, *Eurolegalism: The Transformation of Law and Regulation in the European Union* (Harvard University Press, 2011).

times when the issues before the Court are more controversial, the Court, as an institution, is more socially and politically exposed, and its apparent 'activism' scrutinised.[14]

Yet for all this, it is difficult to pinpoint clear examples of judgments of the Court of Justice which generated the sort of level of political or social controversy that might lead voters to consider that the UK should leave the EU. Indeed, the complaints were more typically about the judgments of the European Court of Human Rights – an organ of the Council of Europe and not of the European Union.

The EU courts were also useful to the UK in two ways. First, a strong compliance machinery increases the functional capacity of the EU to achieve its aims by ensuring that Member States comply with their obligations. Secondly, governments are also litigators before the EU courts. Member States may litigate before the EU courts for a number of reasons but one of those reasons concerns the adoption of EU rules by qualified majority votes. It is one thing for a Member State to accept the primacy of EU rules when those rules require all national governments to agree to them: the power of veto gives each state control over what it will or will not accept. Where primacy doesn't just bite, but hurts, is when EU rules are adopted by a qualified majority of EU states. With successive treaty revisions – and following successive enlargements of the EU –majority voting has become the norm. To be sure, institutional practice is such that where possible, a consensus is sought without the need

---

[14] M Dawson, B De Witte and E Muir (eds), *Judicial Activism at the European Court of Justice* (Edward Elgar, 2013).

for a vote.[15] But, there are instances where EU rules are adopted in the face of opposition by a state and this is where a state may wish to elicit the help of the Court of Justice in striking down the offending rule.

An example of the UK government challenging an EU legislative measure before the Court of Justice concerns the controversial Working Time Directive that set down limits on the number of hours that a worker could legally work. In fact, the UK had not voted against the measure but merely abstained. The Commission had also agreed to water down the directive by allowing derogations to allow individual workers to contract out of the time limits. The Court of Justice rejected the UK's claims that the legislation had an incorrect legal basis in the treaties and was an employment policy measure, rather than one correctly relating to health and safety.[16] But it became a totemic example of claimed EU interference in a sphere of social and employment relations that British Conservative governments sought to insulate from EU control.

In the years leading up to the referendum, the UK government became a more frequent litigator before the Court of Justice in its challenge to EU rules on 'short-selling', the proposal for a Financial Transaction Tax and caps on bankers' bonuses.[17] The UK lost in the first two cases and

---

[15]   F Hayes-Renshaw, W Van Aken and H Wallace, 'When and why the EU Council of Ministers votes explicitly' (2006) 44(1) *Journal of Common Market Studies* 161.

[16]   *United Kingdom v Council (Working Time)*, Case C-84/94, EU:C:1996:431.

[17]   Case C-270/12 ('Short-Selling'), EU:C:2014:18; Case C-29/13 (Financial Transaction Tax), EU:C:2014:283. The litigation in relating to bonuses was abandoned by the UK: Case C-507/13, EU:C:2014:248.

abandoned the third. Outside the legislative context, the UK did win an important case before the EU's General Court challenging a policy of the European Central Bank that would require institutions clearing euro-denominated securities to be based in a Eurozone Member State.[18] But these examples illustrate not just how much post-crisis regulatory responses have heightened tensions between the UK and the EU but also how even sceptical governments in practice rely on EU courts to try and regain what they have lost in the political arena.

Nonetheless, it is misleading to evaluate the impact of EU law on the UK legal order simply through examples of situations of conflict or controversy. Day-to-day, national courts have simply got on with the task of interpreting and applying EU law. If the political task of doing EU business is a routine aspect of national administrative life, then enforcing EU law in national courts may also be regarded as unexceptional. Indeed, discontent with EU law may not be a function of conflict but, on the contrary, the willingness of the judiciary to carry out its responsibilities to ensure the effective enforcement of EU law in the UK. Much like complaints about the application of the European Convention on Human Rights by UK courts, it is a sense of the empowerment of unelected judges that seems to drive antipathy towards 'European' law and which, in part, motivates Brexit.

British workers and citizens have, of course, been the beneficiaries of a capacity to apply and enforce EU law in national courts and tribunals. But, it is not obvious that this

---

[18] *UK v ECB*, Case T-496/11, EU:T:2015:133.

capacity has engendered a wider social affinity between the EU and citizens and, indeed, litigating EU rights may seem like the preserve of the few not the many.

With a future Great Repeal Bill intending to maintain much of EU law within UK law after Brexit, UK courts may well find themselves continuing to apply and interpret rules which have their origins in EU law but without the direct interpretative assistance of the Court of Justice. Yet there will be nothing to prevent UK judges from looking at the published rulings of the Court of Justice as a guide to interpretation. It is one thing to seek to take control over laws by Parliament picking and choosing what laws to keep the same and what to change after 'Brexit Day', but another for politicians to seek to control the behaviour of the judiciary.

10

Control over Trade

When it comes to thinking about what control over trade means in the context of Brexit, there is an obvious ambiguity and tension. Put simply, to what extent is control over trade actually about equipping the UK with greater freedom to conduct its own trade policies – with the outcome of Brexit judged in terms of how much new trade it produces – and how much is 'free trade' a source of political and social contest[1] – and a cause of Brexit – with control oriented towards limiting the UK's exposure to the economic forces of globalisation?

Ambiguities about trade policy defined the UK's post-war relationship with Europe. The UK backed the creation of the European Free Trade Association (EFTA) as a body to promote intra-European trade while allowing members to strike their own free trade deals with other states. EFTA was the intergovernmental alternative to the more supranationalist European Economic Community (EEC) when the latter came into being in the later 1950s. As discussed previously, the UK's departure from EFTA and entry into the EEC followed a realignment of British politics to view closer regional trade integration as being in the UK's best interests. Yet for Conservatives, EEC membership was something of a second-best compared to the bigger prize of

---

[1] ATF Lang, 'Reflecting on "linkage": cognitive and institutional change in the international trading system' (2007) 70(4) *Modern Law Review* 523.

global trade, while for Labour, membership of the EEC risked its capacity to undertake domestic industrial policy objectives as was emphasised by the Labour Party's 1983 election manifesto when it committed to taking the UK out of the EEC. Both parties, however, shared a commitment to trade relations with Commonwealth countries.

But through the 1980s and into the new millennium, the British political mainstream accepted the EU as a powerful promoter of free trade. The drive to complete the Single Market was not only backed by a Conservative government under Margaret Thatcher, its architects included the British European Commissioner Lord Cockfield,[2] as well as many of the senior Commission officials working in what was the Internal Market Directorate of the European Commission. British European Commissioners – Leon Brittan (Conservative) and Peter Mandelson (Labour) – were instrumental in promoting the EU as a global actor pursuing rules-based international trade both through its support of the World Trade Organization (WTO) and through the EU's own capacity to enter into trade deals with non-EU states. The centre ground of British politics aligned itself with trade in a Single Market and globally through membership of the EU.

The 'Single Market' is more than a free trade area in a number of important ways. First, while free trade areas facilitate trade in goods, the EU Single Market also seeks to remove obstacles to cross-border economic activity by facilitating the free movement of workers, the freedom to provide

---

[2] Lord Cockfield, *The European Union: Creating the Single Market* (John Wiley & Sons, 1994).

cross-border services, the freedom to establish businesses and branches across the EU territory and the free movement of capital. Secondly, it tackles not just the obstacles that arise from state policies but through its competition rules it also challenges the trade-distorting activities of companies. Thirdly, if free trade areas are primarily focused on the elimination of tariff (duties) and non-tariff (regulatory requirements) barriers to trade between its members, a customs union goes further in establishing a common external commercial policy, with common tariffs applied to trade between the EU and non-EU states.

The customs union when combined with a free trade area has significant benefits in terms of the ease with which businesses can conduct cross-border economic activity and goods have free circulation. But it also involves constraints. The deeper the level of co-operation between members in removing non-tariff barriers through EU-level harmonisation of regulatory norms and standards, the less autonomy each state has over its capacity to lay down its own rules to regulate the market. And a customs union means that externally, there is also a harmonised trade approach to non-Member States that prevents each Member State from pursuing its own trade policy agenda whether on a bilateral basis or multilaterally through organisations like the WTO.

If the political mainstream was willing to accept the relative balance of benefits and constraints of EU trade, the tensions hardly went away.

For the Left, acceptance of EU membership was tied to the hope that it might buffer the effects of globalisation and help preserve the 'European Social Model'.[3] The Lisbon Agenda of economic, employment and social reform of the 2000s was intentionally constructed by social democratic and centre-Left political leaders as a balanced agenda in which growth and competitiveness would not be at the expense of social inclusion.[4] Yet the EU – and especially the Court of Justice – was open to the critique that EU law prioritised economic objectives over social ones, with certain cases decided by the Court becoming high-profile and stylised illustrations of an apparently asymmetric constitution.[5] Even for those on the Left supporting continuing EU membership, it was hard to reconcile decades of criticism of the EU for the paucity of its social dimension with the claims that the EU, nonetheless, was a strong protector of workers' rights. For the Right, part of the problem was its objection to what the Left wanted, as illustrated by ongoing tensions over the Working Time Directive. But more than these skirmishes, the issue remained whether the costs and limitations of EU member-ship were worth being in the Single Market and participating in its common external trade policy.

Concerns about the effects of free trade were not simply manifestations of abstract or ideological debates about what EU membership meant. They took specific form in the lead up to the 2016 EU referendum in the decision of

[3] A Sapir, 'Globalization and the reform of European social models' (2006) 44(2) *Journal of Common Market Studies* 369.

[4] P Copeland and D Papadimitriou (eds), *The EU's Lisbon Strategy: Evaluating Success, Understanding Failure* (Palgrave Macmillan, 2012).

[5] F Scharpf, 'The European social model: coping with diversity' (2002) 40(4) *Journal of Common Market Studies* 645.

Tata Steel to restructure its European operations, with the threatened closure or sale of the Port Talbot steel works in Wales. The situation highlighted two key issues with a direct linkage to the EU. In terms of the operation of the Single Market, Tata Steel's output supplied the European automotive and construction sectors through plants not just in the UK but also Germany, Netherlands and France. Companies within the Single Market have the freedom to choose where to locate their production, safe in the knowledge that their goods have unrestricted access to the European market. That also means that firms may seek to relocate or consolidate their activities in particular sites. Such a decision has huge economic and social implications for local economies. Indeed, it is easy to forget that a European market has distinctly local qualities.

The second and related issue was the effect on the European steel market of a glut of steel products principally from China, where over-capacity was estimated at 350 million tonnes.[6] The European Union has, at its disposal so-called 'Trade Defence Instruments' (TDIs) that can be deployed to protect the European market from cheap imports. These include the application of duties to the importation of goods from outside the EU. Yet, whereas average EU duties on steel bars and cold rolled flat steel products are in the region of 21–25 per cent, they are between 133–265 per cent in the United States.[7] In determining what duties to impose on dumped

---

[6] European Commission, 'Towards a robust trade policy for the EU in the interest of jobs and growth', COM (2016) 690 (18 October 2016).

[7] Annex to the Communication, 'Towards a robust trade policy for the EU in the interest of jobs and growth', COM (2016) 690 (18 October 2016).

products, the EU has applied what is known as the 'lesser duty' rule. This involves a calculation of two figures – the 'dumping margin' and the 'injury margin' – and applying the lesser figure. This had the effect of significantly capping the duties which the EU had applied to steel imports. It is an approach not taken by the EU's trading partners.

Back in 2013, the European Commission proposed modernising its approach to TDIs not least in light of the threats to the EU market from cheap Chinese steel.[8] But the proposal stalled in the Council as EU countries took different stances on the balance between protectionism and 'free' trade. In February 2016, the UK was one of seven EU states to send a letter to the European Commission urging support for the EU steel industry. But in the same month, a ministerial statement to Parliament made clear that the UK did not back the Commission's proposal to remove the 'lesser duty' rule, stating that it did not strike the right balance between user and producer interests.[9] In March 2016 and as the crisis in the steel sector intensified, the European Commission again called on the Member States to reach an agreement on its proposal to enhance its capacity to adopt stronger TDIs.[10] But the May meeting of ministers in the Trade Council deferred making any decisions, citing the need for further work. It focused instead on preparing the EU–Canada Free Trade Agreement

[8] European Commission, 'Modernisation of trade defence instruments', COM (2013) 191 (10 April 2013)

[9] A Soubry, 'UK's contribution to EU action on steel', House of Commons Written Statement 528 (11 February 2016).

[10] European Commission, Steel: preserving sustainable jobs and growth in Europe, COM (2016) 155 (16 March 2106).

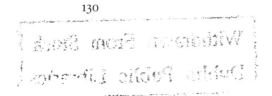

for signature. In these crucial months leading up to the June referendum, the EU could be seen to be further pushing trade liberalisation while failing to protect fair trade, albeit largely because of the blocking position taken by countries like the UK.

Some 56.8 per cent of voters in the Neath Port Talbot constituency voted for the UK to leave the EU.

But the issue of trade was not only being played out in the domestic politics of the referendum campaign. It became a key aspect of the United States presidential campaigns.

The EU and the United States have dominated international trade negotiations and through organisations like the WTO, both parties have exerted their global trade power. Despite this, a trade deal between the two trading blocs has been absent. Negotiations on a EU–US 'Transatlantic Trade and Investment Partnership' (TTIP) were officially launched at a G8 summit under the UK presidency in 2013. By the time of the referendum, thirteen rounds of talks had taken place. But not only were negotiations difficult on issues such as access to services, government procurement and diverging approaches to genetically modified food, they were also a focal point for social movements in the United States and the EU protesting against the effects of trade on standards of living, protection of the environment and labour standards.

The TTIP talks were frequently depicted as secret negotiations, but as Cremona notes, TTIP marked a 'new approach' to providing greater transparency in trade negotiations.[11]

---

[11] M Cremona, 'Negotiating the Transatlantic Trade and Investment Partnership (TTIP)' (2015) 52 *Common Market Law Review* 351.

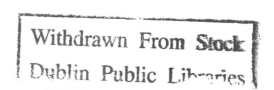

The dispute-resolution mechanism came under fire as arguments were made that they undermined the powers of government to regulate in the public interest, cost governments money in compensation to investors and lined the pockets of an elite group of highly paid private arbitrators. In the UK, the claim that TTIP would open up the UK's health service to competition from US health providers featured in the Scottish independence referendum campaign (the suggestion being that the UK government was all too ready to pursue a trade agenda through TTIP without protecting national and Scottish interests).

In the United States, the negotiation of TTIP and the agreement in 2015 of a US-led multilateral trade deal – the 'Trans Pacific Partnership' (TPP) – became focal points for diverging views on trade not just between Democratic and Republican parties, but within both parties as they selected their candidates to contest the 2016 presidential election. Historically, it was possible to keep both pro free-trade Republicans and sceptical Democrats on the same page by linking efforts to expand trade with the adoption of measures to manage the domestic consequences of international trade competition. President Kennedy's Trade Expansion Act of 1962 authorised a new federal programme known as 'Trade Adjustment Assistance' (TAA). Over the years, the pursuit of new trade deals by different US administrations has been accompanied by efforts to enhance the TAA programme. Yet its effectiveness as a means of supporting workers has long been a matter of controversy with the *Wall Street Journal* describing it as 'everyone's second-favourite option'. For the Right it is an example of unnecessary federal funding, while for the Left its focus on a subset of workers said to be particularly affected by trade deals limited the scope of this social safety net, while doing little to help communities where industry relocation had led to mass lay-offs.[12]

While the US President has constitutional authority to negotiate international treaties, to the extent that these treaties impact on the authority of Congress to regulate commerce – by requiring changes in US law to implement lower tariffs or remove non-tariff barriers – then Congressional approval is required.[13] Through what is known as 'Trade Promotion Authority' (TPA), Congress gives – for a fixed period of time – authority to allow a President to negotiate trade deals in the knowledge that implementing legislation will be subject to a straight 'up-or-down' vote without amendment.[14]

TPA and TAA have always come as a package, with TPA finding support from trade-supporting Republicans and Democrats accepting the 'consolation prize' of compensatory TAA.[15] However, the legislative package that would facilitate

---

[12] N Timiraos, '5 Questions on Trade Adjustment Assistance', *Wall Street Journal*, www.wsj.com (15 June 2015).

[13] On the oversight provided by legislatures on trade deals see: D Jančić, 'Transatlantic regulatory interdependence, law and governance: the evolving roles of the EU and US legislatures' (2015) 17 *Cambridge Yearbook of European Legal Studies* 334; E Fahey and D Curtin (eds), *A Transatlantic Community of Law: Legal Perspectives on the Relationship between the EU and US Legal Orders* (Cambridge University Press, 2014).

[14] DA Gantz, 'The bipartisan trade deal, trade promotion authority and the future of US free trade agreements' (2008) 28 *Saint Louis University Public Law Review* 115.

[15] R Berman, 'A big win for big labor', *The Atlantic* (12 June 2015).

fast-track adoption of TPP became a focal point for organised labour and environmental movements in the United States, and also for presidential-nominee hopeful, Senator Bernie Sanders. While Hillary Clinton had expressed her support for trade agreements like the North American Free Trade Agreement (NAFTA) and for TPP, in May 2015, Senator Sanders publicly and vigorously opposed Congress giving Trade Promotion Authority, citing the number of jobs he believed had been lost to free trade. But the Senate backed TPA and its connected TAA. However, when the Trade Bill moved to the House of Representatives – and in a move by Democrats designed to frustrate the adoption of the TPP – they voted down the TAA part of the legislative package. Only when the TPA and TAA parts were separated did both the House and Senate allow for fast-track authority for TPP.

While Senator Sanders' tactic may have made his Democratic opponent Hillary Clinton shift her stance on trade, the more dramatic change in political positioning was occurring on the Republican side with Donald Trump taking on his own party's pro-trade policy. Like Sanders, Trump viewed global trade as one of the causes of the relocation of jobs outside of the United States, including to lower-wage countries like Mexico. He pledged that if he became president, he would withdraw the United States from the TPP.

The UK's EU referendum campaign and the US's presidential campaigns were, of course, parallel events and one should hesitate before overstating the connection between the two. But in their own ways, each highlighted a collapse of the political centre-ground consensus. In the UK, the consensus on the importance of trade in a Single Market and through

EU membership gave way, while in the United States voters elected a Republican President openly challenging political orthodoxy on trade policies not just of the Obama administration but his own party.

In one way, the trajectories of Brexit and the Trump presidency both assert the need to have greater control over trade. In the UK, that control means having freedom to expand the scope and partners of future trade deals. In her speech to the World Economics Forum in Davos in January 2017 – just days after she outlined her principal negotiating objectives for Brexit – the Prime Minister Theresa May spoke of her ambitions for a post-Brexit 'Global Britain'.[16] It was a speech that avowedly claimed the virtues of 'liberalism, free trade and globalisation'. Yet, the speech also recognised that the 'taken-for-granted' benefits of trade were being called into question by both Left and Right. For Prime Minister May, the task of making post-Brexit Britain the 'most forceful advocate for business, free markets and free trade' is also about showing that 'the politics of the mainstream can deliver the change people need'.

In the United States, the Trump trajectory is towards having greater control over, and limiting the sort of trade deals the United States is willing to have and with whom. The inaugural address of President Trump could not have been clearer. The trade policy ambitions of the new administration will conform to the overriding directive of 'America first', and the imperative to 'buy American and hire

---

[16] T May, 'Davos 2017: Prime Minister's speech to the World Economics Forum', www.gov.uk/government/announcements (19 January 2017).

American'. It is an internationalism controlled, and tamed, by nationalism. Within hours of taking office, the White House website stated that the United States would withdraw from the Trans-Pacific Partnership and seek a renegotiation of the North American Free Trade Agreement, with the threat of withdrawal from the agreement. References to the progress made by the Obama administration on TTIP were simply excised from the website.

In the 1960s, the loss of the option of an encompassing trade deal with the United States pushed the UK closer to its European neighbours and, ultimately to EEC membership. Despite the lure this time of an agreement with the United States to make the process of leaving the EU seem more attractive, it may again prove difficult for the UK to strike a trade deal with a United States administration. This time of Brexit may not be a time of – or for – more trade, and the control which UK voters want is perhaps more of President Trump's style of limits on trade than Prime Minister May's new internationalist aspirations for freer markets and freer trade.

Part III

Time for Brexit

11

Defining Brexit, Redefining Britain

On 2 February 2017, the UK government published a White
Paper, 'The United Kingdom's exit from and new partnership
with the European Union'.[1] It described its aim as being to set
out the 'broad strategy' for a 'new strategic partnership'
between the UK and the EU, but without any 'detail that
would undermine our negotiating position'. The paper built
upon and in large measure replicated the UK position as set
out in Prime Minister Theresa May's Lancaster House speech
on 17 January 2017.[2] It followed a concession made by the
Prime Minister on 25 January 2017 at Prime Minister's
Questions to set out the basis for the UK's negotiations in
a White Paper. Given that the White Paper appeared barely
a week later – its precise moment of completion appeared to
be 04:17 on 02/02/2017 according to the date/time stamp on
the version originally released on the government's website –
it was unlikely to add significantly more detail than the
principles which the Prime Minister had already set out.
Seven months on from the referendum, the government's
direction of travel was becoming clearer. But this was to be
a statement of intent rather than an invitation to explore in

---

[1] HM Government, 'The United Kingdom's exit from and new partnership
with the European Union', Cm 9417 (2 February 2017).
[2] T May, 'The government's negotiating objectives for leaving the EU',
www.gov.uk/government/announcements (17 January 2017).

detail options and choices backed by concrete analysis of the implications of those choices.

The referendum had presented voters with a simple binary choice: Leave or Remain. A vote to remain in the EU was a vote for the status quo. Of course, it would mean the implementation of the 'new settlement' deal and, no doubt, future treaty changes would follow as the EU continued to evolve. But the broad parameters of a vote to stay inside the EU were clear. By contrast, it was always going to be a problem for the government to act on a 'Leave' vote as there would be a range of alternatives for the future relationship between the UK and the EU. Brexit meant Brexit. But what did 'Leave' mean?

In respecting obligations under the European Referendum Act 2015, prior to the referendum, the government of David Cameron had presented to Parliament a report on 'Alternatives to membership'. It set out three principal alternatives to membership, focusing primarily on the UK's future trading relationship with the EU: (1) a model based on Norway's' relationship with the EU through the European Free Trade Association (EFTA) and its European Economic Area (EEA) agreement with the EU; (2) a bilateral free trade agreement; and (3) a relationship based simply on World Trade Organization (WTO) rules. But this document was less about planning a future and more about underscoring why, in the government's view, none of these models had the same balance of advantages and disadvantages as continuing EU membership. The comparison was fundamentally between the status quo of membership and each of these models rather than identifying as between these models which of them would shape the future UK–EU relationship in the event that the country disagreed with the government's position on remaining in the EU. The 'conclusions' to the report do consider the consequences of a Leave vote, and indicate that the government would seek to secure 'the best access for UK companies and consumers to the Single Market'; to undertake the 'slow process of agreeing Free Trade Agreements with countries outside of the EU'; and to keep 'elements of non-economic co-operation'. But it went no further in stipulating how these aims would be achieved.

As subsequently became clear, there was no contingency plan for Brexit. A hastily arranged cross-departmental unit reporting to the then Cabinet Office Minister, Oliver Letwin, was tasked with beginning work on the UK's departure from the EU. But with the then Prime Minister David Cameron announcing his intention to resign following the referendum result, there was a leadership gap and a policy vacuum which made the task of defining a new relationship with the EU impossible until a new premier was in place.[3] Once Theresa May took up her position as Prime Minister, the process of building a new government and defining what Leave would mean could begin.

Into this political hiatus emerged the language of 'hard' and 'soft' Brexit. Much like the referendum itself, it suggested a binary choice. But in reality there are multiple 'varieties of Brexit', reflecting a range of different options.[4] It is a distinction

[3] House of Commons Foreign Affairs Committee, 'Preparing the government for Brexit', 2nd Report (2016–17) HC431 (20 July 2016).

[4] J Worth, 'Varieties of Brexit', www.jonworth.eu (20 December 2016). See also J-C Piris, 'If the UK votes to leave: the seven alternatives to EU membership', www.cer.org.uk (January 2016).

which focuses almost exclusively on the trade dimension of EU membership rather than the wider aspects of policy co-operation on foreign or defence policy. Even in terms of trade, the emphasis lies on different mechanisms of market access rather than the quality of trading relationship whether viewed in economic terms – how much or how little red tape will result or how difficult or easy it will be to resolve trade disputes – or, in non-economic terms, how well or how badly worker and environmental protection will be served. And like many hard/soft metaphors, it is probably better at describing the 'hard' version than the 'soft'.

More specifically, a hard Brexit refers to withdrawing from the EU, from its Customs Union and its Single Market without any sort of trade deal with the EU in place and with future trade conducted under WTO rules. This would leave the UK in the same position as non-EU states like the United States. The most obvious way in which this type of hard Brexit could be softened would be for the UK to conclude an 'association agreement' with the EU in one form or another. Association agreements have been used by the EU as an instrument of its 'external governance' in a range of ways: from facilitating a process of accession to the EU – the so-called 'Europe Agreements' that structured the EU's relationship with Central and Eastern European countries prior to their EU accession – to providing an alternative to membership for European countries within the EU's 'wider Europe' sphere of trade and foreign policy co-operation.[5] In situations where

[5] S Lavenex, 'EU external governance in "wider Europe"' (2004) 11(4) *Journal of European Public Policy* 680.

association agreements are an alternative to membership, nonetheless, they are a mechanism for 'Europeanisation' in the sense of facilitating EU influence within the European neighbourhood beyond the formal boundaries of its Member States.[6]

Given their flexibility as an alternative to EU membership, and given that they provide a basis not just for liberalising trade between the EU and non-Member States but also other forms of policy co-operation, association agreements have an evident utility. During the process of negotiating a draft Constitutional Treaty in 2003, a British MEP Andrew Duff proposed that the status of 'associate member' be created. Had this proposal been adopted, 'associate' membership could have been a vehicle both for states that might ultimately wish to join the EU (using the Article 49 of the Treaty on European Union (TEU) accession process) as well as those wishing to leave (using the Article 50 TEU withdrawal mechanism).The proposal was not accepted but, nonetheless, Duff has extolled the virtues of an association agreement in the context of Brexit.[7]

Under Article 217 of the Treaty on the Functioning of the European Union (TFEU), association agreements can be between the EU and another international organisation, or between the EU and a state. The 'Norway' option is often one identified as a 'soft' form of Brexit, but misleadingly it is not

[6] A Gawrich, I Melnykovska and R Shweikert, 'Neighbourhood Europeanization through ENP: the case of Ukraine' (2010) 48(5) *Journal of Common Market Studies* 1209.

[7] A Duff, 'After Brexit: a new association agreement between Britain and Europe', www.policy-network.net (12 October 2016).

an association agreement between the EU and Norway but instead refers to the association agreement between the EU and EFTA. The EU and its Member States participate in this EEA agreement on the EU side, while three EFTA states (Norway, Liechtenstein and Iceland) participate on the EFTA side (Switzerland has a separate bilateral free trade agreement with the EU). The EEA agreement is extensive, providing not just for tariff-free movement of goods, but for full participation in the Single Market (including free movement of workers) as well as involvement in EU programmes such as its Horizon 2020 research funding and collaboration programme. The agreement does not extend the EU's common agriculture and fisheries policy to the three EFTA states although it does deal with certain aspects of trade in these goods.

Significantly, the EEA model does not include a Customs Union. In a Customs Union, not only are tariffs eliminated as between the states that form the Customs Union, the participating states also agree to apply a common external tariff to the goods imported into the Union from non-participating states. The EU – as well as being a Free Trade Area – is also a Customs Union, with EU states adopting a Common Commercial Policy and a Common External Tariff. As a consequence, in terms of trade with states that form part of the WTO, the EU has common tariff rates that apply regardless of the Member State into which goods are imported. Once a product is imported and customs formalities and duties are applied, goods can then go into free circulation within the EU as if they had been produced in the EU.

Because the EEA agreement does not create a Customs Union, this leaves the EFTA states free to pursue their own trade policy and through EFTA, a large number of free trade agreements have been concluded. However, as the EEA agreement only gives tariff-free movement to goods produced in the participating states, there needs to be compliance with 'rules of origin' which allow any relevant tariffs to be applied within the EU to goods which have been imported into a participating EFTA state and then imported into an EU state. Given the significant trade between Norway and Sweden and given their geography and their histories of co-operation, arrangements are in place between the two countries to minimise the formalities when goods cross borders.[8] The absence of a Customs Union necessarily adds costs and red-tape for firms and companies but this is softened considerably by the access to the Single Market which participation in the EEA brings.

All of which then begs the question of whether the UK could leave the EU but find a way to participate in the EEA as if it were a country like Norway. As chapter 15 explains, it has been argued that the UK is a signatory to the EEA agreement and has not triggered the mechanism for withdrawing from that agreement in terms of Article 127 of the agreement. For the reasons explained later, even if it could be contended that the UK remained a contracting party to the agreement, its withdrawal from the EU renders the application of the EEA agreement either entirely devoid of

---

[8] R Milne, 'Norway model offer Britain food for thought on post-Brexit trade', *Financial Times* (28 October 2016).

purpose, or so partial as to be meaningless. The better approach would be to consider whether the UK could seek to participate in the EU Single Market and other EU programmes via the EEA agreement as if it were not currently a signatory to the agreement as an EU Member State.

The first step would be for the UK to return to its pre-1973 position and rejoin EFTA. Article 56 of the EFTA Convention would require the EFTA Council to consider an application for membership by the UK and if the four EFTA states agreed then an instrument of accession could be adopted. That alone would bring the UK into a free trade relationship with the other EFTA states – and it could seek access to the free trade agreements concluded between EFTA and other non-EU states – but in order to participate in the EEA, all the parties to the EEA agreement would need to agree, with ratification or approval by all parties.

Nonetheless, the obstacles to this form of soft Brexit are not merely procedural. It would entail accepting free movement of workers; it would mean accepting the application of EU rules and regulations without having a vote on their adoption; it would mean making budgetary contributions to the EU for participation in EU programmes; and it would also mean accepting the jurisdiction not just of the EFTA Court but also the continuing influence of the European Court of Justice in its interpretation of EU law because of the aim of seeking 'homogeneity' in the application of the agreement between the EU and EFTA states.[9] The choice for the UK government would be

---

[9] H Haukeland Frederiksen, 'The EFTA court 15 years on' (2010) 59(3) *International and Comparative Law Quarterly* 731.

between pursuing an EFTA/EEA form of 'soft Brexit' that would minimise some of the economic risks of Brexit; would enhance the potential for political support at UK and sub-national levels; and would likely also be welcomed by EU partners, and a 'hard Brexit' that would view the EFTA/EEA approach as not so much a 'soft Brexit' as a 'Leave lite' option which would be difficult to reconcile with the main themes of the Leave campaign in terms of taking back control.

Even if this soft Brexit approach had been a desirable outcome for the UK, any attempt by the UK to rejoin EFTA and to participate in the EEA could not just be viewed through the lens of what the UK might think was in its own interests. There is much in the EU–EFTA relationship that is itself problematic given the complex task of continually updating the annexes to the EU agreement to keep the legislative framework up to date with EU legislative changes.[10] Moreover, UK membership of EFTA would change the political dynamics of that grouping of states. All in all, the attempt to manage Brexit would itself shine a light on a range of other political, institutional and legal dynamics in the EU–EFTA relationship.

Of course, there would be nothing to prevent the UK entering into its own association agreement with the EU. The obvious model to consider would be the EU–Ukraine 'Deep and Comprehensive' trade agreement signed on 27 June 2014. As a style of agreement it extends much further than a normal

[10] European Commission, 'A review of the functioning of the European Economic Area', Commission Staff Working Document, SWD (2012) 425 (7 December 2012).

EU bilateral trade agreement with wide-ranging political and policy co-operation. Significantly, the EU–Ukraine association agreement does not create automatic rights of free movement of people. Title III of the agreement ensures that Ukrainians present on the labour markets of EU states are entitled to freedom from discrimination as regards working conditions, remuneration and dismissal. But access to the labour market is a matter for the laws of the Member States and any relevant EU legislation. Outside of the area of workers there is a commitment to working towards visa-free movement.

Nonetheless, the experience of the EU–Ukraine agreement also shows the risks that association agreements entail. Association agreements require the unanimous agreement of the governments of the EU Member States and, additionally, require national ratification before they enter into force. These procedural rules not only make reaching an agreement potentially quite slow and difficult, there is always the possibility that ratification will also be delayed or indeed fail. The ratification of the EU–Ukraine agreement was initially derailed in the Netherlands when – following the adoption of a new law allowing citizen-initiated referendums – the electorate voted not to agree to the approval of the Dutch ratification of the agreement, throwing the agreement into legal turmoil.[11] In an interesting twist – and copying the model used for David Cameron's 'new settlement' agreement – the Heads of State and Government of the EU States meeting

---

[11] G Van der Loo, 'The Dutch referendum on the EU–Ukraine association agreement', www.ceps.eu (8 April 2016).

within the European Council at the December 2016 summit adopted a decision, binding in international law, specifying *inter alia* that the association agreement did not confer on Ukraine the status of 'candidate country' for EU accession and nor did the provisions on the movement of workers confer any right to reside and work freely in the EU or limit the capacity of Member States to limit numbers. While designed to respond to the concerns of Dutch voters, one can easily see how this sort of language, if it formed part of a UK–EU association agreement, might soften (for the UK) a form of Brexit that would otherwise entail a 'deep and comprehensive' future relationship between the UK and the EU.

However, these options apparently have been ruled out by the Prime Minister in her Lancaster House speech. Brexit is not to be softened by any type of association agreement but through a free trade agreement. The UK will not be a participant in a Single Market or a Customs Union but rather will seek 'the best possible access' to that market. Existing models – whether in full or in part – are to be rejected in favour of a 'bespoke Brexit'.

The 2 February 2017 White Paper was not produced to allow Parliament to consider a range of options from which to cut a template for its version of a bespoke Brexit. There is only one tailor and that is the Prime Minister. Whatever may the advantages of other models, and however the national interest may be perceived by elite political and economic interests, the Prime Minister is cutting her Brexit cloth to fit the British body politic as she understands its shape and needs following the referendum. It is a Brexit intended to fit with the narrative of taking back control rather than what might otherwise be thought to be in the UK's wider political, economic and constitutional interests. Tellingly, it is the unwillingness of the UK government to consider and debate alternative forms of Brexit which has added fuel to the fire of the Scottish government's claims that it is being ignored and its demands for another independence referendum.

That the Prime Minister and her government could shape the outcome of the referendum in this way is, perhaps, also due to the lack of any contingency planning by her predecessor and his government. Had there been a more detailed plan setting out the UK's future relationship with the EU, this would have set the benchmark and defined the political conversation about what Leave meant. Indeed, had such a plan repeated the 2015 Conservative Party manifesto commitment to the UK remaining part of the Single Market, Theresa May might have found she had rather less room for manoeuvre. That would have been especially so had David Cameron followed through on his earlier statement that Article 50 would be triggered immediately after the referendum. Had that happened, there would have been little time to look for alternative strategies. Instead, the new Prime Minister immediately filled the power vacuum and then took advantage of the Brexit policy vacuum – assisted by the legal challenges which provided convenient legal cover while she took charge of government and the political process – to define her Brexit course. It is a course which fits a narrative about the UK's future as champion of free trade. For the Prime Minister, this is not about defining Brexit; it's about redefining Britain. Global Britain.

12

Future Trade: Deals and Defaults

In her 17 January 2017 speech at Lancaster House,[1] and two days later, at the World Economics Forum in Davos,[2] Prime Minister Theresa May placed the negotiation of new trade deals at the heart of her 'Global Britain' strategy for post-Brexit Britain. The starting point for that strategy, nonetheless, has to be the definition of the UK's future trade relationship with the EU. However desirable it may be to conclude new bilateral trade agreements with non-EU states, the UK's economic relationship with the EU will remain its primary relationship for the foreseeable future. In terms of timing, unless and until it is clear what future trading relationship the UK will have with the EU, and given the limited resources – both human and time – available to the UK to conduct multiple trade negotiations in parallel, it is unlikely that significant process can be made on this wider Global Britain strategy until the foundations of the UK's trade relationship with the EU are laid.

The UK's future trade relationship with the EU will not be forged in a legal vacuum. The UK and the EU are both members of the World Trade Organization (WTO). Indeed,

---

[1] T May, 'The government's negotiating objectives for leaving the EU', www.gov.uk/government/announcements (17 January 2017).

[2] T May, 'Davos 2017: Prime Minister's speech to the World Economics Forum', www.gov.uk/government/announcements (19 January 2017).

the UK was one of the founding members of the WTO and an original signatory to its General Agreement on Tariffs and Trade (GATT) 1947, prior to the existence of the European Economic Community (EEC). However, during its period of membership, it has been the EU that has been the primary actor within the WTO given that the EU takes over the exercise of its Member States trade policy competences. Once the UK leaves the EU, the UK will, nonetheless, remain a member of the WTO and that membership has legal consequences for the type of deal that the UK might seek with the EU.[3]

Both the UK and the EU will be bound by the discipline of membership in two senses. First, failure to reach any sort of trade deal will mean that trade will be conducted according to the principles of the GATT, the General Agreement on Trade in Services (GATS) and other WTO agreements. This is the penalty default of leaving the EU without a trade deal.[4] Secondly, in order to escape the default situation where tariffs become applicable to trade between the UK and the EU, any agreement – including any transitional

---

[3] L Bartels, 'The UK's status in the WTO after Brexit', https://ssrn.com/abstract=2841747 (23 September 2016).

[4] The concept of 'penalty default' is one developed in the context of contract law to explain judicially created rules designed to induce parties to more fully negotiate and bargain their contracts given that the alternative is to fall back onto a less desirable judicially created 'default'. In the context of the WTO, the idea is that the penalty default of the imposition of tariffs is an inducement to the EU and UK to bargain more fully a better set of trading arrangements. On penalty defaults see: S Baker and KD Krawiec, 'The penalty default canon' (2004) 72(4) *The George Washington Law Review* 663.

or interim agreement – must be compliant with WTO requirements.

Defining what will be the default position under WTO rules is key to establishing a baseline for any UK–EU deal. Using harmonised customs codes applicable to goods, a member of the WTO produces schedules setting out the legal ceilings on tariffs ('bound rate') which it will apply (the actual 'applied rate' may be lower than the bound rate). These rates apply to a country's trade with other WTO member countries on a 'Most Favoured Nation' (MFN) basis. If a country wishes to reduce or eliminate tariffs it cannot (subject to exceptions) discriminate between countries but must offer the same treatment to the others.

As a Member State of the EU, the tariff schedules and tariff rate quotas (important in respect of agricultural products) applied by the UK to trade with non-EU countries, are those that are common to all EU states. On leaving the EU, the UK will need to adopt its own schedules of commitments and concessions to be applied to commerce between the UK and WTO members. Were the UK to leave the EU without a preferential trade agreement with the EU, both the UK and EU will be obliged to impose tariffs on trade between themselves in line with their tariff rate schedules. Through successive rounds of multilateral negotiations, average EU tariff levels have been falling. Nonetheless, EU tariffs on trade in motor vehicles – which is both an important part of intra-EU trade as well as trade between the UK and non-Member States – are around 10 per cent.

Bartels has argued that the schedules of tariff concessions made by the EU are already those of the UK, with the EU standing in the shoes of the UK in the exercise of its rights.[5] This would mean that the UK would not be starting with a blank sheet in negotiating its WTO schedules of concessions and commitments. In a written statement to Parliament on 5 December 2016, the UK's International Trade Secretary Liam Fox indicated that the UK would seek to 'replicate as far as possible' its existing WTO schedules and commitments.[6] And in a subsequent blog post, the UK's representative at the WTO explained that this policy of replicating the schedules currently shared with the EU is a strategy to ensure a 'smooth transition' within the WTO and to minimise the risk of objections from any of the other WTO members when the UK adopts its own schedules.[7] But what remains unclear is how long this might take and what obstacles lie ahead.[8] If the idea of a future Great Repeal Bill is to keep UK law compliant with EU law in the immediate aftermath of Brexit, then it appears that as far as its trade with non-EU states is concerned, taking back control also means keeping things the same.[9]

However, one area where things will need to change in some ways is in the agricultural sector. Once the UK leaves the EU and its common agricultural policy, its approach to

---

[5] Bartels, 'The UK's status in the WTO after Brexit'.

[6] L Fox, 'UK's commitments at the World Trade Organization', House of Commons Written Statement 316 (5 December 2016).

[7] J Braithwaite, 'Ensuring a smooth transition within the WTO as we leave the EU', www.blogs.fco.gov.uk (23 January 2017).

[8] P Ungphakorn, 'Second bite – how simple is the UK–WTO relationship post-Brexit?', www.tradebetablog.wordpress.com (27 August 2016).

[9] I Dunt, 'Very quietly, Liam Fox admits the Brexit lie', www.politics.co.uk (6 December 2016).

FUTURE TRADE: DEALS AND DEFAULTS

agricultural subsidies will come under WTO scrutiny. This is also a sector where each WTO member's 'tariff rate quotas' allow certain quantities of agricultural products to enter the market duty-free or at a rate below the bound rate. These quotas apply as between the EU and WTO members. Determining what should be the UK's share of the EU's tariff rate quota is not without its difficulties. One way would be to look at actual trade patterns over a period of time and try to allocate on that basis. Nonetheless, it will be a challenge to maintain the status quo and while the normal bound rate that applies above the quota level will apparently remain the same, if too great a share of the quota is allocated to the UK, then an exporter to an EU country may find that the EU's quota share has been exhausted leading to the imposition of the necessarily higher bound rate. As Downes argues, the issue is not as simple as slicing up the EU quota, its value for exporters – including the value that comes from access to an EU market in which goods enter into free circulation – may be diminished.[10] The suggestion made by Holmes, Rollo and Winter that the UK and the EU take a joint approach to any modifications to their tariff concessions seems wholly sensible.[11]

The idea that the UK and the EU might need to work together is also relevant to the UK's future trading relationship with those states with which the EU has already concluded preferential trade arrangements. As will be discussed

[10] C Downes, 'The post-Brexit management of EU agricultural tariff rate quotas', www.ssrn.com (21 November 2016).
[11] P Holmes, J Rollo and LA Winters, 'Negotiating the UK's post-Brexit trade arrangements' (2016) 238 *National Institute Economic Review* 822.

further below, the EU's trade policy has been characterised by increased use of bilateral trade deals. Once the UK leaves the EU, it will need to put in place its own arrangements with those states with which the EU has bilateral agreements. Working with the EU and those states to seek to 'grandfather' and, thereby, retain, the existing arrangement would again emphasise a UK strategy of seeking continuity of trade as a post-Brexit default.

Given the penalty default of MFN tariffs, there is an incentive to seek to eliminate those tariffs in future UK–EU trade. However, any removal of tariffs would then need to be extended to other WTO members in line with the MFN principle. The WTO rules allow for an exception to the MFN principle where regional or other groups of WTO members enter into customs unions or free trade agreements that give preferential treatment to the parties to those agreements. The EU's treaties establishing a Single Market comprising not just a customs union, but also an internal market, is one such arrangement permitting tariff-free trade between its Member States. Free trade agreements between the EU and non-EU states are also examples of this exception to the MFN principle.

But as an exception to the MFN principle, these arrangements must comply with the requirement in Article XXIV(8) of the GATT namely that they eliminate tariffs and trade restrictions 'with respect to substantially all the trade' between the participating states. Article V of GATS contains an analogous requirement in respect of the removal of discrimination in an agreement with 'substantial sectoral coverage'. It is only comprehensive customs unions and free trade deals that are permissible exceptions to the MFN principle. Evaluation of compliance with this requirement is far from straightforward and in the context of Brexit even more so. Normally the issue would be whether the outcome is one in which tariffs and other barriers are lower than they were before the agreement. Of course, in the context of Brexit, there were no tariffs in trade between the UK and the EU. The comparison is instead between what the default would be and what any agreement achieves. Also significant is the scope of the agreement in terms of the sectors that are covered. An agreement that sought to eliminate barriers only in a particular sector would essentially constitute the sort of trade discrimination that the MFN principle prohibits. A differentiated UK–EU arrangement that focused solely on key economic sectors would be unlikely to meet the requirements of comprehensiveness, although the exclusion of the agriculture sector is relatively common in regional trade agreements.[12] It also seems clear than any transitional or interim agreement that might bridge UK withdrawal and the conclusion of a new comprehensive trade deal would also need to be notified to the WTO and assessed for its compliance with WTO rules.[13]

It is in this legal context that the Prime Minister's assertion that she would prefer to leave the EU without a deal rather than conclude a bad deal, needs to be evaluated.

---

[12] M Schaefer, 'Ensuring that regional trade agreements complement the WTO system: US unilateralism as a supplement to WTO initiatives' (2007) 10(3) *Journal of International Economic Law* 585.

[13] P Ungphakorn, 'The case of the two UK-EU "interim" deals – is the one in the WTO really "Plan B"?', www.tradebetablog.wordpress.com (20 March 2017).

The no-deal baseline is one that means the application of tariffs in trade between the UK and EU after more than forty years of tariff free trade. When combined with the depreciation in the value of Sterling, the cost of imports will increase. All of this on top of new customs formalities. A bad deal would need to be particularly bad to make no deal preferable.

As to the legal form of any deal, for all the talk about a 'bespoke Brexit' – a deal that does not conform to any existing model of EU trade relations – UK negotiators will be confronted with, and challenged by, the EU's legal and bureaucratic default settings that dictate how it engages with non-Member States. It is, perhaps, the irony of Brexit, that the EU is not a state with complete sovereignty and freedom to do what it wants, how it wants. It remains an international organisation and the powers of its institutions are defined in, and limited by, its founding treaties. That legal context shapes the form of its legal relationships with non-EU states, including its approach to trade deals.

As described in the previous chapter, the option of an 'association agreement' with the EU under Article 217 of the Treaty on the Functioning of the European Union (TFEU) is unlikely to be pursued by the UK for both substantive and procedural reasons. That leaves the EU to pull together its external legal competences in trade and elsewhere to put in place an agreement. In that regard, it is worth highlighting recent EU experiences of trade deals with non-Member States not just because they usefully illustrate the legal challenges and political risks associated with such deals but also because this is an area where the EU rather than its Member States has trade policy competence and negotiation expertise.

The EU has recent experience of concluding bilateral trade deals. With multilateral approaches to trade policy stalling and with new trade powers emerging, the EU has had to confront a changed and changing political, economic and legal environment for its external trade policy.[14] In the mid 2000s, the European Commission continued to emphasise the importance it attached to multilateral trade policy development through the WTO. Nonetheless, the Commission's *Global Europe* strategy began to identify candidate countries with which to conclude bilateral free trade agreements. For the EU, any such agreements 'must be comprehensive in scope, providing for liberalisation of substantially all trade and go beyond WTO disciplines'.[15] At the same time, protection of fundamental rights, labour and environmental standards have become focal points for social movements keen to ensure that free trade is also fair trade, something reflected in the European Commission's 2015 new trade policy strategy.[16] The first bilateral trade agreement to be concluded in terms of the *Global Europe* strategy was a free trade agreement with South Korea. Although substantive negotiations were finalised in just over two years, it took a further five years from the date of formal conclusion of the agreement for it to enter into full force (although it applied provisionally for four years). The difficulty lies in the nature of EU competence.

---

[14] SM McGuire and JP Lindeque, 'The diminishing returns to trade policy in the European Union' (2010) 48(5) *Journal of Common Market Studies* 1329.

[15] European Commission, 'Global Europe: competing in the world', COM (2006) 567 (4.10.2006).

[16] European Commission, 'Trade for all: towards a more responsible trade and investment policy', COM (2015) 497 (14 October 2015).

Article 3 TFEU states that the EU's Common Commercial Policy (CCP) shall be an area of exclusive EU competence. That means that for negotiations falling with the scope of the CCP, individual EU states no longer have the power to enter into deals with non-Member States. Determining how far the CCP extends is a function both of what the treaty says and its interpretation by the Court of Justice. Article 207 TFEU defines the CCP as including trade in goods and services, the commercial aspects of intellectual property rights and foreign direct investment. In a ruling due in 2017, the Court of Justice will have the opportunity to determine more precisely the scope of the CCP when it considers the EU–Singapore free trade agreement.[17]

The difficulty comes where agreements extend beyond the EU's exclusive competence. Matters that are wholly or partly within the remaining powers of the Member States require domestic ratification. So whereas trade issues within the scope of CCP could be agreed without domestic ratification (voting in the Council can also be by qualified majority voting), those that fall outside the zone of exclusive competence require unanimous agreement and domestic approval so increasing the chances of veto and delay. Agreements that combine fields of exclusive and non-exclusive competence are known as 'mixed' agreements.[18]

[17] Opinion 2/15, request for an opinion submitted by the European Commission pursuant to Article 218 (11) TFEU; application lodged 10 July 2015. Advocate General Sharpston delivered her view of the scope of the CCP on 21 December 2016: EU:C:2016:992.
[18] C Hillion and P Koutrakos (eds), *Mixed Agreements Revisited: The EU and its Member States in the World* (Hart Publishing, 2010).

Despite its protestations, the Commission has reluctantly accepted the practice of concluding mixed agreements on the basis that the Commission would rather have a deal done that can be provisionally applied pending its formal entry into force. Depending on the outcome of the EU–Singapore case, one strategy could be to allow the exclusive competence tail to wag the Brexit dog. In other words, a Brexit trade deal could be structured around the scope of the EU's exclusive competence so as to avoid national ratification processes. Even if less encompassing than might be desired – and perhaps requiring further and future negotiations on other aspects of UK–EU relations – it could help soften the hardness of a Brexit that would otherwise see the UK and EU simply failing to reach an agreement and falling back on WTO rules.

The risk of domestic approval problems in respect of mixed agreements was dramatised most clearly by the Canada–EU Trade Agreement (CETA). The EU and Canada began trade negotiations in May 2009 and the European Council President and Canadian Prime Minister formally announced that an agreement had been reached in September 2014. It took to July 2016 for the European Commission to propose to the Council the signature and conclusion of the agreement. At a press conference just two weeks after the EU referendum, EU Commissioner Malmström reiterated that while in the opinion of the European Commission the agreement fell within the scope of the exclusive competence of the Union under the CCP, nonetheless, the Commission was prepared to accept the conclusion and ratification of the deal as a 'mixed' agreement. In other words, the entry into force of the deal would be further delayed by domestic approval processes. The risks relating to national approval soon materialised.

Proceedings were brought before the German Constitutional Court seeking an interim injunction to prevent the German federal government from signing any act to formally conclude CETA and to halt its provisional application pending full ratification. In rejecting these applications, the German Constitutional Court expressly noted that to grant an injunction even on a temporary basis would interfere with the capacity of Germany and the EU to conduct trade policy. Indeed, the inability of trading partners to rely on the EU and its Member States to formally conclude the agreements they signed would, in the view of the Court, have a 'permanently negative impact' on global trading relations.[19]

However, the threats to EU trade deals are very real. Echoing the wider debates about the risks from globalisation and free trade, CETA and other such agreements have served as focal points for national and pan-European activists seeking to stop or limit free trade. The complex system for national approval of mixed agreements creates spaces and opportunities for such activism to garner support to delay, amend or veto EU trade agreements at national and even sub-national level. That the European Parliament (EP) gives consent to agreements also acts as another focal point for activism.

---

[19] Federal Constitutional Court judgment of 13 October 2016 in applications: 2 BvR 1368/16, 2 BvR 1444/16, 2 BvR 1823/16, 2 BvR 1482/16, 2 BvE 3/16. An English language summary of the Court's Press Release in the case can be found at www.bundesverfassungsgericht.de.

Ahead of a meeting in Luxembourg on 18 October 2016 in which the Council and EU Member States were expected to adopt decisions approving the CETA deal and its provisional application, the parliament of the Walloon region of Belgium voted on 15 October 2016 to withhold consent to Belgium's approval of CETA. It cited the need for stronger safeguard clauses in the agreement to protect labour and environmental standards and raised concerns voiced elsewhere in Europe about the proposed 'investment court system'.

On 27 October 2016 a joint EU–Canada 'interpretative text' was agreed with a view to clarifying the text of the agreement and so respond to the concerns raised by the Walloon parliament.[20] Consequently, CETA was formally signed on 30 October 2016. Nonetheless, the full entry into force of the agreement requires domestic ratification and so the risks of problems remain, including future domestic legal challenges,

CETA could be a model for a future trade deal between the EU and the UK. Yet the problems associated with such a deal demonstrate the risks that lie ahead.[21] But already, CETA and Brexit are intertwined in time. Coinciding with the aftermath of the referendum, the difficulties in securing ratification appeared to confirm the critique of EU membership that, when it came to promoting trade liberalisation globally, the need to secure agreement with twenty-eight

---

[20] Council of the EU, 'Joint Interpretative Instrument on the Comprehensive Economic and Trade Agreement (CETA) between Canada and the European Union and its Member States', Doc 13541/16 (27 October 2016).

[21] D Kleimann and G Kübek, 'After the "CETA drama", towards a more democratic EU trade policy', www.politico.eu (1 December 2016).

national governments and then secure domestic approval simply meant that the EU was a problematic bilateral trade partner. Indeed, as Canadian Prime Minister Justin Trudeau remarked at a joint press conference with the then French Prime Minister Manuel Valls on 13 October 2016, if the EU could not conclude a trade deal with Canada 'with whom will Europe do business in the years to come?' Echoing that remark, when asked during a press conference whether the earlier failure to finalise the CETA deal had wider implications, including for any future trade deal with the UK, EU Trade Commissioner Malmström quipped, 'If we cannot make it with Canada, I'm not sure we can make it with the UK. But jokes aside . . .' No one laughed. But it becomes clear why, for some, taking back control over trade is a realistic alternative for the UK than pursuing trade liberalisation through the EU.

Nonetheless, given that concluding a trade deal has to be the foundation of the UK's future relationship with the EU, perhaps the important point is that there is a political penalty default in play as much as the financial and legal defaults previously described, because for the UK as much as the EU, its credibility as a trade partner is also at stake. So a failure to come to any sort of agreement will harm the credibility of the UK every bit as much as it will the EU. And for both sides, their failure to reach an agreement would send a terrible signal to the world about the capacity of two important global actors to co-operate and work effectively on the global stage.

13

Differentiated Brexit

In her Lancaster House speech setting out her government's negotiating objectives for Brexit, the Prime Minister said that Brexit would not result in the UK being 'half-in, half-out'. Yet, Brexit could have a more differentiated quality to it geographically, sectorally and, unsurprisingly, temporally.

Geographically, the extent of the territorial application of EU law can be varied where, as in the case of Denmark, for example, territories like Greenland and the Faroe Islands were excluded or removed from the reach of EU obligations. Conversely, the unification of Germany saw the territorial reach of EU membership expand. Brexit raises the issue of whether the same sort of flexibility might be achieved but in the very different context of a Member State leaving the EU.

Certainly, the referendum result showed different patterns of voter sentiment across the UK, and particularly in the constituent nations of the United Kingdom. Northern Ireland constituted a single counting area for the referendum and 56 per cent of the electorate voted for the UK to remain in the EU. In Scotland, every one of the thirty-two counting areas returned a majority vote for Remain with 62 per cent of the electorate in Scotland voting for continuing UK membership of the EU. If, as described in the preceding chapters, the post-referendum period has been an exercise in trying to translate voter concerns into a blueprint for Brexit, then an outcome negotiated by a UK government for the whole of the

UK was open to the accusation of failing to respect the wishes of different parts of the UK.

The position in Scotland is made more poignant given the backdrop of the 2014 independence referendum. In the paper on 'Scotland in the European Union' published by the Scottish government to accompany its White Paper on independence, the Scottish government asserted:[1]

> under the current constitutional arrangements, it is a
> real possibility that in less than four years' time Scotland
> could be forced out of the EU even if a majority of people in
> Scotland want to retain membership.

This was a risk that the electorate was apparently prepared to contemplate given that they also voted for Scotland to remain part of the United Kingdom in the 2014 referendum. But how then to reconcile the two referendums separated by less than two years: a vote for Scotland to stay in the UK but a vote in Scotland for the UK to stay in the EU?

Following the June 2016 referendum, the Scottish government made much of its assertion that it would push for a Brexit outcome that respected the wishes of the Scottish electorate. The Scottish First Minister detected an inconsistency between, on the one hand, the UK government's willingness to consider the distinctive positions of Northern Ireland and Gibraltar in the context of Brexit as well as pursuing differentiated 'sectoral' arrangements, and on the other hand, a perceived reluctance to consider a differentiated

---

[1] Scottish Government, 'Scotland in the European Union', www.gov.scot/Resource/0043/00439166.pdf (November 2013).

Brexit for Scotland.[2] However, a differentiated Brexit risks creating a 'trilemma'. In a trilemma three different sets of interests need to be reconciled but, at any one time, only two of those sets of interests are compatible to the exclusion of the other. The challenge of a differentiated Brexit is whether the interests of the EU, the UK and Scotland can overcome this trilemma.

In terms of the shape of such a differentiated Brexit, a couple of options were floated. One suggestion was dubbed the 'reverse Greenland' option in which the continuing application of EU law was retained by participating devolved territories.[3] The obvious difficulty with this approach is that it would treat the UK as remaining in the EU, just that its scope of territorial application would not extend to those parts of the UK that 'opted-out'. But unlike the situation when Denmark's EU membership was redefined to exclude Greenland, the effect would be to leave a sub-state entity with only limited devolved powers as the entity claiming to exercise sovereign powers on behalf of the UK. This was never really going to be an option because even if the EU might be persuaded to pursue such an approach (itself quite unlikely), the UK government would not accept a situation in which the UK effectively remained in the EU.

Other options were presented by the Scottish government in December 2016 with the publication of its vision of

---

[2] N Sturgeon, speech to the David Hume Institute, www.davidhumeinstitute .com (28 February 2017).
[3] UP Gad, 'Could a "reverse Greenland" arrangement keep Scotland and Northern Ireland in the EU?', www.blogs.lse.ac.uk (7 July 2016).

'Scotland's place in Europe'.[4] The document deliberately positioned itself as a set of proposals that were not premised upon Scotland being independent, although the conclusion might be drawn that the high aspirations were unlikely to be met, providing a pretext for independence to protect Scottish interests.

The central proposition of the Scottish government was that Scotland, while remaining in the UK, should be permitted to participate in the Single Market through the European Economic Area (EEA) agreement in the event that the UK as a whole chose not to seek to retain access to the Single Market through the EEA agreement. The example of the Faroe Islands was highlighted. The Faroe Islands has a unique status and following a negotiated settlement with Denmark in 2005, exercises autonomous internal powers of government and certain external powers. It has entered into trade agreements with the European Free Trade Association (EFTA) states and membership of EFTA itself has been mooted.

There are obvious difficulties with the Faroe Islands analogy. A post-war referendum in the Faroe Islands backed independence, with the 2005 agreement with Denmark seeking to settle the position of the Faroe Islands without prejudice to the issue of independence. In 2014, a referendum in Scotland rejected independence. While more powers have been devolved to Scotland following that referendum it does not exercise full internal powers of governance and issues of

[4] Scottish Government, 'Scotland's place in Europe', www.scot.gov (20 December 2016).

foreign policy are expressly reserved to the UK. A significant internal constitutional change would be required to put Scotland on a similar footing to the Faroe Islands.[5] It would be a significant leap for Scotland – as a sub-state nation – to be permitted EFTA membership and then for all the other EU states to agree to it becoming a party to the EEA agreement.

But the debate about whether a differentiated form of Brexit might be possible soon morphed into a demand for a second independence referendum. During the 2015 General Election campaign, the First Minister Nicola Sturgeon suggested that a material change in circumstance might make a second independence referendum likely. Brexit would certainly constitute a material change. In its manifesto for the 2016 elections to the Scottish Parliament, the SNP indicated that if it was clear that a majority of people in Scotland favoured independence, a second independence referendum should be held. Although the SNP formed a government following the election, it lost its overall majority in the Scottish Parliament. Nonetheless, it is clear that the First Minister Nicola Sturgeon believed the election result gave the Scottish government an electoral mandate for another independence referendum should the conditions be fulfilled. Amidst increasing tension between the Westminster and Scottish governments over the shape of Brexit, on 13 March 2017, Scotland's First Minister announced that her government would seek to hold a referendum on independence to

---

[5] J Hartmann, 'The Faroe Islands: possible lessons for Scotland in a new post-Brexit devolution settlement', *Edinburgh Law Review*, forthcoming, https://ssrn.com/abstract=2909543 (1 February 2017).

give voters a 'choice between a hard Brexit and becoming an independent country'.[6]

Time and timing are at the heart of this linkage of Brexit and another Scottish independence referendum. Even without Brexit, for some, too little time has passed since the 2014 referendum for another to be conducted. The uncertainties of Brexit will also be compounded by an independence referendum. Yet for others, if Brexit is not the time for another independence referendum it is difficult to see when would be the right time. Even if the prospect of another independence referendum is accepted, there is also a crucial question of timing: should it take place before the UK leaves the EU – the preference of the Scottish government – or after Brexit? But even assuming that a referendum was held and that a vote for independence was the result, there would still be uncertainty over whether, and how, an independent Scotland should seek EU membership.

Many of the arguments about an independent Scotland's route to EU membership were rehearsed during the 2014 independence referendum campaign. It was claimed that an independent Scotland could avoid the normal EU accession process under Article 49 of the Treaty on European Union (TEU) and instead could experience a continuity of effect of membership, to be achieved through a renegotiation of the treaties under Article 48 TEU. It was said that a normal revision of the treaties could be used to change the territorial

---

[6] Scottish Government Press Release, 'Scotland must have choice over future', http://news.gov.scot/news/scotland-must-have-choice-over-future (13 March 2017).

reach of EU law as happened when Germany unified and when Greenland removed itself from the application of EU law to Denmark. It was never entirely clear why the pursuit of treaty change under Article 48 TEU was preferable to an accession process under Article 49 TEU given that the same requirements of the unanimous consent of all the other Member States – and hence the risk of veto by one or more of them – applied to both provisions. The primary explanation was time: the fear that an accession process would take time and leave Scotland outside of the EU after independence.

In the context of Brexit, if an independent Scotland could succeed to the UK's membership of the EU, this might also be a means of avoiding a formal Article 49 TEU accession process. This would again raise the issues explored in the context of the 2014 referendum, of who could succeed to the UK's international obligations in the event of a break-up of the UK.[7] While the claim that an independent Scotland could succeed to the UK's EU membership might have had some political appeal, as a matter of law it was more doubtful. First, as was suggested during the independence referendum, if Scotland split from the rest of the UK, it was highly likely that the latter would be treated in international law as the successor state to the rights and obligations previously exercised by the UK as a whole. If Scotland gained independence prior to Brexit, it would be the rest of the UK that

---

[7] On which see: J Crawford and A Boyle, 'Opinion: referendum on the independence of Scotland – international law aspects' in HM Government, 'Scotland analysis: devolution and the implications of independence' (Annex A) (11 February 2013).

would be the successor state to EU membership and not Scotland. If secession occurred after Brexit, there would be no UK membership of the EU to which to succeed.

Secondly, to arrive at the conclusion that an independent Scotland could be the successor state to the UK for the purposes of EU membership, it would also have to be accepted that for all other treaties and international obligations, the rest of the UK would likely be regarded as the successor state. This would reduce successor state attribution to a divorce-like dividing up of possessions. Thirdly, even if it was to be accepted that Scotland could act as the successor state to the UK, it would acquire not just the rights of EU membership but also any of the UK's liabilities. While that might be convenient for the UK in potentially reducing its liabilities to the EU when it leaves the EU, it would be much less convenient for a newly independent Scotland.

Although it is clear that there was a strong vote in Scotland in 2016 for the UK to remain in the EU, it may not be so obvious either that this necessarily translates into support for independence or that voters would unquestionably support an independent Scotland's membership of the EU. Indeed, the option of EFTA membership and, through EFTA, access to the EU Single Market through the EEA might have considerable advantages over EU membership at least in economic terms (it would not entail joining the Eurozone, it would exclude agriculture and fisheries and it would allow an independent Scotland to conduct its own trade policy). A period in EFTA could also smooth a future path to EU membership.

However, even if the interests of Scotland and the EU (and for that matter the EFTA states) aligned, this is clearly a road down which the UK government is not prepared to travel. Indeed, the Scottish government's version of nationalism is on a collision course with a new nationalism that views the post-Brexit United Kingdom through distinctly unionist lenses.

Looking beyond territorial differentiation, as discussed in the previous chapter, a wholly sectoral approach to the negotiation of a post-Brexit trade deal would seem unlikely given that such an arrangement would not meet the requirement for a World Trade Organization (WTO)-compliant trade deal. Which is not to say that a comprehensive trade deal between the UK and EU would not have sectoral specificity within it, not least because of the importance of certain sectors to the UK economy including financial services and car production. But even leaving aside the WTO dimension, and assuming that the interests of the UK and the devolved administrations converged on a more differentiated approach to Brexit (whether geographically or sectorally), it is simply less clear that the Brexit trilemma can be overcome on the EU side. In evidence to the House of Common Select Committee on Exiting the EU, the former UK Permanent Representative to the EU, Sir Ivan Rogers stated that all his instincts told him that the EU27 would shy away from a sectoral approach to future trade negotiations with the UK.[8]

If a Brexit differentiated by place and by sector may turn out to be much less likely, a Brexit differentiated in time

---

[8] H Mance, 'Former UK top diplomat warns EU will oppose sectoral Brexit deals', *Financial Times* (22 February 2017).

is, however, a more plausible scenario. The idea of putting in place transitional arrangements has an obvious appeal not least because of the tight timeframe for negotiations once Article 50 is triggered. It may simply not be possible to conduct and conclude all relevant negotiations within that period.

In one sense, the appeal of transitional arrangements is that it acts as a hedge against a failed 'hail Mary' strategy of seeking to negotiate everything all at once within two years. Being able to deploy a transitional arrangement, would allow negotiations to continue but without Brexit leading to the parties falling off a cliff-edge without any sort of deal at all. More proactively, putting in place a transitional arrangement might itself structure the timing and phasing of negotiations, allowing the parties to focus energies on the main items for immediate resolution – principally the terms of the withdrawal agreement and a broad framework and roadmap for future co-operation – but allowing time to develop the substantive future trade and co-operation deal beyond the two-year Article 50 process. This would also echo sentiments expressed by EU actors that negotiations on a future trade arrangement would need to follow the negotiations on a withdrawal agreement and a framework for future co-operation.

Yet there are equally obvious concerns against transitional arrangements. Certainly, for the most ardent Brexiteers, the desire was always for as quick an exit as possible. To their ears, talk of transition sounds a lot like foot-dragging or an attempt to block or derail the UK's departure from the EU. For those less ideologically committed to Brexit, nonetheless, there are the linked questions of what transition would look like and, more importantly, to what end would transition be aimed?

For some, an obvious transitional model would be to secure UK access to the Single Market on tariff-free terms by exercising rights under the EEA agreement.[9] It would be important that this would have to be on the basis that the UK was no longer a Member State of the EU and so its participation would be on the EFTA-state side and would likely have to entail membership of EFTA itself. Although the EEA covers all four freedoms, Article 112 of the Agreement does permit safeguard measures to be put in place and it might be that the UK would also want a Protocol like that afforded to Liechtenstein which permitted it – on a transitional basis – to demand that migrant labour from the EU and other EFTA states seek prior authorisation before seeking entry, residence and employment. The difficulty with the EEA as a transitional arrangement is that it would seem to entail precisely the same steps to get into on a transitional basis as it might on a more permanent basis. Once inside this arrangement – and with certain benefits flowing from a relationship based on an association agreement rather than a free trade agreement – it would also be more difficult to transition then to another form of non-EU membership. In short, the combined entry and exit barriers would likely make the EEA an endpoint rather than a transitional model.

Instead of deploying a particular model as a transitional arrangement, the logic of a 'bespoke' Brexit might also be extended to the formulation of transitional arrangements.

---

[9] Adam Smith Institute, 'The case for the (interim) EEA option', www
.adamsmith.org (22 July 2016).

The problem, however, is that the actual detail and structure of this sort of transition may be rather hazy, tending to identify more the things that such a deal would need to avoid, or conversely might ideally want, but without real clarity on how any of these things might come about.[10] And as acknowledged even by proponents, there are significant obstacles to such an approach, not least the danger that it could take as long and be as difficult to negotiate a bespoke interim Brexit as a bespoke final Brexit.

There is also a connection to be drawn between the discussion of a sectoral approach to Brexit and a temporal approach. Particularly in respect of services which constitute a significant part of the UK economy, the issue is less about the increased costs of market access if the UK were to default to WTO rules in the absence of an agreement between the UK and EU, and much more about denial or restriction of market access due to the UK acquiring a third-country status within regulatory frameworks. It is here that the future of UK financial services is at stake.

Firms established in the EU can legally set up branches and agencies in other Member States or can offer cross-border services from the home state in which they are established and regulated. Through authorisations granted in compliance with EU law, EU-based firms can conduct a wide variety of financial services in their home states and through the required recognition of authorisations already granted in other Member States of the EU ('passporting'). Non-EU-based financial service

---

[10] D Chalmers and A Menon, 'Getting out quick and playing the long game', OpenEurope Briefing, www.openeurope.org.uk (25 July 2016).

providers can set up headquarters in one of the EU Member States and use this as a means of accessing the EU financial services market. According to a research report for the EP, London is the European headquarters for half of the world's financial firms.[11] Once the UK leaves the EU, financial services firms established in the UK will no longer have automatic rights of passporting, but will seek to rely instead on the Commission adopting 'equivalence decisions' as it does with third-country firms.[12] Given the degree of conformity that arises as a result of the UK's EU membership, equivalence should be achievable, but it also then requires that this conformity is maintained after Brexit and that it is subject to continuing oversight and assessment by the European Commission.

However, even the possibility of non-EU based firms gaining access to the Single Market through equivalence decisions varies depending on the financial sector and the relevant legislation. Moreover, even where equivalence is provided for, the extent to which it grants market access on terms similar to passporting is also variable. In both wholesale and retail banking, the limited reach of equivalence decisions has little resemblance to the passporting that UK-based banks enjoy with the UK in the EU and its Single Market.[13] One

[11] Economic Governance Support Unit, 'Brexit, the United Kingdom and EU financial services', PE 587.384, www.europarl.europa.eu (9 December 2016).

[12] European Commission, 'EU equivalence decisions in financial services policy: an assessment', Commission Staff Working Document, SWD (2017) 102 (27 February 2017).

[13] Economic Governance Support Unit, 'Third country equivalence in EU banking legislation', PE 587.369, www.europarl.europa.eu (9 December 2016).

commentator suggests that passporting alone is worth around £10 billion to the UK economy annually.[14]

Evidence presented to the House of Lords European Union Committee inquiry into Brexit and financial services strongly supported a transitional arrangement for financial services to stop the industry falling off a cliff-edge in the event that an encompassing bespoke Brexit deal was not negotiated within the period of the Article 50 negotiations.[15] Nonetheless, while there may be some consensus that such a transitional arrangement may be desirable to allow financial services firms to adjust to the new and changing realities of Brexit, there remains a distinct lack of clarity as to the form and nature of this, and any other, sort of sectoral transitional arrangement.

To the extent that Brexit is differentiated in time, it will be in terms of the sequencing and timing of different phases of the negotiations. The focal point for the initial phase will be the withdrawal agreement and the settling of the key issues of citizens' rights and determination of liabilities. Thereafter, the relatively limited time left to negotiate and conclude other issues will require the UK and EU to decide on certain priorities. With that in mind, the Prime Minister's belief that transitional arrangements only refer to a phase of implementation occurring after a deal is struck during the Article 50 negotiations seems like particularly wishful thinking.

---

[14] F de la Peña, 'Gentle Brexit, a very British exit: EEA membership as the most favourable model to secure financial services passports' (2016) 27(7) *European Business Law Review* 1057.

[15] House of Lords European Union Committee, 'Brexit: financial services', 9th Report (Session 2016–17) HL81 (15 December 2016).

14

Taming of Control: The Great Repeal Bill

The rhetoric of taking control which surrounded the referendum vote for the UK to leave the EU spoke to a new nationalism and a new internationalism. Yet, change which voters might have expected to follow Brexit seems unlikely to transpire in the short to medium term. As the preceding chapters have indicated, there may be a significant taming of control when it comes to the UK's post-Brexit international trade given the emphasis which has continually been placed on seeking continuity in the UK's trade relationships. Similarly, in respect of control over national laws and the freedom to enact rules without the scrutiny or intervention of EU political or judicial institutions, the UK government's aim is to maintain the corpus of existing EU law – the *acquis communautaire*, as it is known – through the adaptation of domestic legislation. A Great Repeal Bill, no less, is to be introduced to Parliament in 2017 with the aim of repealing the European Communities Act 1972 (and other enactments that will no longer be required), but also with the goal of preserving the effects of EU law within domestic law.

In her Lancaster House speech, Theresa May stated:[1]

> The same rules and laws will apply on the day after Brexit as they did before. And it will be for the British Parliament

---

[1] T May, 'The government's negotiating objectives for leaving the EU', www.gov.uk/government/announcements (17 January 2017).

to decide on any changes to that law after full scrutiny and proper Parliamentary debate.

This statement expresses two of the Prime Minister's principles for Brexit first announced in her speech and elaborated in the subsequent White Paper: the principles of certainty and of taking control over laws. In respect of taking back control over laws, this is clearly something which will be displaced to another time: a time after Brexit. And so the immediate effect of leaving the EU is not going to be substantive in terms of a bonfire of directives and regulations. Rather, it is a statement of principle, namely that it will be for future Parliaments to decide what laws to repeal, amend or retain. Yet, the White Paper also states that this principle of the sovereignty of Parliament never actually went away:

> Whilst Parliament has remained sovereign throughout our membership of the EU, it has not always felt like that.

If correct, the taking of control over laws is, again, not about making substantive changes to how the UK is governed after Brexit, but rather about changing voter sentiment about how it feels to be governed. The idea that things will stay the same on 'Brexit Day' is intended, no doubt, to be reassuring and to offer 'certainty' to those anxious about how Brexit will impact on their lives and businesses. However, if the point of voting for the UK to leave the EU was that things would be different outside the EU, then the government's intentions may be anything but reassuring to 'Leave' voters. Unsurprisingly, some have argued that the retention of EU law in domestic law after Brexit should be time-limited through a 'sunset clause' in the Great Repeal Bill.[2]

But there is also an important legal point about what can and should remain the same. EU law is not like domestic law. In order to be applicable, it requires circumstances to fall within the scope of EU law. Typically that entails some form of cross-border activity with the aim of ensuring that obstacles to that activity are removed if they are discriminatory or otherwise create restrictions which cannot be justified. This legal framework assumes membership of the EU and gives effect to its aims. It simply does not make sense to replicate this in UK law after Brexit. If domestic law will be required it will be to implement whatever agreement is negotiated between the UK and the EU. Where EU law is more like domestic law – indeed, where it has been adopted to take over individual state's responsibilities to regulate in the public interest in areas of worker, environmental, health and safety, social and consumer protection – then there is more reason to consider retaining or replicating this in domestic law. Paradoxically, it will be all the regulatory aspects of EU law that will be protected in UK law after Brexit more than the deregulatory, liberalisation aspects. In other words, what will be maintained within, or incorporated into, UK law will be highly asymmetric and will emphasise giving domestic legal effect to the much-derided 'Brussels red tape'.

Leaving aside whether the ambition to keep the rules and laws the same is the correct aspiration, the technical

---

[2] M Littlewood, 'Why the Great Repeal Bill must include a sunset clause', www.brexitcentral.com (6 October 2016).

challenge of delivering that goal is a significant one. EU law is found in a variety of sources each with different legal characteristics. It is a law that changes over time. It is also interpreted, elaborated, amended and applied in a complex administrative system that operates at, and between, EU and national levels as well as across national administrations. Merely replicating the rules will not be enough. Moreover, the means of achieving all of this will expose the UK's own political and legal system to the type of critical evaluation about its density and democratic quality as was applied to EU law during the UK's membership.

To appreciate the scale of the task of 'legislating for Brexit',[3] it is useful to think about how EU law has been applied in the UK during its membership. To give domestic legal effect to the UK's membership of the EU, section 2(1) of the European Communities Act 1972 ensured that rights and obligations created by the EU treaties, or the legislation and rules made by the EU's institutions, would be given legal effect in UK law. Once the UK leaves the EU the source of those rights will be cut off. The task of domesticating EU law – to give EU law a domestic legal source – will depend on the particular source in question.

The EU treaties contain provisions which are capable of being applied directly in national law, including: provisions abolishing customs duties and charges; rules prohibiting obstacles to free movement; requirements for non-discriminatory internal taxation; and competition rules that prohibit cartels

---

[3] J Simson Caird, 'Legislating for Brexit: the Great Repeal Bill', House of Commons Library Briefing Paper 7793 (23 February 2017).

and abusive exercises of market power. Leaving to one side the competition rules where domestic legislation already replicates EU law, future changes in domestic law will be focused on implementing any new negotiated trade arrangements and not on replicating the existing treaties which contain obligations that assume continuing EU membership. Indeed, there will be other provisions of the treaties – on the common agricultural policy, on economic and monetary union – that the UK would not seek to reproduce in domestic law. Rather the focal point of any domestication of EU law is more likely to be at the level of EU regulations and directives.

One of the unique qualities of the EU as an international organisation is that its rules are not just to be found in the treaties which establish the organisation or which that organisation enforces like the World Trade Organization (WTO) agreements. It has the capacity to generate legislative rules as well as non-legislative delegated and implementing acts that amend, supplement or facilitate the uniform implementation of legislative rules. This is the world of EU regulations and directives. In legal terms, regulations share similar qualities to treaty provisions: they can be applied directly in national law without the need for domestic legislation. Once the UK leaves the EU, this supply of law within UK law will be stopped. Measures will need to be taken to incorporate these directly applicable rules into UK law and the White Paper states that:

> The Government's general approach to preserving EU law is to ensure that all EU laws which are directly applicable in the UK (such as EU regulations) ... remain part of domestic law on the day we leave the EU.

183

It is one thing to incorporate into UK law, EU regulations which set out the main legislative rules governing a field in a general way. But, one of the primary uses of regulations at EU level is in the continual implementation and application of these legislative frameworks. Whereas legislative action is relatively episodic – and as will be seen, more likely to be done through directives, rather than regulations – the production of delegated and implementing regulations is a daily occurrence. In the first few months of 2017 alone, the European Commission authored fifty regulations and the Council of Ministers authored another thirty-three. Not only is there an existing enormous corpus of EU law to be incorporated into UK law, it is one that is continually changing and being updated. The very notion that at a moment in time – Brexit Day – the same rules will apply as they did when the UK was a Member State is both an illusion and a delusion.

EU directives pose a different technical challenge. They are very different legal instruments from regulations in that they require Member States to introduce or amend national laws to meet the requirements specified in the directives. In one sense that ought to make the government's task much easier in that UK law has already transposed directives into UK law. It does so via primary legislation enacted by Parliament but also by the mechanism provided in section 2(4) of the 1972 Act whereby – through powers exercised by government ministers – domestic statutory instruments incorporate EU directives into domestic law without the need for primary legislation to pass through the normal Westminster parliamentary process. The difficulty is that once the 1972 Act is repealed, there will no longer be a legal basis in primary law for all the statutory instruments adopted under the 1972 Act and so they will no longer be valid. Accordingly, one of the key tasks of the Great Repeal Bill and any other Brexit-related legislation will be to create the necessary power in primary law to retain these statutory instruments in force.

However, the challenge facing the Great Repeal Bill is not simply technical it is constitutional. Given the scale of domesticating EU law into UK law, there will be significant pressure to avoid time-consuming primary legislation and, instead, to use the mechanism of delegating powers to ministers to adopt regulations. While an essential feature of modern government, nonetheless, delegated powers require parliamentary supervision and oversight. Indeed, it would be ironic if the consequence of taking back control over law-making was to shield rule-making from parliamentary scrutiny. Of course, UK constitutional law does insist on the application of procedures to give Parliament oversight over such delegated rule-making. Nonetheless, the scale of the operation may make meaningful oversight difficult to achieve. In any event, recent evidence shows how little parliamentary time is devoted to debating delegated rules. According to the Hansard Society, in the session 2015–16, MPs spent less than eight hours debating statutory instruments in the Commons Chamber.[4]

Moreover, the Great Repeal Bill may not only delegate powers to ministers to enact rules incorporating EU law

---

[4] Hansard Society, 'Westminster lens: Parliament and delegated legislation in the 2015–16 session', www.hansardsociety.org.uk (2017).

into UK law, but may also empower ministers – by the same means – to amend both existing primary legislation passed by Parliament as well as to amend future legislation.[5] These so-called 'Henry VIII' clauses in statutes threaten to undermine parliamentary control over law-making as well as the rule of law.[6] Indeed, one of the complaints about the operation of the European Communities Act 1972 was precisely that it empowered ministers to amend laws passed by the UK Parliament in order to give continuing effect to EU law. Of course, it is possible to design regimes of delegation in such a way as to ensure accountability and oversight and even to require renewal of the delegation over time (another use for 'sunset' clauses). The point is to highlight the risk that it may not be Parliament deciding on which laws to change after 'full scrutiny' and 'Parliamentary debate', but rather ministers exercising the sort of executive power which voters appeared to reject when they complained about the powers of the European Commission.

There is also an important devolution dimension to the constitutional challenge of domesticating EU law. On the one hand, the repatriation of competences back to the UK will also mean that the devolved governments will also acquire new tasks and responsibilities because the issues fall within their sphere of competence. But on the other hand, the Great Repeal Bill – as a legislative act of the Westminster

---

[5] NW Barber and AL Young, 'The rise of prospective Henry VIII clauses and their implications for sovereignty' (2003) *Public Law* 113.

[6] Bingham Centre for the Rule of Law, 'How can Brexit be done under the rule of law?', www.biicl.org (24 October 2016).

Parliament – will include provisions which will have an impact on the exercise of devolved legislative competences. By constitutional convention – the Sewel Convention – Westminster is obliged to seek the consent of the devolved parliaments before it legislates on matters within devolved competence and so it was expected that legislative consent motions (LCM) would need to be passed.[7] In January 2017, the Secretary of State for Scotland, David Mundell confirmed that a LCM was likely to be sought. However, the Sewel Convention's formal reach is only in respect of primary legislation passed by Westminster like the Great Repeal Bill itself, and not the delegated rules enacted through it or other primary legislation. The risk might then be that UK ministers could exercise delegated rule-making powers in areas within the competence of the devolved administrations. This is an obvious gap in the Sewel framework and one which Brexit exposes.[8]

In terms of timing, the Great Repeal Bill will be enacted prior to the UK's withdrawal from the EU, albeit without coming into effect until the UK ceases to be a Member State of the EU. In other words, and contrary to some of the claims made by those supporting the UK leaving the EU, the UK could not simply leave the EU by repealing the European Communities Act 1972 but will need to use the Article 50 mechanism. The point of the Great Repeal Bill is

---

[7] S Douglas-Scott, 'The "Great Repeal Bill": constitutional chaos and constitutional crisis?', UK Constitutional Law Blog, www .ukconstitutionallaw.org (10 October 2016).

[8] A Page, 'Brexit: the implications for the devolution settlement', www .centreonconstitutionalchange.ac.uk (27 September 2016).

to synchronise withdrawal as a matter of both EU and domestic law.

Time will not stop at the moment the UK leaves the EU and the Great Repeal Act (as it will then be) swings into effect. The rule-making structures of the EU will not shup up shop just because the UK has withdrawn from the EU. In the days, weeks and months afterwards, new legislation, delegated rules and implementing measures will be adopted at EU-level which will change the *acquis*. The extent to which UK law will remain in conformity with EU law after Brexit Day is unclear but it seems highly likely that the Great Repeal Bill will includes mechanisms to allow UK law to be revised, particularly through its delegated rule-making mechanisms. However, what is particularly significant is that – unlike maintaining the *acquis* to which the UK was already bound while a Member State – the domestication of future EU law would entail adapting UK law to rules adopted when it has ceased to be a Member State. This would not merely keep UK law the same, it would be to continue to keep UK law compliant with EU law but without any of the rights of representation and influence over the content of those rules which the UK enjoyed while it was a Member State. To draw a comparison, under the terms of the European Economic Area (EEA) agreement, the three participating European Free Trade Association (EFTA) states agree to align their laws with new EU measures through the EEA Joint Committee. Although the EFTA states do not have voting rights in the Council of Ministers, nonetheless, the EFTA states are allowed to participate as observers. If one reason for the apparent rejection of an EEA-approach to Brexit might be that it would lead to the

UK complying with swathes of EU law post-Brexit, it is perfectly conceivable that a Great Repeal Act could achieve much the same regulatory outcome. Indeed, if there was no trade agreement in place to establish tariff-free access to the Single Market, but the UK continued to apply and update the *acquis* as a matter of domestic law, then it would end up in the rather unusual position in which non-tariff barriers might be avoided but tariffs would be applied.

But the difficulties are not restricted to the practicalities and effects of seeking to mirror the EU's *acquis* at an instrumental level. Indeed, there is a real danger that our attention is drawn simply to the visible tip of the regulatory iceberg. All these regulatory frameworks require to be implemented and applied and enforced, with businesses capable of being able to have legal certainty in practice and not just in theory. A Great Repeal Bill that focused only on formal domestication of EU rules would not deal with some of the most crucial issues that will face businesses seeking to operate in the EU after Brexit. These issues relate to applications for, and recognition of, authorisations to place products on, or offer services in, the Single Market. This is the complex, multi-level world of European administration and the networks, committees and agencies which makes this all operate across the EU. This is what lies hidden beneath the waterline, and which risks causing businesses based in the UK to founder as they seek to navigate a way into the Single Market from outside.

The issue of the UK's future relationship with EU agencies is an important manifestation of concerns about how continuous economic life will be in practice after

Brexit. The UK government's Brexit White Paper identified regulatory co-operation with such agencies as something to be resolved:

> There are a number of EU agencies, such as the European Medicines Agency (EMA), the European Chemicals Agency (ECHA), the European Aviation Safety Agency (EASA), the European Food Safety Authority (EFSA) and the European (Financial Services) Supervisory Authorities (ESAs), which have been established to support EU Member States and their citizens. These can be responsible for enforcing particular regulatory regimes, or for pooling knowledge and information sharing. As part of exit negotiations the Government will discuss with the EU and Member States our future status and arrangements with regard to these agencies.

There are six 'executive' EU agencies and over thirty 'decentralised' agencies. Executive agencies play a significant role in implementing EU programmes that involve the financing of projects and so have relevance to the UK education and science communities that often engage with such agencies when making applications for research funding and research collaborations with partners based in the EU. These agencies can, and do, work with non-EU Member States but the extent and nature of the relationship depends not just on a background international agreement between the EU and the third country but also the type of the agreement. At its simplest, an 'association agreement' allows a state's institutions to participate in these research-funding programmes as if they were based in an EU Member State. However, the UK government is looking instead to negotiate a trade deal which could include negotiation of a science and technology agreement similar to the one the EU has with Canada. The crucial difference is that both sides bring their own money to the collaboration.

However, it is the work of decentralised agencies which has featured more prominently in post-referendum discussions, particularly the work of the agencies identified in the White Paper. Nonetheless, it is important to recognise that agencies vary enormously in their functions, and also remain connected to, and embedded within, both national and EU institutional structures. Determining the future relationship with EU agencies is, therefore, a necessary but not a sufficient condition for ensuring continuity in economic and legal relationships post-Brexit. There is a far more complex and multi-level administrative landscape to be traversed.

For instance, there is an important distinction to be drawn between EU regulatory frameworks that decentralise authorisation procedures down to the Member States and those that decentralise them to EU agencies for EU-wide approval. Where economic undertakings seek a national approval for certain biocides, for example, the application is made to a competent national authority based in a Member State to place the product on the market of that state. In order to seek access to the markets of other Member States, companies can make 'recognition' applications – either at the same time or subsequently – based on the authorisation granted by the original Member State. After Brexit, while companies may continue to make applications to the UK Health and Safety Executive for authorisation based on the *acquis*, as an authorisation will no longer be from a competent authority of a Member States, the procedures on recognition in other Member States will not automatically be available.

Certain biocides benefit from EU-wide authorisation from the ECHA. The same is true for certain new medicines approved by the UK-based EMA. The extent of the authorisation granted is the whole territory of the EU, making it much more likely that companies will seek to place their products first on the EU market and only then see what stance UK regulatory authorities take. A former UK medicines regulator was reported to have warned this might lead to new cancer drugs being approved in the EU with delayed approval in the UK.[9] However, in some key sectors, an EU-wide authorisation can only be granted to a firm based in an EU Member State. An EU-wide medicines authorisation can only be held by a firm established within the EU. Credit agencies seeking EU-wide authorisation from the European Securities and Markets Authorities (ESMA) also need to be established in an EU state. Firms based in non-EU states must seek an 'equivalence' decision from the European Commission pursuant to an agreement between ESMA and the non-EU state. In other words, maintaining the *acquis* in UK law will not be enough to ensure continuity in market access for UK-based businesses without some type of agreement between the UK and the EU and even then, it may not be on the same basis as before Brexit.[10]

[9] 'Cancer drugs may be delayed after Brexit, says experts', www.bbc.co.uk /news (10 February 2017).

[10] See the evidence contained in House of Commons Foreign Affairs Committee, 'Article 50 negotiations: implications of "no deal"', 9th Report (Session 2016–17), HC1077 (12 March 2017).

It is not enough to make UK law formally symmetrical to EU law on Brexit Day. Laws are made effective by the administrative apparatus that puts it into practice. With or without an agreement between the UK and the EU, businesses will need to know who they need to approach for authorisations to carry out their activities and whether these will be recognised in EU states. And they will also want to know what mechanisms will exist to resolve disputes. It is unclear what form any future dispute-resolution mechanism with the EU will take, and no enlightenment can be found in the White Paper. But it is important to keep in mind that the administrative system of the EU is itself a means of managing disputes and conflicts in the first instance. Administrative co-operation – especially in the context of systems of mutual recognition of licences, author-isation and qualifications – is vital to the effective operation of, and compliance with, EU legal frameworks. A Great Repeal Bill on its own cannot produce that.

There is also the vital question of the authoritative interpretation of law and the role of UK courts after Brexit.[11] Leaving the jurisdiction of the EU courts is a central plank of Brexit. There will be no possibility for UK courts to seek authoritative interpretations of the *acquis* from the Court of Justice under the preliminary ruling mechanism. But it would seem odd to take strenuous efforts to ensure the continued application of EU law in the UK – unless and until Parliament decides otherwise – only then for the interpretation of that law by UK courts to drift. If there is to be a homogeneity of

---

[11] R Gordon QC, 'The UK courts after Brexit' (2016) *Butterworths Journal of International Banking Law and Financial Law* 511.

interpretation as well as a symmetry of rules, UK courts will have to have regard to the rulings of the EU courts. What is not clear is what instructions to courts – if any – will be contained in the Great Repeal Bill to guide their future interpretation of national rules that replicate EU law. Under the European Communities Act 1972, which will be repealed, there is a specific instruction to UK courts to interpret EU law in accordance with the principles laid down by the Court of Justice. Absent such a provision, it may simply be the case that UK courts will continue to consult judgments of the Court of Justice albeit that UK courts will be no longer bound by such rulings.

To return to where we began in exploring the 'Time for Brexit', the debate about whether Brexit will be hard or soft is a question of how much things will be the same or different for the UK after Brexit. For voters who wanted the UK to remain in the EU, the risk was how much would change after the UK leaves. For those who wanted the UK to leave the EU, the hope was that, indeed, much would change. Both sets of voters may be surprised at the efforts being placed on seeking continuity in governance. For Remain voters, while this may afford some comfort, it will simply reinforce the view that the better way of keeping things the same was for the UK to remain a Member State of the EU. For Leave voters, the outcome may be more ambiguous. On the one hand, post-Brexit continuity would seem to be a rebuttal of 'Project Fear' claims about the risks from leaving the EU. On the other hand, the taming of control rather than the taking of control may well lead some to conclude that Brexit is an incomplete political project. For them, Brexit Time keeps ticking.

Part IV

Time to Brexit

15

Article 50 TEU: How to Withdraw from the EU

On 1 December 2009, the Lisbon Treaty entered into force. For the first time, an EU treaty expressly provided – in Article 50 of the Treaty on European Union (TEU) – for a Member State to withdraw from the European Union. The United Kingdom's withdrawal from the EU following the 2016 referendum is the first test of the new treaty article. What it says – and significantly, what it omits to say – is the subject not just of legal analysis, but also of public and media attention. It is hard to conceive of any other article of the EU treaties which is now as well-known as Article 50.

The Lisbon Treaty was negotiated following the failure of the Treaty establishing a 'Constitution for Europe'. So if we are to understand the origins of Article 50 it is to the process surrounding the Constitutional Treaty that we need to look.

Having in mind, in particular, a future enlargement of the EU that would greatly increase the number of EU states (following the accession of central and eastern European countries), the European Council met in Laeken in December 2001 to set out a roadmap for the future of the EU. A Convention on the Future of Europe was established to address a range of constitutional and institutional issues. However, the work of the Convention ranged beyond mere legal house-keeping, and it became clear that it had ambitions to prepare a Constitution for Europe to be adopted as a single document to replace the much-amended treaties.

A preliminary draft of the Constitutional Treaty was published on 28 October 2002 setting out the broad constitutional architecture of the document.[1] Article 46 of the preliminary draft identified a possible mechanism for voluntary withdrawal but contained no specific text. However, earlier that month, the UK government's representative to the Convention, Peter Hain, had presented a text it had commissioned from academic lawyers led by the then Professor of European Law at Cambridge University, Alan Dashwood.[2] What became known as the 'Cambridge text' included a relatively simple article providing for a Member State to withdraw from the EU, as an entirely voluntary process that did not require authorisation from any other EU state or institution. Procedurally, the text envisaged that once notified, it would be for the Member States meeting as an international intergovernmental body – the Heads of State and Government – and deciding by unanimity, to make any consequential amendments to the treaties.

Draft language for Article 46 was presented to the Convention by the 'Praesidium' – the body steering the work of the Convention – in April 2003.[3] It departed from the 'Cambridge text' in significant ways. First, it stipulated that

---

[1] On the idea of a 'constitutional architecture' and its application to the Constitutional Treaty see: P Craig, *The Lisbon Treaty: Law, Politics and Treaty Reform* (Oxford University Press, 2010), ch 1: 'Reform, Process and Architecture'.

[2] Document CONV 345/1/02 (16 October 2002)

[3] Document CONV 648/03 (2 April 2003).

a state's decision to withdraw had to be 'in accordance with its own constitutional requirements'. Secondly, it provided for the Council of Ministers – an EU institution – to conclude an agreement on behalf of the Union, setting out the arrangements for the state's withdrawal. Thirdly, such an agreement could be reached by a qualified majority vote of the members of the Council, meaning that no single state would have a veto right. However, the assent of the European Parliament (EP) would be required. Finally, and in recognition that withdrawal would be voluntary and not subject to an agreement being reached, it specified that the Constitution would cease to apply to the withdrawing state two years following notification, or at the date of entry into force of any withdrawal agreement.

The Praesidium described the text as being 'partly based on the procedure under the Vienna Convention on the Law of Treaties', supplemented by a capacity to conclude a withdrawal agreement. But in important ways, the text shifted the emphasis away from merely expressing a right under international law to withdraw from a treaty, towards a more bespoke Union process with procedural, institutional and temporal qualities. This shift accelerated as the text was refined. It became clear that notification would be given to the European Council – the meetings of the Presidents and Prime Ministers – and not the Council of Ministers. Recognising the role of the European Council in giving strategic leadership to the Union, it would also have responsibility for setting out guidelines for the negotiation of any withdrawal agreement. The European Council was also given the possibility – acting by unanimity – to extend the time period for negotiating a withdrawal agreement. All in all, the drafting process indicated that once a state decided to exercise a right to withdraw, the practice would be governed by EU institutional law.[4]

The inclusion of the withdrawal clause was not without controversy as evidenced by the amendments proposed – but not accepted – to the clause as it was being drafted in the Convention.[5] Joschka Fischer – then Germany's foreign minister and representative on the Convention – tabled an amendment for its deletion, as did a number of others. For Fischer the clause was unnecessary but for others the clause was also in tension with the fundamental commitments which Member States had entered into, including the idea that economic and monetary union was an 'irreversible' process.[6] For the then French foreign minister Dominique de Villepin, the draft text ought to be amended to limit its use to circumstances in which a Member State would withdraw following a failure of that state to ratify a future amendment to the treaties/constitution. He and others had also proposed turning the unilateral right to withdraw into a negotiable right to request a withdrawal.

---

[4] On which see C Hillion, 'Accession and withdrawal in the law of the European Union' in A Arnull and D Chalmers (eds), *The Oxford Handbook of European Union Law* (Oxford University Press, 2015).

[5] Document CONV 672/03 (14 April 2003) summarises the amendments proposed to the part of the draft Constitutional Treaty containing the withdrawal clause. Details of all amendments can be found on the archived website of the Convention on the Future of Europe, www.european-convention.europa.eu.

[6] Following agreement on the Maastricht Treaty, Protocol 24 was annexed to the European Community Treaty declaring the 'irreversible' character of economic and monetary union.

The withdrawal clause expressed something of the uncertainty of the EU's future integration path and, indeed, of the capacity of an EU form of 'constitutionalism' to accommodate and animate a Union with a growing number of Member States and increasingly heterogeneous peoples.[7] The clause signified a contradiction in the very process which gave rise to it: a process of integration seeking to draw states closer and more loyally into a dense set of institutions, rules and co-operative procedures derived from EU law – yet, at the same time, providing a procedural mechanism through which a state could decide to turn its back on the EU and unburden itself from the demands of membership.

The failure of the Constitutional Treaty to be ratified following its rejection in referendums in France and the Netherlands, and the subsequent abandonment of the 'constitutional concept' in favour of a reforming and amending Lisbon Treaty, can also be interpreted as symptomatic of a limited capacity of EU law to engender a form of 'constitutional patriotism' capable of channelling, or alternatively compensating for, deeper social anxieties about political, economic and social changes affecting the lives of the EU's citizens.[8]

---

[7] For an analysis of the different dimensions of 'constitutionalism' and the extent to which the EU possesses a truncated form of constitutionalism see: N Walker, 'EU constitutionalism in the state constitutional tradition' (2006) *Current Legal Problems* 51.

[8] For an introduction to the concept of 'constitutional patriotism' and its association with the work of the German theorist Jürgen Habermas, see: J-W Müller and KL Scheppele, 'Constitutional patriotism: an introduction' (2008) 6(1) *I-CON: International Journal of Constitutional Law* 67.

With the failure of the Constitutional Treaty, the withdrawal clause was rescued by the Lisbon Treaty, becoming Article 50 TEU. In so doing, the Union had done more than merely equip itself with legal language reflecting rights under international law; it had sought to take control over a withdrawal process by rendering the right to withdraw and the process of withdrawal subject to EU procedural and institutional norms.

The text of Article 50 suggests a sequential, phased process that begins when a Member State takes the decision that it wishes to withdraw from the EU. So Article 50(1) TEU states:

> Any Member State may decide to withdraw from the Union in accordance with its own constitutional requirements.

This suggests that a decision to withdraw is not merely a unilateral and voluntary act by a government, it is one that EU law presupposes has been taken in accordance with a state's own constitutional requirements. It is not for EU law to dictate what those requirements are. Whether or not referendums are held is purely a matter for the Member State itself. The other provisions of Article 50 simply proceed on the assumption that such a decision has been made and they regulate the consequences of that decision as a matter of EU membership and of EU law.

Nonetheless, the inclusion of the words 'in accordance with constitutional requirements' creates some confusion. Had those words been omitted – as in the 'Cambridge text' – it would still have been for the legal system of a Member State to impose whatever constitutional requirements were necessary to make such a decision lawful from a domestic point of view. There is also a difficult temporal dimension. Put simply, when is such a 'decision' actually made? One way of looking at the UK's withdrawal is to say that the decision was given to the electorate to make, and a referendum was held for which Parliament enacted legislation to ensure the proper conduct of the vote. Yet, the legislation did not stipulate what was to happen after the referendum and so the decision to leave is a matter of continuing political choice exercised in the light of the referendum result. It could be said once the UK notified its intention to withdraw then the process is in the hands of the EU and a decision has effectively been take. But it is notification of the 'intention' and not the decision. It may also be said that the decision to withdraw isn't simply an event but an ongoing political process. And as the need for constitutional legality regarding that decision is a matter of domestic law rather than imposition via Article 50(1), every aspect of political choice and decision relating to Brexit – decision, notification, withdrawal – remains subject to domestic legal controls. In that respect, the procedures laid down in Articles 50(2) and (3) regarding the process of withdrawal once the UK notifies its intention to withdraw, continue to be supplemented by whatever constitutional requirements UK law does or does not impose, as a matter of domestic law.

In order for the process to start at EU level, the UK must notify its intention to withdraw: Article 50(2) TEU. The treaty is silent as to what form this takes, or when such a notification should be made following a 'decision' to withdraw being made, or whether such an intention, when notified, can be changed and the notification revoked. Not surprisingly, one commentator has described Article 50 TEU as not just lacking clarity, but as 'incomplete'.[9]

However, the treaty does elaborate somewhat on the institutional process for negotiating an orderly departure from the EU. As indicated, the procedure laid down in Article 50(2) TEU suggests that the UK is not simply leaving an intergovernmental club, but withdrawing from a European institutional apparatus that seeks to control the withdrawal process. Article 50(2) TEU states:

> In the light of the guidelines provided by the European Council, the Union shall negotiate and conclude an agreement with [the withdrawing state], setting out the arrangements for its withdrawal, taking account of the framework for its future relationship with the Union.

This indicates that a withdrawal agreement will also be accompanied by another agreement which will set out at least the framework for the future relationship with the EU, if not all its details. But what is not clear is how comprehensive these agreements can be either individually or taken together. A minimalist version would see a simple withdrawal agreement dealing with the immediate priorities – timing of withdrawal, personnel implications, financial and budgetary matters, citizens' rights, transitional arrangements on market access – supplemented by a roadmap style of framework

---

[9] H Hofmeister, '"Should I stay or should I go?" – a critical analysis of the right to withdraw from the EU' (2010) 16(5) *European Law Journal* 589.

agreement setting out the areas and timetable for future negotiations. A maximalist version would treat the Article 50 negotiations as the entirety of what would need to be agreed both for the immediate consequences of withdrawal as well as the future relationship.

The scope and extent of negotiations may be determined by the procedural rules governing the negotiation of the agreements. Article 50(2) TEU continues:

> [The withdrawal agreement] shall be negotiated in accordance with Article 218(3) of the Treaty on the Functioning of the European Union. It shall be concluded on behalf of the Union by the Council, acting by a qualified majority, after obtaining the consent of the European Parliament.

These procedural rules have two implications. First, as Hillion observes, the withdrawal agreement is treated institutionally as if it was the negotiation of an 'external' agreement between the EU and a non-EU state rather than an intra-EU state accord.[10] This brings such an agreement firmly within the orbit of the EU's constitutional and institutional law. Secondly, the conclusion of the agreement by a qualified majority – and without any mention of domestic approval by the other EU states in accordance with their constitutional requirements – suggests that the scope of the agreement could be limited to matters falling with the exclusive competence of the EU. Yet most comprehensive EU external agreements are 'mixed' in that they also include matters within the powers of the EU's Member States

---

[10] Hillion, 'Accession and withdrawal in the law of the European Union'.

and so require the consent of all the Member States' governments and domestic approval through national ratification processes. As a legal basis, Article 50 TEU could prove to be legally limiting on what might be negotiated within its terms.

Where Article 50 TEU is most obviously limiting is in terms of time. Article 50(3) states:

> The Treaties shall cease to apply to the State in question from the date of entry into force of the withdrawal agreement or, failing that, two years after the notification referred to in paragraph 2, unless the European Council, in agreement with the Member State concerned, unanimously decides to extend this period.

It is this timeframe which shapes Brexit. Given the desirability of withdrawal before the next elections to the EP in June 2019, a notification of intention to withdraw would need to be made in spring 2017. The UK Prime Minister had made clear that notification would be made before the end of March 2017 at the latest.

Subsequent chapters explore how and when the withdrawal process will unfold. But it is worth reflecting on what might have happened had Article 50 TEU never been introduced into EU law by the Lisbon Treaty. After all, the Lisbon Treaty, like the Constitutional Treaty could also have failed.

As an amending treaty, the Lisbon Treaty required ratification by all Member States of the EU in accordance with their respective constitutional traditions. 'Ratification' is the expression by a state of its willingness to be bound by a treaty. States differ as to the domestic constitutional requirements which precede such an expression, including the use (or not) of referendums.[11]

Following a judgment of the Irish Supreme Court,[12] it has been the practice of Ireland to conduct mandatory referendums to approve constitutional amendments giving effect to EU treaty revisions. The Lisbon Treaty was initially rejected in a referendum in Ireland on 12 June 2008. A meeting of the Heads of State and Governments of the Member States adopted a decision intended to address Irish concerns.[13] A second referendum in Ireland on 2 October 2009 – as the full force of the financial and banking crisis was being felt – resulted in Irish ratification of the Lisbon Treaty.

The German Constitution, by contrast, does not mandate the use of referendums and instead it has been in the German Constitutional Court (GCC) that the key challenges to EU treaties have been fought. A legal challenge to Germany's ratification of the Lisbon Treaty followed in the footsteps of other significant constitutional judgments of the GCC on Germany's EU membership, including its famous judgment on the Maastricht Treaty. In upholding the legality of Germany's ratification of the Maastricht Treaty, the GCC

---

[11] See F Mendez, M Mendez and V Triga, *Referendums and the European Union* (Cambridge University Press, 2014).

[12] *Crotty v An Taioseach* [1987] IR 713.

[13] This decision – not an act of an EU institution but an agreement binding in international law between the then twenty-seven EU states – was to be the precursor to a Protocol to be attached to the treaties at the next occasion at which the treaties were amended. This was, of course, the legal template borrowed by David Cameron and his European Council colleagues in creating a 'legally binding' vehicle for the UK's 'new settlement' in advance of the June 2016 EU referendum.

had positioned itself as the gatekeeper of German sovereignty, ensuring that Germany's participation in European integration met constitutional standards laid down in the constitution as interpreted by it.

In its Lisbon judgment, the GCC was, therefore, able to draw on a consistent theme in its judgments that the binding nature of Germany's EU obligations derives from its express consent to be bound rather than from a distinct legal and political authority inherent in EU law itself. The capacity of the German government to consent to further expansions in European integration is, according to the GCC, limited by requirements of the German constitution to respect the democratic principle – expressed by the involvement of the German parliament – and the 'constitutional identity' of the federal state itself. Nonetheless, having staked out apparently significant domestic constitutional limits to European integration – limits which David Cameron's 2015 Chatham House Europe reform speech intimated might be worth copying[14] – the GCC found that the Lisbon Treaty did not transgress these limits, allowing ratification to be completed. Remarking on its ruling, Joseph Weiler noted that the GCC 'has a well-earned reputation of a Dog that Barks but does not Bite'.[15]

It would have been ironic if the fate of the Lisbon Treaty – and with it Article 50 – had been decided by either

---

[14] See www.gov.uk/government/speeches/prime-ministers-speech-on-europe (10 November 2015)

[15] J Weiler, 'The "Lisbon Urteil" and the fast food culture' (2009) 20(3) *European Journal of International Law* 505.

the British courts or the British people. Legal challenges have been brought in UK courts over the years seeking variously to prevent the UK's initial membership of the then European Economic Community (EEC),[16] through to complaints concerning the ratification of various amending treaties.[17] The Lisbon Treaty was no exception. A member of the United Kingdom Independence Party (UKIP) brought legal proceedings in 2008 arguing that as much of the Lisbon Treaty replicated the Constitutional Treaty, and as the Labour government had promised in its 2005 manifesto that a referendum would be held before ratifying the Constitutional Treaty, a legitimate expectation had been created that a referendum would be held and that failure to respect a manifesto commitment constituted a breach of contract. The argument failed on the grounds that manifesto and other political commitments to holding referendums cannot be enforced by the UK courts. With ratification proceeding without a referendum in the UK and with ratification complete in all other Member States the Lisbon Treaty finally entered into force. The provision on withdrawal from the EU became live in Article 50 TEU. It is this provision – its procedural, institutional and temporal requirements – that shapes the UK's withdrawal from the EU.

Immediately after the referendum, the Vote Leave campaign attempted to cast doubt on the use of Article 50

---

[16] *Blackburn v Attorney General* [1971] 2 All ER 180; *McWhirter v Attorney General* [1972] CMLR 882.

[17] *R v Foreign Secretary ex parte Rees-Mogg* [1994] QB 552; *McWhirter v Foreign Secretary* [2003] EWCA Civ 384

TEU as the sole legal means of effecting the UK's withdrawal. It suggested that general provisions of international law, including the Vienna Convention on the Law of Treaties might be invoked: after all this would seem consistent with the view that the Lisbon Treaty had simply recognised a right of states in international law to withdraw from treaties. However, the Vienna Convention acknowledges that treaties may provide the means and mechanisms by which withdrawal occurs. More specifically, Article 5 of the Convention is clear that as regards the treaties governing international organisations, the provisions of the Convention apply 'without prejudice to any relevant rules of the organisation'. All of which directs us towards the EU treaties and to Article 50 TEU in particular. While Article 50 TEU is not constitutive of a right to withdraw it does, nonetheless, lay down binding EU legal norms and procedures for the exercise of that right by a Member State.[18]

That Brexit will be conducted through Article 50 TEU is to accept the continuing political and legal authority of the EU until withdrawal has occurred. And so perhaps the paradox of Article 50 is that its invocation is also an act of fidelity at the moment of divorce. While decades of legal and political integration may not have been enough to keep the UK in the EU, the EU's legal order and institutional mechanisms may be sufficiently attractive to facilitate the UK's departure.

---

[18] See: C Hillion, 'This Way Please! A legal appraisal of the EU withdrawal clause' in C Closa (ed), *Troubled Membership* (Cambridge University Press, 2017).

Two other issues presented themselves after the referendum in terms of the adequacy of notification under
Article 50 TEU as a means of disentangling the UK from the
EU. One issue was participation in 'Euratom'. The original
European Communities which the UK joined included the
European Atomic Energy Community, constituted by a distinct treaty. This Community provides the forum for nuclear
research and co-operation among the Member States and it
exists as a distinct entity albeit one whose institutions are
shared with the EU and whose treaty makes reference to the
EU treaties. Article 106(a)(1) of the Euratom Treaty lists the
provisions of the EU treaties which shall also apply to
Euratom and this includes Article 50 TEU. In that way,
triggering Article 50 TEU would lead to withdrawal from
Euratom. The UK government had made clear that this was
its intention when Article 50 was triggered and indeed, the
UK's Article 50 letter expressly referred to the UK's withdrawal from Euratom.

The second issue relates to the agreement between
the European Union and its Member States and three of the
European Free Trade Association (EFTA) states in the form
of the European Economic Area (EEA) agreement. Given
that the UK is listed as one of the contracting parties, it was
suggested that in order for the UK to withdraw from that
agreement it would also need to trigger the withdrawal
mechanism laid down in Article 127 of the agreement by
giving twelve months' notice. On 29 December 2016, two
members of the think-tank 'British Influence' lodged
a judicial review application to test whether the Article 127
mechanism also needed to be triggered, but at a permission

hearing on 3 February 2017, permission to proceed with the application was not granted.[19] The issue remains unresolved, but the more plausible argument would be that once the UK leaves the EU, the EEA agreement would not be a proper legal means of managing the UK's relationship with the EU27, and would have relatively limited, if any, application to the UK's relationship with the three EFTA states.[20] Article 126 of the EEA agreement also limits its territorial application to the territory of the participating EFTA states and the EU: once the UK leaves the EU, it will not be within the territorial scope of application of the agreement, frustrating its enforcement.

Yet it would be to the courts that others would turn to seek clarification of what domestic legal steps would be required before Article 50 TEU could be triggered. Time to litigate.

[19] *Yalland and Wilding v Secretary of State for Exiting the European Union* (unreported).
[20] See also DS Tynes and EL Haugsdal, 'In, out or in-between? The UK as a Contracting Party to the European Economic Area Agreement' (2016) 41(5) *European Law Review* 753.

16

Litigating Brexit

It is one of the remarkable features of membership of the European Union, that much of the enforcement of EU law takes place in the national courts of the EU's Member States.[1] Although the treaties establish a mechanism for the European Commission to bring legal actions against Member State for their breaches of EU law, they also create rights and duties enforceable by individuals and companies in their national courts. As the Court of Justice made clear, the treaties do not just create obligations between states, they create rights for individuals which become part of their legal heritage.[2] Individuals, through their national courts, hold the exercise of public authority to account to ensure that it is compatible with EU law obligations. This mirrors forms of legal redress against exercises of public power when judged against domestic legal standards.

An important part of the legal story of EU membership is this connection between European integration, national courts, EU rights and individuals. The implications of this phenomenon – documented and described by Kelemen as

---

[1] For analysis of the different patterns of litigation among the Member States see: KJ Alter and J Vargas 'Explaining variation in the use of european litigation strategies' (2000) 33(4) *Comparative Political Studies* 452.
[2] *Van Gend en Loos*, Case 26/62, EU:C:1963:1.

'Eurolegalism' – are varied.[3] On the one hand, and like the phenomenon of litigation more generally, it may be seen as a tool of privileged elites seeking to maintain or acquire power and influence. On the other hand, it opens up new avenues for the expression of claims that may be marginalised or suppressed by normal political processes, and ensures that political power respects the rule of law. Litigation reveals where power lies while also having to determine where it ought to lie and what is legitimate to be decided by governments, parliaments and courts.

But if the process of enforcing EU rights in the national courts has deepened the experience of EU membership, domestic litigation has also been a means of seeking to contest membership. Legal actions before the German Constitutional Court challenging the ratification of new EU treaties have illustrated that domestic courts are locations for struggles over the meaning and effects of EU membership. The judgments of the Constitutional Court have placed limitations on what the federal government can and cannot do without parliamentary consent.[4] As noted in the previous chapter, the UK courts have been locations for failed attempts to shape the UK's membership of the EU.

The litigation which followed the 23 June 2016 referendum was in part about rights created by EU law and made available in, and protected by, national courts and in part it

---

[3] RD Kelemen, *Eurolegalism: The Transformation of Law and Regulation in the European Union* (Harvard University Press, 2011).

[4] D Thym, 'In the name of sovereignty statehood: a critical introduction to the Lisbon judgment of the German Constitutional Court' (2009) 46 *Common Market Law Review* 1795.

was about contestation around membership of the EU with litigation used to control the process of ending EU membership. It was also litigation with different strands. The central strand concerned whether the UK government had the legal power to trigger the withdrawal process under Article 50 in the absence of statutory authorisation. Another strand related to the impact of withdrawal from the EU on the constitutional positions of Northern Ireland and the other devolved governments. Proceedings were also commenced to consider whether a notification of an intention to withdraw under Article 50 could be revoked. [5]

The main strand of litigation – later to be known as the *Miller* case – followed the publication of a post on the UK Constitutional Law Association's blog on 27 June 2016, just days after the referendum result. Its authors – Nick Barber, Tom Hickman and Jeff King – argued that before notification was given under Article 50, authorisation from Parliament was required.[6] Having set out the argument, it was then a question of whether it might be taken up by litigants and lawyers. On 3 July 2016, the law firm Mischon de Reya announced that it was supporting a legal challenge

---

[5] It is also worth noting the litigation that didn't happen, including complaints that assertions and statements made during the referendum campaign amounted to a 'fraudulent device or contrivance' contrary to section 115 of the Representation of the People Act 1983. For extended commentary see: R Clayton, 'The Brexit case that never was', UK Constitutional Law Association Blog, www.ukconstitutionallaw.org (22 March 2017).

[6] N Barber, T Hickman and J King, 'Pulling the Article 50 "trigger": Parliament's indispensable role', UK Constitutional Law Blog, www .ukconstitutionallaw.org (27 June 2016).

by – at the time – unnamed clients and that Lord Pannick QC, as well as one of the authors of the blog, Tom Hickman, had been retained as counsel. Meanwhile, an application for judicial review had already been lodged on 28 June 2016 by a named claimant, Deir Dos Santos, a UK citizen. At an administrative hearing on 19 July 2016, it was agreed that Mr Dos Santos's action would be joined to the proceedings being spearheaded by Mischon de Reya, now brought in the name of Ms Gina Miller – a wealth manager – as the lead claimant. The hearing before the Divisional Court was scheduled for 13, 17 and 18 October 2016. To this action, other interested parties were joined including the 'People's Challenge', a crowd-funded action to protect rights of EU citizens led by Grahame Pigney and others.

The unanimous judgment in *Miller* given on 3 November 2016 by the three-judge panel of the Divisional Court concluded that the statutory authority of Parliament was required before Article 50 was triggered.[7] The ruling was greeted with outrage by sections of the British media, branding the judges as 'enemies of the people' and declaring that the courts were defying the will of the majority who had voted for the UK to leave the EU. The lead claimant Gina Miller was also subject to intense media scrutiny and received threats including through social media.

As the litigation in London was getting underway, in Belfast, Raymond McCord had lodged an application for judicial review on 11 August 2016 to ask the High Court to

---

[7] *R (Miller) v Secretary of State for Exiting the European Union* [2016] EWHC 2768 (Admin).

consider the compatibility of the UK's withdrawal from the EU with aspects not just of the devolution of powers to Northern Ireland but also the Belfast 'Good Friday' peace agreement. He brought his action as 'a British and European citizen and a resident of Northern Ireland' and as a peace campaigner (following the murder of his son by Loyalist paramilitaries). A week later, on 19 August 2016, a group of politicians led by Steven Agnew MLA also initiated proceedings in the Belfast High Court. The claims were rolled together, and the court made clear that to the degree that their arguments replicated those also being litigated before the High Court in London, proceedings would be stayed pending the outcome of that litigation. Therefore, the cases would proceed solely by reference to the specific constitutional and legal context of Northern Ireland.

Some days prior to the Divisional Court in London's ruling, on 28 October 2016, the Belfast High Court had dismissed arguments that the government's power to trigger Article 50 of the Treaty on European Union (TEU) had been excluded or limited by either the Northern Ireland Act 1998 or the Belfast 'Good Friday' Agreement.[8] There was, in its view, no requirement for an Act of Parliament before Article 50 TEU notification could proceed. Any impact on future individual rights and the operation of institutions was, in its view, speculative and not an immediate consequence of notification under Article 50(2) TEU. In the event that it was found that an Act of the UK Parliament was necessary before Article 50 TEU

---

[8] *In the matter of an application by Raymond McCord and Steven Agnew and others for leave to apply for judicial review* [2016] NIQB 85.

could be triggered, at least in Northern Ireland, this would not bring into play a constitutional convention requiring prior consent from the Northern Ireland Assembly. Claims that a 'section 75' equality impact had to precede a triggering of Article 50 were also dismissed.[9] Finally, the contention that any change to the constitutional position of Northern Ireland required the consent of the people in terms of the Belfast 'Good Friday' Agreement was rejected.

The rulings from the Divisional Court in London and the courts in Belfast were appealed, with permission given for both cases to be heard together before the UK Supreme Court – leap-frogging the Court of Appeal – to avoid further delays. Government lawyers had previously given assurances that Article 50 would not be triggered until the outcome of the litigation was known, but given the Prime Minister's intention to trigger Article 50 before the end of March and given that if the Divisional Court's judgment was upheld, legislation would need to be introduced to Parliament, time was pressing.

Four days of hearings and submissions took place between 5 and 9 December 2016. Prior to the hearings, the 'skeleton' arguments of the parties had been published. Together with the judgment of the Divisional Court, this facilitated an extensive academic analysis of the core issues before and during the Supreme Court hearing. Indeed, in its majority judgment, the Supreme Court noted the influence of

[9] Section 75 of the Northern Ireland Act 1998 imposes duties on public authorities in Northern Ireland to assess the impact of policies on the equality of opportunity of different social groups.

this analysis – much of it in the form of blogs on the same site as the original Barber, Hickman and King blog – in the shaping of the submissions presented to the Court. The Attorney General Jeremy Wright and First Treasury Counsel James Eadie led the appeal on behalf of the Secretary of State for Exiting the EU. Given that the case also involved the appeals from the Northern Irish courts on the issues raised in the Agnew and McCord cases, the Attorney General for Northern Ireland led on that aspect of the appeal. Counsel was also instructed to represent the Scottish and Welsh governments (as interveners on the devolved competence issues). As well as counsel for the principal claimants in the cases, other interested parties – particularly parties concerned about losses of citizenship rights – were represented.

The hearing before the Supreme Court was televised and transcripts of the proceedings were available on the Supreme Court's website. This transparency was important given not just the significance of the issues to be decided by the Court but also because of the strong press reaction to the Divisional Court's ruling. The broadcast of the hearings showed just how legally technical the issues were. This was not to be a rerun of the referendum campaign. Instead, lawyers and judges spent four days engaged in the slow, often tedious task of citing and debating legal authorities presented to the Court in huge tabbed bundles of documents. It was grindingly dull viewing except for the odd moment of levity when counsel and the bench debated the correct pronunciation of *De Keyser* (one of the legal authorities being debated). Yet this was all rather helpful in illustrating what was – and importantly, what was not – at issue, and when the judgment was eventually delivered on 24 January 2017, the external response to the ruling was muted.

By a majority of eight to three, the Supreme Court concluded that Parliament was required to legislate to authorise ministers to give the notification under Article 50(2) TEU to begin the process of withdrawing the UK from the EU.[10] For the majority, the main issue to be decided was the authority of the government under prerogative powers and its relationship to the European Communities Act 1972 which gave domestic legal effect to EU law consequent to the UK's membership of the European Economic Community (EEC – now EU) effected by its 1972 Treaty of Accession.

The majority first considered whether there were limitations on the effects that the exercise of prerogative powers could have. They concluded from the authorities of the *Case of Proclamations* (1610) and *The Zamora* (1916) that ministers of the Crown could not exercise prerogative authority to change domestic law.[11] While there is a power delegated to ministers to make rules, including rules which can amend primary statutory provisions (so called 'Henry VIII' powers), such a power only exists where it is created by Parliament through statute. Absent such a statutory authorisation, the government cannot by its own actions change domestic law.

The majority then considered the scope of the prerogative power claimed by the government. Clearly, if the

[10] *R (Miller) v Secretary of State for Exiting the European Union; Reference by the Attorney General for Northern Ireland in the matter of an application by Agnew and others; Reference by the Court of Appeal (Northern Ireland) in the matter of the application by Raymond McCord* [2017] UKSC 5.

[11] *The Case of Proclamations* (1610) 12 Co Rep 74; *The Zamora* [1916] 2 AC 77.

scope of the prerogative is limited in the first place, then the government might not have the power it wished to exercise. The Royal Prerogative is a residual power that may be exercised in a limited range of circumstances and where there is no more specific power in common law or in statute. In a situation that was previously covered by a prerogative power but is now subject to a statutory scheme, the exercise of the prerogative power is pre-empted to the extent that it is now covered by statute: the principle in *De Keyser* (1920), *Fire Brigades Union* (1995) and *Laker Airways* (1977).[12] This kind of example of substantive pre-emption or material conflict-avoidance is quite straightforward: the more specific scheme Parliament has put in place should not be undermined by general claims to exercise a residual inherent prerogative power. But it is much harder to determine whether the 1972 Act had limited the scope of application of the prerogative when applied to the activities of the government on the international level. Indeed, the point of the 1972 Act might have been said to facilitate the continuing and ongoing exercise of that prerogative by ensuring that whatever resulted from international negotiations could then be applied within domestic law as required by section 2(1) of the 1972 Act. In other words, unlike *De Keyser* there was no obvious substantive conflict.

However, for the majority there was a clear conflict, namely that the purpose of the 1972 Act was to provide a legal

---

[12] *Attorney General v De Keyser Royal Hotel* [1920] AC 508; *R v Secretary of State for the Home Department ex p Fire Brigades Union* [1995] 2 AC 513; *Laker Airways Ltd v Department of Trade* [1977] QB 643.

'conduit' between domestic law and the international level, allowing EU law into UK law, with the effect of notification under Article 50 TEU – if it led to the UK's withdrawal from the EU – being to shut off the supply of EU law. This would then change the domestic legal position. This was what Lord Pannick QC – counsel for Miller – had in mind when he presented the Court with the analogy that once Article 50 was triggered, the bullet would hit the target and the loss of EU rights was the inevitable consequence.

The majority recognised that EU law was an independent source of law exterior to domestic law. However, this did not mean that it escaped the principle established in the *Case of Proclamations* and *The Zamora*. Although normally such an exterior source would not have direct domestic legal effects and so changes in the exterior source would not immediately lead to changes in domestic law, the 1972 Act had created a mechanism allowing EU law to immediately flow into UK law. Shutting off the pipe would change domestic law.

Nonetheless, the obvious objection to this line of argument was that EU law changes all the time and this changing body of law results – in UK constitutional terms – from the exercise of prerogative power on the international level. The 1972 Act facilitates rather than constrains that. However, the majority drew a distinction between the normal changes arising from the exercise of rule-making powers at EU level (negotiated and adopted in accordance with the decision-making rules of the EU) and a unilateral action by the UK government that would bring about a 'fundamental change in the constitutional arrangements of the United Kingdom' (para 78 of the judgment). The effect of withdrawal from the EU would be more than the change in the content of law from time to time as it evolved at EU level, it would be to cut off completely a source of law and a source for which Parliament had expressly provided in the 1972 Act.

In his dissenting judgment, Lord Reed considered that no such distinction could be drawn. If the specific function of section 2(1) of the Act was to regulate the flow of EU law into the UK – which the majority recognised could change over time – that effect was itself conditional on the Act giving domestic legal effect to the UK's international obligations under the treaties creating the European Communities. If the UK relinquished its obligations under EU law, there would simply be no international obligations to which to give effect. This reasoning depicts the domestic statute as being a response to international obligations rather than something conditioning or limiting the exercise of the prerogative on the international level. Moreover, for Lord Reed, any change in rights and obligations at EU level did not change the fundamental sources of rights constitutionally recognised in domestic law.[13]

Nonetheless, for the majority, while the 1972 Act had made it possible for the exercise of prerogative powers to change domestic law in a manner that did not violate constitutional principles, this did not extend to authorising the complete withdrawal of EU law as a source of law available and applicable in domestic law. The only question would be whether subsequent statutory changes had

---

[13] See also M Elliott, 'Analysis: the Supreme Court's judgment in *Miller*', www.publiclawforeveryone.com (25 January 2017).

given authorisation for such a change. After all, the 1972 Act had been amended to include the Lisbon Treaty as one of the treaties to be recognised in UK law, and the Lisbon Treaty included the amendment which introduced Article 50 into the Treaty on European Union. However, the majority rejected any suggestion that section 2(1) of the 1972 Act could be interpreted as giving the government the authority to trigger Article 50. It noted that the right to withdraw under Article 50 TEU was exercised at EU level and not, as section 2(1) stipulates, a right to be given 'legal effect or used in the United Kingdom' (para 79 of the judgment).

The majority also recognised that while it was true that other statutory enactments – particularly the European Union Act 2011 – had placed limitations on the exercise of prerogative powers in respect of EU treaties by making the approval of treaties by UK ministers subject to domestic requirements to pass legislation or hold a referendum, this did not mean that outside their scope, the prerogative was unrestricted. In other words, restriction on the scope of prerogative powers can occur in three principal ways:

- where statute expressly seeks procedurally to regulate the exercise of a prerogative power (eg the European Union Act 2011)
- where the exercise of a prerogative power is substantively pre-empted by a statutory scheme (eg *De Keyser*)
- where the exercise of the prerogative would frustrate a fundamental constitutional feature which – given the nature of the UK's unwritten constitution – is created or

otherwise recognised in statute, especially a statute which the UK courts have recognised as 'constitutional' in nature (the essence of the *Miller* ruling).[14]

Given the failure of the European Union Referendum Act 2015 to regulate the outcome of the referendum, no assistance could be found from the silence in this legislation, leaving the Supreme Court to conclude that where 'a referendum result requires a change in the law of the land and statute has not provided for that change, the change in the law must be made in the only way in which the UK constitution permits, namely through Parliamentary legislation' (para 121 of the judgment).

What remained to be determined was whether the exercise of legislative powers by Parliament to authorise the triggering of Article 50, would also then trigger a require-ment to obtain the legislative consent of the devolved parlia-ments. This question exposed a different feature of the UK's constitution, namely the operation of constitutional conven-tions. Since the devolution of powers to Scotland, Wales and Northern Ireland, it remains the case that the UK Parliament has not lost its sovereignty to legislate in areas that have been devolved. Nonetheless, by convention, if the UK govern-ment wishes to propose legislation in a devolved field, it will seek the consent of the devolved institutions. This is the so-called Sewel Convention. In the case of Scotland, the con-vention was reflected in statute in amendments made by the Scotland Act 2016. Nonetheless, the Supreme Court held unan-imously that the UK courts were observers of conventions and

---

[14] F Ahmed and A Perry, 'Constitutional statutes' (2016) *Oxford Journal of Legal Studies* (advance access, 24 December 2016).

not enforcers and it was not for the Supreme Court to determine whether legislative consent was required or ought to be sought. It was a matter for politics and not law.

As for the distinct issues raised from the Northern Ireland appeal, the Supreme Court did not find any overlap or conflict between the provisions of the Belfast Agreement or the Northern Ireland Act, and the procedures governing the UK's withdrawal from the EU. Which is only to say that the significance of the UK's withdrawal from the EU and its impact on Northern Ireland – and indeed the Irish Republic – is also to be understood in political rather than legal terms.

The cases before the Divisional Court and Supreme Court were decided on the assumption that, once triggered, the Article 50 process would lead to the UK's withdrawal from the EU. The issue of whether an Article 50 notification could be revoked was consciously not debated.[15] To do so would have inevitably meant that a reference to the Court of Justice would be required to give an authoritative interpretation of Article 50. For both sides, it was preferable to assume the worst-case scenario under which the triggering of the process led to the UK's withdrawal from the EU, and then consider whether there were domestic constitutional constraint applicable to that scenario. As ever, time shaped key decisions and choices.

However, on 12 January 2017 a letter was sent to the Irish Attorney General indicating that proceedings would be

---

[15] See Jean-Claude Piris, 'Article 50 is not for ever and the UK could change its mind', *Financial Times* (1 September 2016).

brought in the Irish courts in a crowd-funded case seeking to establish whether Article 50 TEU was indeed revocable. On 27 January 2017, papers were filed in the High Court in Dublin with Steven Agnew and other Green Party politicians named as the claimants together with a British QC Jolyon Maugham who had led the initiative and the crowd-funding. The claim hinges on certain alleged breaches of the EU treaties said to have arisen through meetings held between the EU27 to the exclusion of the UK. Nonetheless, the linkages between these arguments, additional claims about losses of rights and the interpretation of Article 50 are far from clear. Even if the case were to give rise to a reference to the Court of Justice,[16] the Court may not end up answering the key issue of whether Article 50 is unilaterally revocable either because an answer to that question is not necessary to resolve the issues raised or because the Court might consider the case to be contrived in order to seek an essentially 'advisory' opinion, contrary to the aim of the preliminary reference procedure.[17]

What is striking, however, is that litigation is a way of managing the silences in statutes and treaties. The 2015 Act was silent as to how a vote for the UK to leave might be given effect. Article 50 is silent as to whether a notification given can be revoked. Litigation seeks to fill these silences, completing incomplete legal texts across time. [18]

---

[16] See E O'Dell, 'There's no guarantee Ireland's new Brexit case will get the referral it wants', www.cearta.ie (11 December 2016).

[17] *Foglia v Novello (No 2)*, Case 244/80, EU:C:1981:302.

[18] See also D. Howarth, 'On Parliamentary Silence', UK Constitutional Law Blog, www.ukconstitutionallaw.org (13 December 2016).

Yet this process is driven by the accidents of litigation, of what does, and does not get litigated. At moments in time, opportunities are presented that can be taken and which allow issues to be explored. But as one of the barristers for Gina Miller has written subsequently and poignantly, the vast majority of people cannot bring judicial review proceedings in UK courts with legal costs starting in the tens of thousands of pounds.[19] It is this reality check which also helps explain why many voters didn't buy the legal story of an EU membership that endowed them with rights and entitlements and included them in the integration project. It helps explain why people may have resented the capacity of Miller to bring her claim to court, perhaps more than they objected to the outcome. If the referendum was an opportunity for people to express their dislike of political elites, then responses to the post-referendum litigation also warns of anxieties about legal elites and the influence they have over politics. Indeed, the more that law either displaces politics or limits politics the more that a distrust of law and courts is created. This was, perhaps, one of the failures of European law itself.

[19] T Hickman, 'Public law's disgrace', UK Constitutional Law Blog, www.ukconstitutionallaw.org (9 February 2017).

17

Time to Organise

In the statutory documents presented to Parliament prior
to the referendum, the UK government repeatedly asserted
that in the event of a vote in favour of leaving the EU, 'the
British people would expect [the withdrawal] process to start
straight away'.[1] That the Article 50 notification was not made
immediately following the referendum was no bad thing.
Indeed, one of the more specific effects of the Article 50
litigation was that it bought the UK and devolved governments a valuable amount of time to organise to prepare for
Brexit.

With the departure of David Cameron as Prime
Minister, the primary task of his successor Theresa May was
to form a new government. It would be a Brexit government in
two specific senses. First, a new government department – the
Department for Exiting the EU (DExEU) – was created
to lead the process for withdrawal from the EU. A new
Department for International Trade (DIT) was created to
lay the foundations for the negotiation of future trade
deals. Secondly, personnel that were prominent in the
'Leave' campaign were placed in key ministries. The new
departments for Exiting the EU and International Trade
were headed by key Eurosceptics, David Davis and Liam

---

[1] HM Government, 'The process for withdrawing from the European
Union', Cm 9216 (February 2016).

Fox respectively, while Boris Johnson was appointed as Foreign Secretary. The philosophy seemed to be that those who had pushed for Brexit would now be expected to deliver it, at least in the short term.

The negotiating objectives for Brexit would be defined by this new government. In forming her team the Prime Minister brought into Downing Street two close allies – Fiona Hill and Nick Timothy – as her joint chiefs of staff. The Lancaster House speech which set out the Prime Minister's principles for the Brexit negotiations was reported to have been the product of a close group of advisors based within Downing Street, including Nick Timothy who had publicly advocated Brexit.[2] While the shape of Brexit will be closely controlled within Downing Street, the formulation of the content and approach to negotiations engages multiple levels of government.

First, there is the work that will be done within Whitehall through the ministries with the new Department for Exiting the EU acting as a central hub for co-ordinating the government's position. The new department's Permanent Secretary, Oliver Robbins also acts as the Prime Minister's EU advisor and 'sherpa' in EU negotiations.[3] In organisational terms, the new department created three policy directorates to reflect the broad substantive areas for negotiation: (1) trade and partnerships; (2) market access and budget;

[2] G Parker, 'Loyal aides helped to draft May's defining speech', *Financial Times* (19 January 2017).

[3] J Owen and R Munro, 'Whitehall's preparation for the EU's exit from the EU', Institute for Government Briefing Paper, www.instituteforgovernment.org.uk (14 December 2016)

and (3) justice, security and migration.[4] As well as a 'Cross-Government Policy Coordination' Directorate within DExEU, cross-departmental 'boards' were created – mainly chaired by DExEU officials but with DIT leading on trade issues and the Treasury on budgetary issues – to obtain input from across Whitehall. A new 'Brexit' Cabinet Committee, chaired by the Prime Minister was created with twelve ministerial colleagues equally split between the Remain and Leave sides of the referendum. A revised Cabinet Committee structure introduced by the new Prime Minister was viewed in some quarters as a return to a more traditional style of Cabinet government after a period of less formal 'sofa' government.[5] Yet, with DExEU acting as the secretariat and providing the papers for the Brexit Cabinet Committee it is less clear that the Committee exercises influence over the negotiations rather than simply sharing ownership of the government's position.

For the UK, Brexit requires a fundamental reorganisation of government not just to prepare the negotiations, but also to prepare for the repatriation of tasks and responsibilities in readiness for the UK's departure from the EU. All of which is happening in the wake of years of austerity-driven cuts and civil service staff reductions right across Whitehall. The challenge for the civil service should not be

---

[4] Department for Exiting the EU, 'Senior Management Team', www.gov.uk /government/publications/department-for-exiting-the-european-union-senior-management-team (19 January 2017).

[5] N Allen and N Siklodi, 'Theresa May asserts control in a revamped cabinet-committee system', http://blogs.lse.ac.uk (31 October 2016).

underestimated.[6] In the context of Brexit, Lord Kerslake, the former head of the UK Civil Service concluded that government 'is unprepared and under-resourced for the tasks it faces in the immediate future and for some years to come'.[7] It is these sorts of asymmetries of resources in personnel and experience between the UK and the EU, when combined with the finite resource of time under Article 50, that will shape the Brexit negotiations.

Two other relevant dimensions of political communication need to be considered: upwards between Whitehall and the UK's representation in Brussels, and downwards between Whitehall and the devolved administrations.

The UK's Permanent Representative to the EU – the UK's EU ambassador – has a direct reporting line back to DExEU on Brexit issues, rather than reporting primarily to the Foreign Office. In the period between the referendum and the start of the negotiations, Sir Ivan Rogers resigned as the UK's ambassador to the EU. It was Sir Ivan who had helped pilot David Cameron's 'new settlement' renegotiations. His stint as EU ambassador was due to end during the Brexit negotiations. Nonetheless, it wasn't merely his early departure which made news in January 2017, but the content of an email sent to colleagues announcing his resignation.

In his email, Sir Ivan highlighted a need for civil servants to provide 'unvarnished' advice to ministers and to

---

[6] A Menon, 'Brexit: the biggest challenge the civil service has ever faced?', www.prospectmagazine.co.uk/politics/brexit-the-biggest-challenge-the-civil-service-has-ever-faced (6 January 2017).

[7] Lord Kerslake, 'Rethinking the Treasury' (February 2017).

challenge 'muddled thinking'. This was widely interpreted as a criticism of overly optimistic expectations of what Brexit would look like among Brexit-supporting ministers. Yet, for others this was precisely the sort of pessimism which had meant that David Cameron's renegotiations had lacked ambition, and pro-Brexit supporters were not disappointed by Sir Ivan's departure. The former UKIP Leader, Nigel Farage lamented the replacement of Sir Ivan by 'another career diplomat' – Sir Tim Barrow – thereby extending his populist critique of political elites to the civil service itself. Indeed, UKIP suggested that it was important that Sir Ivan's successor was pro-Brexit. However, the more fundamental point is that Sir Tim Barrow – a man with limited past experience of the EU – together with Oliver Robbins will be pivotal in managing the negotiations on the UK side.

Looking beyond Whitehall, as the Supreme Court reiterated in its judgment in *Miller*, the UK's relationship with the EU is a 'reserved' or 'excepted' matter and so does not fall within the legislative competence of the devolved parliaments. Insofar as Brexit might entail legislation by Westminster in an area that was within devolved legislative competence, the Supreme Court also declined to enforce the 'political' convention that requires the legislative consent of the devolved parliaments before Westminster legislates. In this way, any influence the devolved governments might have over the formulation of the UK government's negotiating objectives would derive from political pressure unaided by the threat of veto.

In the month preceding the June 2016 referendum, elections to the devolved institutions were held. In Scotland, the Scottish National Party's Nicola Sturgeon remained as First Minister, leading an SNP minority government. With the SNP committed to EU membership, and with a strong vote in Scotland for the UK to remain in the EU, unsurprisingly the issue of protecting Scottish interests in the Brexit negotiations was something continually reiterated by the Scottish government, as was the need for the UK government to include the devolved administrations in formulating its negotiation objectives. Equally unsurprisingly, Brexit was bound up with the SNP's ambitions for an independent Scotland, notwithstanding the result of the 2014 referendum rejecting Scottish independence. The threat of another independence referendum was certainly one means of seeking leverage over the UK government. The announcement of a draft independence referendum bill by the Scottish First Minister Nicola Sturgeon to her party conference in October 2016 was no doubt intended to pressure the UK government to work more closely with the Scottish government on the terms of Brexit.[8] The appointment of Michael Russell as the First Minister's Brexit co-ordinator was, initially, interpreted as an indicator that the First Minister's more immediate priority was Brexit rather than a second independence referendum.

Following the June 2016 referendum, the Scottish First Minister established a 'Standing Council on Europe', composed *inter alia* of academics, politicians and former civil servants to advise on Scotland's priorities and the

---

[8] Scottish Government, *Consultation on a Draft Referendum Bill*, www.gov .scot/Resource/0050/00507743.pdf (20 October 2016).

Article 50 negotiations. The potential for Scotland to seek a differentiated Brexit outcome was discussed in this forum. In December 2016 – and before the UK government set out its objectives in the Prime Minister's Lancaster House speech and subsequent White Paper – the Scottish government produced its own paper setting out its ambition for the UK to remain in the Customs Unions, or alternatively for Scotland to remain in the Single Market.[9]

In Wales, following the May 2016 elections and resulting from an agreement between the Labour Party and the Welsh nationalist party Plaid Cymru, a minority Labour government was formed under the leadership of Labour's Carwyn Jones. A European Advisory Group was established to provide confidential advice to the Welsh government on the UK's withdrawal from the EU. One important difference with the situation in Scotland was that while the major political parties in Wales had all backed the UK remaining in the EU, the electorate had voted with the majority for the UK to leave the EU. Despite voter rejection of EU membership, key concerns lie with how EU payments to farmers and to disadvantaged areas will be preserved or replicated post-Brexit.[10] In a paper produced by the minority Labour government and supported by Plaid Cymru, the Welsh government set out its key priorities, noting that the repatriation of powers to the UK and devolved

---

[9] Scottish Government, 'Scotland's place in Europe', www.gov.scot (20 December 2016).

[10] J Hunt, R Minto and J Woolford, 'Winners and losers: the EU referendum vote and its consequences for Wales' (2016) 12(4) *Journal of Contemporary European Research* 824 (www.jcer.net).

governments after Brexit would render existing mechanisms for intergovernmental dialogue not 'fit-for-purpose'.[11]

The UK's position in or out of the Single Market is of particular significance to Northern Ireland, not least in its relationship with the Irish Republic. Any imposition of tariffs and customs formalities would be especially disruptive to cross-border trade. Maintaining the Common Travel Area between the UK and Ireland will also be a key aspect of negotiations but raises the obvious problem that the border will also be a border into and out of the EU.[12] Given the particular constitutional, economic and practical issues that are raised for Northern Ireland, the collapse in January 2017 of the power-sharing agreement that allowed devolved government to function threatened to limit the capacity of Northern Ireland's distinct interests to be channelled into the Brexit negotiations. In a bid to resolve the political crisis, new elections took place on 2 March 2017. The result was that the Democratic Unionist Party – which backed Brexit – lost its majority, with Sinn Féin coming within one seat of parity of members with the DUP. Nonetheless, power is shared and talks to form a new government had failed to produce a settlement by the time that the UK government triggered its withdrawal from the EU. The return of 'direct rule' from Westminster was not inconceivable and, in some quarters,

---

[11] Welsh Government, 'Securing Wales' future: transition from the European Union to a new relationship with Europe', www.beta.gov.wales /brexit (23 January 2017).

[12] For a fuller discussion of the issue see House of Lords European Union Committee, 'Brexit: UK–Irish relations', 6th Report (2016–17) HL76 (12 December 2016).

was viewed as a way of making the UK government responsible for the effects of Brexit on Northern Ireland.

In formal institutional terms, two structures are available as mechanisms through which to feed in the views of the devolved administrations: the 'Joint Ministerial Committee' and the 'British–Irish Council'. The Joint Ministerial Committee served as a forum for discussions between the UK government and the governments of the devolved administrations following the devolution of powers to Scotland, Wales and Northern Ireland. It met in plenary sessions annually until 2014. It was revived by Theresa May because of Brexit, and on 24 October 2016, the First Ministers of the devolved administrations met with the Prime Minister in Downing Street to discuss how the devolved administrations would be involved in Brexit. As well as agreeing to meet in a further plenary session early in 2017, it was decided to establish a subcommittee – JMC (EN) – to be chaired by the Secretary of State for Exiting the European Union, David Davis, and with representation from the devolved administrations. As the accompanying press release explained, the intention was to give the devolved administrations a 'direct line to the Brexit secretary.' The subcommittee met for the first time on 9 November 2016 and agreed to meet monthly thereafter.[13]

On 25 November 2016, a summit of the British–Irish Council was convened in Wales to discuss Brexit. Set up

---

[13] Prime Minister's Office, 'Devolved administrations vital to our success in the future', www.gov.uk/government/news/pm-devolved-administrations-vital-to-our-success-in-the-future (24 October 2016)

under the Good Friday Agreement, it brings together not just the UK and Irish governments but the devolved governments, and those of the Isle of Man, Jersey and Guernsey. Differences of views between the Scottish and Welsh First Ministers were reported with the latter suggesting that proposals for Scotland to have a separate deal on Single Market access were unworkable.[14] The meeting was also attended by the Irish Taioseach Enda Kenny, but Theresa May did not attend.

Despite these institutional devices for consultation with the devolved administrations, they had no obvious impact on the formulation of the UK government's negotiating objectives. Had the Supreme Court ruled that formal legislative consent motions were needed in the parliaments of the devolved administrations, that might have changed the political landscape. Instead, following the judgment, the Scottish government decided not to press for a formal consent motion. Subsequent to the introduction of the bill to authorise the triggering of Article 50 into the UK Parliament, the Scottish government's Minister for UK Negotiations on Scotland's Place in Europe, Michael Russell, lodged a motion for debate in the Scottish Parliament that the notification bill not proceed.[15] On 7 February 2017, the

[14] S Morris, L Brooks and H McDonald, 'First ministers clash over separate Brexit deal for Scotland', *The Guardian* (25 November 2016).
[15] Motion S5M-03858 (6 February 2017):

> That the Parliament agrees with all but one of Scotland's MPs that the UK Government's European Union (Notification of Withdrawal) Bill should not proceed, as the UK Government has set out no provision for effective consultation with the devolved administrations on reaching an agreed UK approach

Scottish Parliament supported this symbolic motion by a vote of ninety to thirty-four.

In evidence presented to the Commons Select Committee on Exiting the EU on 8 February 2017, Michael Russell indicated that the Scottish government had not been consulted on the UK government's White Paper and had only received sight of it forty minutes before its publication. Given that the White Paper was published two days before the JMC (EN) was due to discuss the Scottish government's paper on 'Scotland's place in Europe', and given the UK government's emphasis on the constituent nations of the UK 'facing the future together' it is simply not evident that the JMC performed any real substantive policy-formation or policy-influencing function in the definition of the UK's government's negotiating objectives. Indeed, the JMC was always a more formal means of channelling information than a functional means of influence or decision-making.[16] Instead, Brexit would be orchestrated in the corridors of Whitehall and be driven by Downing Street.

> to the negotiations on implementing Article 50, has refused to give a guarantee on the position of EU nationals in the UK, has left unanswered a range of detailed questions covering many policy areas regarding the full implications of withdrawal from the single market, and has provided no assurance that a future parliamentary vote on the outcome of the negotiations will be anything other than irrelevant, as withdrawal from the EU follows two years after the invoking of Article 50 if agreement is not reached in the forthcoming negotiations, unless they are prolonged by unanimity.

[16] N McEwen, 'Negotiating Brexit in a devolved state: the dynamics of intergovernmental relations', www.constitution-unit.com (1 December 2016).

Having failed to attain any political leverage through the formal institutional channels of political communication, on 13 March 2017, Scotland's First Minister Nicola Sturgeon announced that she would be seeking another independence referendum before the UK withdrew from the EU. Despite the UK Prime Minister's insistence that 'now is not the time' for a second independence referendum, on the eve of the triggering of Article 50, by sixty-nine votes to fifty-nine, MSPs backed the First Minister's proposal to begin a process of obtaining consent for another referendum. The UK government's time to organise is the Scottish government's time to mobilise.

18

The Parliamenterisation of Brexit

The European Union (Notification of Withdrawal) Bill was introduced to Parliament on 26 January 2017, two days after the UK Supreme Court decided that the government did not have legal authority to trigger Article 50 of the Treaty on European Union (TEU) and would instead require statutory authorisation.[1] The outcome of the litigation increased expectations that the UK Parliament would take a decisive role in the Brexit process. Indeed, for supporters of the litigation and of its result, putting Parliament back at the heart of the decision-making process was the correct constitutional response to the referendum.

Yet, despite all the attention which the *Miller* case had attracted, on the face of it, its outcome was simply to require Parliament to legislate to authorise the triggering of the notification of intention to withdraw under Article 50. The Supreme Court indicated that Parliament could 'content itself with a very brief statute' (para 122).

Moreover, if the bill to authorise the triggering of Article 50 TEU was to become a vehicle for enhancing parliamentary oversight it would have to overcome the

---

[1] Whereas there was no contingency plan for the referendum result, the government had made contingency plans for a defeat in the courts, with different drafts of the bill reported to have been prepared: 'Government preparing four versions of Brexit law as Supreme Court ruling looms', *The Independent* (22 January 2017).

obstacles facing parliamentarians in the amendment of government bills.

The forces that were pushing for greater parliamentary oversight of Brexit pre-dated the Article 50 litigation and pre-dated the referendum itself. In the run up to the referendum, both the House of Lords European Union Committee and the House of Commons European Scrutiny Committee prepared reports on the UK's negotiation of the 'new settlement' deal with the EU.[2] What is striking is their concerns about parliamentary scrutiny of the renegotiation process; concerns that would later manifest themselves again in the context of the Brexit negotiations. In particular, the Lords European Union Committee had demanded that Parliament not be presented with a *fait accompli* at the end of David Cameron's renegotiations, while accepting that the government would not be willing to provide a 'running commentary' on the negotiations. The unwillingness to provide a running commentary became a defining characteristic of the first six months of the post-referendum period.

The idea that the most Parliament might hope for would be a 'downstream' retrospective endorsement of any international deal reflects the historic power of the Executive to conduct foreign policy with limited parliamentary control. The Constitutional Reform and Governance Act 2010 (CRAG)

---

[2] House of Lords European Union Committee, 'The referendum on UK membership of the EU: assessing the reform process', 3rd Report (Session 2015–16), HL30 (21 July 2015); House of Commons European Scrutiny Committee, UK 'Government's renegotiation of EU membership: parliamentary sovereignty and scrutiny', 14th Report (Session 2015–16), HC458 (15 December 2015).

was enacted to ensure that Parliament did have an opportunity to express a view on the ratification of a treaty. Once a treaty has been negotiated, the text is to be laid before Parliament for 21 days and can be ratified unless either House of Parliament resolves that the treaty not be ratified. As Paul Craig describes, there is a constitutional 'belt and braces' approach at work.[3] It is for Parliament to enact into domestic legislation any rights and obligations arising from any international agreements, consistent with the UK's 'dualist' constitutional approach to international agreements. In order to prevent the Executive entering into international agreements which Parliament may be reluctant to give effect to, it makes sense to give Parliament sight of the agreed treaty text prior to its formal ratification. Nonetheless, this serves to highlight the *fait accompli* retrospective endorsement approach to the role of Parliament. It is a take-it-or-leave-it option.

Executive supremacy in international negotiations is not a feature unique to the UK. Indeed, when it came to the negotiation of international trade agreements at EU level, the executive 'tandem' of the European Commission and the Council traditionally dominated. Working to a mandate defined by the Member States in the Council, the European Commission negotiated trade deals on behalf of the EU with regular reporting back to a committee of national representatives. Following the Lisbon Treaty, the European Commission is now also obliged to report regularly to the

---

[3] P Craig, 'Brexit: a drama in six acts' (2016) 41(4) *European Law Review* 447.

European Parliament (EP) on the progress of negotiations: Article 207(3) of the Treaty on the Functioning of the European Union (TFEU). However, the EP has succeeded in defining a more substantive role in international negotiations given that in most circumstances the consent of the EP is required at the end of the process: Article 218 TFEU. It is this effective power of veto 'downstream' that has enhanced the EP's voice 'upstream'. Indeed, Jančić describes the EP as engaged in 'parliamentary diplomacy' with increasing influence over the substance of international negotiations.[4]

More precisely the role of the EP is set out in a 2010 'Framework Agreement' between the EP and the European Commission. It states that the EP 'shall be immediately and fully informed at all stages of the negotiation and conclusion of international agreements, including the definition of negotiating directives'. It also entails providing the EP with information – including confidential information – in sufficient time for it to express its views and for the Commission to take those views into account. While MEPs do not participate directly in negotiations, the Commission may agree to grant them observer status. More detailed procedural rules are set out in Annex III of the Framework Agreement and, in respect of the negotiation of international agreements, they require the Commission to provide the EP:

- during the negotiation process, 'all relevant information that it also provides to the Council'

---

[4] D Jančić, 'The role of the European Parliament and the US Congress in shaping transatlantic relations: TTIP, NSA surveillance and CIA renditions' (2016) 54(4) *Journal of Common Market Studies* 896.

- draft amendments to negotiating directives, draft negotiating texts, agreed articles and the text of the agreement to be initialled
- relevant documents received from third parties (subject to the originator's consent)
- information about the development of the negotiations including how the Parliament's views have been taken into account.

It is against this background of the enhanced constitutional position of the EP that attempts by the UK Parliament to enhance its own influence over the Brexit process needs to be understood. National parliamentarians sought to bootstrap their own claims for enhanced parliamentary influence based directly on the experience of the EP.

Drawing on evidence given by Professor Derek Wyatt about the role of the EP in international negotiations, the House of Lords European Committee published a report on 20 October 2016 setting out a basis for enhancing parliamentary scrutiny of Brexit.[5] The report sought a middle way to scrutiny that would be more than the government's preference for scrutiny at the end of the process but less than the type of parliamentary 'micromanagement' that the government wished to avoid. Highlighting statements made by the Secretary of State for Exiting the EU that, in its dealings with Parliament, it would 'certainly match and, hopefully, improve on what the European Parliament sees', the Lords report

---

[5] House of Lords European Union Committee, 'Brexit: parliamentary scrutiny', 4th Report (Session 2016–17), HL50 (20 October 2016).

identified four core principles which it suggested should underpin parliamentary involvement:

- Parliamentary committees should have access – including on a confidential basis – to a wide range of relevant documents.
- Documentation should be supplied in sufficient time for committees to express their views and for government to take those views into account.
- There should be a 'comply-or-explain' approach to any recommendations made by parliamentary committees.
- There ought to be procedures to safeguard confidential information.

These principles are analogous to the procedures agreed between the Commission and the EP. But in seeking to repli-cate these principles of European constitutionalism within domestic constitutional practices, the difficulty would be in translating these aspirations into concrete commitments and statutory requirements.

In its White Paper, the government repeated its assurance that 'the UK Parliament receives at least as much information as that received by members of the European Parliament'. But while pointing to the multiple parliamentary inquiries, written parliamentary questions and parliamentary debates on Brexit that had occurred even before the EU (Withdrawal) Bill had been introduced to Parliament, it stated that 'to enable the Government to achieve the best outcome in the negotiations, we will need to keep our positions closely held'. The only concrete pledge contained in the White Paper was to put the final deal agreed between the EU and the UK to a vote in both Houses of Parliament. Yet it was unclear whether this was anything other than what the government would be required to do under CRAG and would continue to reflect a minimal, downstream take-it-or-leave-it approach to Brexit.

One can begin to see how the outcome of the *Miller* litigation might have been harnessed towards the ends of turning aspirations for enhanced parliamentary involvement into prescribed legislative processes. Unsurprisingly the government's EU (Withdrawal) Bill adopted a minimalist approach to what would be required to trigger the Brexit process. In two clauses, the bill sought to do nothing more than meet the requirements of the Supreme Court judgment in terms of providing the barest legal clothing to authorise the Prime Minister to trigger Article 50. But also unsurprisingly, Opposition parties attempted to clothe this bare Brexit with procedural amendments designed to give Parliament greater oversight of the Brexit negotiations. The success or failure of these strategies would be a function of party discipline, procedural rules on the selection and debate of amendments, and necessarily of the limited parliamentary time set aside to rush the legislation through Parliament to meet the Prime Minister's self-imposed deadline of triggering Article 50 by the end of March 2017.

On each of the three days of the Committee Stage of the bill (6–9 February 2017) a series of amendments were proposed and either debated and voted upon, or not called. Proposed amendments included:

- regular reporting to Parliament on the progress of negotiations
- giving a statutory basis to the composition, and consultation, of the Joint Ministerial Committee (through which devolved administrations are consulted)
- requiring Parliament to be provided with documents which either the European Commission or European Council provided to the EP during negotiations
- arrangements for parliamentary scrutiny of confidential documents
- a requirement that Parliament vote on the text of any new agreement with the EU before its agreement with the European Commission and before its presentation to the EP for approval.

All these amendments – together with a proposal for a second referendum on the terms of a future EU deal – were defeated and not just because the governing party had a majority in the Commons. MPs found themselves caught between, on the one hand, their own preferences about whether the UK should remain in the EU and, on the other hand, the demands of party discipline – with both Conservative and Labour MPs expected by their party leaders to vote through the Article 50 legislation – as well as the expectations of their constituents, whether they voted for the UK to remain in or leave the EU.

However, and amidst rumours of a potential rebellion by some Conservative MPs, during the debate on amendments relating to the role of Parliament in approving any final deal, the Minister of State at the Department for Exiting the EU, David Jones intimated that:

> I can confirm that the Government will bring forward
> a motion on the final agreement, to be approved by both
> Houses of Parliament before it is concluded. We expect
> and intend that this will happen before the European
> Parliament debates and votes on the final agreement.[6]

The minister clarified that this would be a vote on the final draft text before its presentation to the EP and it would be the text of both a withdrawal agreement and any agreement on future co-operation with the EU. This might have been thought to be simply a restatement of the pledge in the White Paper to involve Parliament at the end of the Article 50 process and, in any event, to be in accordance with the provisions of CRAG. However, CRAG sets out the procedure following the agreement of a treaty but prior to its ratification, whereas the government's announcement was to give Parliament a vote on the draft texts and prior to their transmission to the EP for its consent.

Nonetheless, this may end up being a distinction without a difference and, either way, parliamentarians will be faced with a *fait accompli* at the end of the negotiation process. Given that the clock will be ticking down to the UK's withdrawal from the EU, a vote to veto risks the UK leaving the EU without a deal in place. Time will play an important role as there will simply be no time to reopen negotiations unless the other Member States unanimously agree to extend the timeframe for discussions to continue.

Just as the bill was making its way to the Lords for their consideration, a new twist was added by the release of

---

[6] D Jones, Hansard, Vol 621, Col 264 (7 February 2017).

a paper known colloquially as the 'Three Knights Opinion'.[7] Authored by three highly respected (and knighted) legal figures as well as some of the barristers in the Article 50 case, it was claimed that Parliament had to have not just oversight of the withdrawal process and a vote at the end but had to legislate to authorise any loss or variance of rights that would flow from a final withdrawal decision or, indeed, withdrawal without an agreement. The Opinion suggested that in terms of Article 50(1), a decision to withdraw had to be in accordance with 'constitutional requirements' and, as the Supreme Court made clear in *Miller*, the loss or variance of rights that had been made available in domestic law by Parliament required statutory approval. It was said that because it would only be clear at the end of the process what rights would be changed, it was at this point that Parliament had to have control.

Although focusing on the 'constitutional requirements' aspect of Article 50(1) is a bit misleading – as a matter of Article 50 itself, this only applies as regards the taking of a 'decision' to withdraw – nonetheless, the Supreme Court's judgment in *Miller* does make clear that the exercise of prerogative powers are subject to constitutional requirements. These include, of course, the procedural parliamentary processes laid down in CRAG. But as Craig notes, the provisions of CRAG are a constitutional 'default' rule and do not prevent the operation of other constitutional rules.[8]

---

[7] Sir Francis Jacobs, Sir David Edward, Sir Jeremy Lever, Helen Mountfield QC and Gerry Facena QC, 'In the Matter of Article 50 of the Treaty on European Union', www.bindmans.com (10 February 2017).

[8] Craig, 'Brexit: a drama in six acts'.

The Supreme Court in *Miller* established that removing EU law as a source of law capable of being given effect through the European Communities Act 1972 triggered a constitutional rule that Parliament had to give statutory authorisation for such an exercise of prerogative power. If Parliament is required to legislate for a withdrawal agreement or for withdrawal without an agreement, it could only be because the requirements of statutory authorisation imposed by the Supreme Court extend from notification to withdrawal. This might be considered to be less a 'belt and braces' approach to constitutional requirements and more about constraining the Executive within a legal straightjacket.

However, there are three good reasons to cast doubt on the claim advanced in the Opinion. The first is that the more one considers that it is at the end of the process that the loss of rights becomes concrete, the less obvious it is why statutory authorisation for notification of withdrawal was required. The answer would be that once the process is triggered then the withdrawal of rights becomes inevitable. But if that's the case then it is not obvious why one would then need statutory authorisation at the end of the process. Secondly, the Opinion rests on the claim that it is only at the end of the process that it will be clear exactly which rights will be lost or varied. But the Supreme Court was very clear that its ruling was based on the loss of a source of rights and not the loss or variance of any particular right. Statutory authorisation is required before notification under Article 50 because the source of rights in EU law will be lost. As the Court made clear, during its membership the content of EU rights changed all the time without the need for the UK to legislate in advance of every new EU rule and regulation. Thirdly, while it is true that the provisions of CRAG are default provisions and more specific requirements could be provided for, as things stand CRAG does represent the constitutional framework which Parliament has chosen to make for oversight of the negotiation and approval of treaties. It would be for Parliament – including during the passage of the EU (Notification) Bill – to make different arrangements.

If the dominance of the governing party in the Commons often means that MPs' amendments to government bills fail, the passage of a bill to the Lords affords alternative opportunities for amendments. It is not uncommon for amendments that fail in the Commons to be resurrected in the Lords as a strategy to maintain pressure on government to make concessions.[9] Procedures in the Lords are somewhat different from in the Commons and at committee stage there are not the same controls over amendments or the time allowed for discussing amendments as apply in the Commons. Moreover, the Conservative Party does not have a majority in the Lords, creating more possibilities for Opposition parties and cross-benchers to work together if amendments are put to a vote.

On 1 March 2017, the Lords inflicted a defeat on the government when it passed an amendment to the EU (Notification) Bill to protect the rights of EU/EEA citizens and family members legally resident in the UK on the day

---

[9] M Russell, D Gover and K Wollter, 'Does the Executive dominate the Westminster legislative process? Six reasons for doubt' (2016) 69 *Parliamentary Affairs* 286.

that the Act passed. Importantly, given the potential of the bill to act as a mechanism for increasing parliamentary oversight of the Brexit process, an amendment to the bill requiring parliamentary approval prior to the Prime Minister concluding an agreement – or deciding that the UK should leave the EU without an agreement – was also passed two days later.

The bill returned to the Commons on 13 March 2017. By a vote of 331 to 286, the bill was stripped of the Lords modifications. The Lords did not insist on their amendments allowing the bill to pass unamended. Parliament had done what the Supreme Court said needed to be done: no more, and no less.

The parliamentary process was an important point in Brexit Time. At the point when parliamentarians were being asked to undertake the formal task of creating a legislative framework to authorise the triggering of Article 50, it was also becoming clear what the consequences of leaving the EU would be and what particular form of Brexit the UK government intended to pursue. For some MPs this might be a time to defy party discipline and to vote with their own conscience over beginning the withdrawal process. For others, this was a time and an opportunity to enhance parliamentary scrutiny and oversight over the Brexit deal, not least to ensure that ministerial statements about parliamentary engagement were given procedural bite. For those who had brought legal actions to demand that Parliament provide statutory authorisation for the triggering of Article 50, the introduction of the bill was a time to put parliament back in the centre of political decision-making.

That the bill was passed unamended, however, dramatised how little the Supreme Court litigation had achieved. It is one thing for a court to say that the Executive requires parliamentary approval before it can act, but what it cannot do is change the Executive's control over parliamentary process. A government with a majority in the Commons can usually get its way even when faced with a Lords in which opposition parties constitute a majority given that the unelected House bends to the will of the elected chamber. But more than that, had the litigation never occurred and had the government exercised its prerogative powers, then responsibility for Brexit would lie firmly with the government. Requiring Parliament to put the bullet in the barrel to allow Article 50 to be triggered made it responsible not just for the referendum, it made it complicit in Brexit.

The European Union (Notification of Withdrawal) Act received Royal Assent on 16 March 2017. At 12.30 pm (BST) on 29 March 2017, the UK's ambassador to the EU, Sir Tim Barrow, delivered a letter signed by Prime Minister Theresa May notifying the European Council of the UK's intention to withdraw from the European Union.

Time to leave.

Time to negotiate.

19

Negotiation Time

On one side of the Brexit negotiations stands 'the EU'. Not only is the EU a Union of twenty-seven states for the purposes of the Article 50 negotiations – the UK does not participate on the EU side – it is a Union of institutions. Over time, the power of these institutions has evolved with the European Council – the summit meeting of the leaders of EU states meeting with the President of the European Commission – assuming an ever more central role in shaping European integration.[1] At the same time, it has traditionally been the European Commission which has negotiated international agreements on behalf of the EU. And as a sign of its increasing influence, the European Parliament (EP) has also acquired an institutional role in respect of the EU's international agreements.[2] All of which makes the Union a complex beast with which to do business even in favourable times, let alone at the moment when one of its states decides to pull the plug on its membership.

Following the referendum result, on 28 June 2016 European Commission President Jean-Claude Juncker

---

[1] C Bickerton, D Hodson and U Puetter, 'The new intergovernmentalism: European integration in the post-Maastricht era' (2015) 53(4) *Journal of Common Market Studies* 703.

[2] C Eckes, 'How the European Parliament's participation in international relations affects the deep tissue of the EU's power structures' (2014) 12(4) *I-Con* 904.

circulated an internal note within the Commission stating that there would be no negotiation – formal or informal – with the UK until the notification under Article 50 had been received. On 7 October 2016, a group called 'Fair Deal for Expats' brought a legal challenge before the EU courts arguing that Juncker's missive had no legal basis, was discriminatory against the UK and its citizens, violated their fundamental rights and was a breach of the principle of sincere co-operation.[3] Given the time that the EU's General Court takes to hold hearings and give a ruling – many years – the legal action would, however, have no practical effect.

In terms of the Article 50 procedure, the withdrawing state notifies the European Council of its intention to withdraw, with the European Council then setting out the guidelines for the withdrawal negotiations. Following the announcement that the UK would trigger Article 50 on 29 March 2017, European Council President Donald Tusk called a meeting of the European Council for 29 April 2017 to adopt the guidelines for the Brexit negotiations. This would be the first formal Brexit negotiations among the EU27 within the European Council.

For the Union, a negotiator is appointed. The default position, consistent with other EU international agreements, is for the European Commission to conduct negotiations on behalf of the EU.

In July 2016, Commission President Juncker announced that from 1 October 2016, the former French foreign minister

---

[3] *Fair Deal for Expats and others v European Commission*, Case T-713/16: [2016] OJ C428/20.

and ex-EU Commissioner Michel Barnier would head the Commission's Task Force on Article 50 negotiations and take on the role of its chief negotiator. Barnier's Task Force Deputy, Sabine Weyand, has significant trade negotiation experience including a spell in the Cabinet of Pascal Lamy when he was EU Trade Commissioner. In a press briefing on 6 December 2016, Barnier noted that the time for negotiations would be short. With the need for the EP – and indeed the UK Parliament – to vote on a withdrawal agreement, he concluded that there would be less than eighteen months available for negotiations. If notification was received before the end of March 2017 as indicated by the Prime Minister – and desirable to ensure that withdrawal took place before the June 2019 elections to the EP – an agreement would need to be reached by October 2018. Barnier also outlined the key principles that would guide the EU's negotiations:[4]

- the preservation of the unity and interests of the EU27
- non-membership not to have the same benefits as membership
- no negotiation before notification
- the indivisibility of the four freedoms.

On 15 December 2016, an informal meeting of the leaders of the EU27, together with the presidents of the European Council and European Commission agreed to appoint the European Commission as its Brexit negotiator.

The Member States have retained significant influence over the negotiations in five key ways. First, the

---

[4] M Barnier, Press Briefing, www.ec.europa.eu (6 December 2016).

European Council establishes the guidelines that define the framework of the negotiations to be conducted on behalf of the EU by the Commission. Secondly, the General Affairs Council – the meetings of the Foreign Affairs ministers – takes the decision to authorise the opening of the negotiations and agrees the negotiating directives that deal with issues of substance as well as further procedural aspects. With the European Council set to agree guidelines for negotiations in April 2017, the next General Affairs Council meeting was scheduled for 16 May 2017. The European Council made clear that the negotiating directives could be amended and supplemented throughout the negotiations to reflect the evolving position of the European Council. Thirdly, as well as a representative from the rotating Council presidency – each Member State takes it in turn to organise the meetings of the Council of Ministers for six months – the President of the European Council also has his own representative present and participating in all negotiation sessions. European Council President Donald Tusk had already appointed Didier Seeuws to head up a special Brexit Task Force within the Secretariat-General of the Council.

Fourthly, a Working Party attached to the Council is to ensure that negotiations are conducted in accordance with the European Council guidelines and the Council's negotiating directives as well as giving guidance to the Commission. Finally, 'sherpas' from the Member States are involved in the preparation of the work of the European Council. It is crystal clear that while the Commission is formally the negotiator – a move designed to give a single voice to the EU's position and to prevent disunity among the Member States – the European

Council and the Member States have sought to retain overall control.

The publication of the European Council's negotiating framework immediately drew a robust response from the outgoing President of the European Parliament, Martin Shultz who complained that the institutional role of the EP was not reflected in the proposed framework. The Parliament had appointed Guy Verhofstadt to act as the EP's 'negotiator'. After all, the consent of the EP is required for a withdrawal agreement negotiated under Article 50. However, the EP's position in the Article 50 process is ambiguous because the process conflates the issue of termination of EU membership – the divorce – with issues consequential to that termination – the post-divorce relationship.

Had Article 50 of the Treaty on European Union (TEU) simply have stated that a Member State may withdraw from the EU by serving notice of its intention to withdraw, it is not obvious that there would be any need to involve the EP at all in that process. Moreover, if the EU is viewed as a Union of states, and if the right to withdraw reflects a right of a sovereign state in international law as regards treaties and international organisations of which it is a member, then it would be appropriate that the European Council act as the focal point for a Member State's departure from the EU, assisted from a technical point of view by the European Commission.

However, Article 50 identifies that the consent of the EP is required and that a withdrawal agreement shall be negotiated following the procedure in Article 218 of the Treaty on the Functioning of the European Union (TFEU).

Nonetheless, the EP's role is an oversight and scrutiny role rather than a 'negotiating' role. According to the European Council's negotiating framework, representatives from the EP will be present at preparatory meetings of the European Council alongside national sherpas. The Commission is required to keep the Parliament closely and regularly informed throughout the negotiations, while the Council presidency exchanges views with the EP before and after meeting of the national foreign ministers. As is the norm in any event, the President of the European Parliament – while not a member of the European Council – would be invited to be heard before meetings of the European Council.

For Schulz, writing on behalf of the Conference of Presidents (the leaders of the Parliament's political groups), the EP had been relegated to a secondary role. And in a warning to the European Council, he noted that the consequence of a failure of a withdrawal agreement – which could result from an EP veto – was not the status quo but the UK being forced to leave the EU without an agreement: 'the very hardest of Brexits'. He demanded that representatives of the EP be present at negotiations alongside the European Commission, and that EP sherpas be present in meetings of national sherpas.

Subsequent press reports suggested that assurances about the EP's involvement had been given by the Commission President to Martin Schulz's successor as EP President, Antonio Tajani.[5] In evidence to the House of

---

[5] D Boffey, 'EU Parliament will be "very difficult" in Brexit talks, says leading MEP', *The Guardian* (25 January 2017).

Lords European Union Committee, one British MEP Richard Corbett suggested that the EP's representative Guy Verhofstadt would be invited by the Commission negotiator Michel Barnier to join meeting but not to participate directly unless invited to. Mr Verhofstadt would report back to the EP through the Conference of Presidents and the Conference of Committee Chairs. However, the MEP noted that as the Conference of Presidents included representatives from Eurosceptic parties like the United Kingdom Independence Party (UKIP), it was unlikely that much would be divulged at these meetings with more informal briefings by Mr Verhofstadt likely to feature.[6] The EP's stance on the negotiations would be defined in a resolution scheduled to be debated a week after the triggering of Article 50.

If this is the institutional context for the Article 50 negotiations, then what remains to be analysed is how negotiations might proceed. Article 50 is relatively unclear on what is or is not within its scope as a legal basis for a withdrawal agreement. Indeed, there are likely to be multiple elements related to the withdrawal process including:

- the agreement settling the terms of the withdrawal
- a framework for the future co-operation between the withdrawing state and the EU
- one or more substantive agreements including the free trade deal which the UK wishes to secure and any transitional agreement or additional side agreements for foreign and security policy co-operation.

[6] House of Lords European Union Committee, 'Oral evidence', www.parliament.uk (18 January 2017).

An agreement to revise the treaties to remove references to the UK and to decide on new voting rules and allocation of MEPs will also be required, although that will likely be part of the wider reflection on the future of the EU after Brexit.

Although the withdrawal agreement can be agreed by a 'qualified majority' vote of the Member States it would go against the principle of the unity of the EU27 to end up with an agreement that didn't command a consensus. As for the other agreements, different procedural rules apply. In general, the more comprehensive any EU–UK agreement the more likely it will be to require unanimous consent of the governments of the EU27 and also domestic approval by each state in accordance with domestic constitutional requirements. What is remarkable is how little legal clarity had been achieved in the period following the referendum on exactly how these different negotiations would be sequenced. For the UK, the ambition was always to conduct parallel negotiations on the formal terms of withdrawal and an ambitious free trade agreement. However, on the EU side the language was different tending to see the withdrawal agreement and trade negotiations as sequential. For the UK, it would not make sense simply to decide on the terms of exit without knowing what the future would look like. For the EU, it would not wish to open talks on the future without resolving the terms of exit.

All of which means that one of the first issues for resolution is the extent of any outstanding UK liabilities to be paid to the EU. The history of UK relations with the EU – from Wilson's pre-referendum renegotiation to Thatcher's rebate negotiations – suggests that getting an agreement on the finances is crucial to allowing other aspects of these or future negotiations to take place. In the context of Brexit, initial estimates of between €20 billion and 40 billion escalated to a figure closer to €60 billion.

Yet for four reasons the financial aspects of the Brexit negotiations could provide difficult. First, it is hard to get a clear figure on what percentage share of any outstanding liabilities would be the correct proportion. Secondly, quantifying what those liabilities might be – and what they might or might not include – is equally open to interpretation. Thirdly, the same can be said for determining what share of assets might be attributed to the UK. Finally, there is a more specific issue of whether there is a legal obligation on the UK to meet whatever liabilities may have accrued when the UK withdraws and the treaties cease to apply, and if so, how that might be enforced.

Within the scope of the Multiannual Financial Framework, spending is agreed for the period 2014–20. While the UK's withdrawal would take place before the expiry of this period, nonetheless, the funds would already have been committed to projects and the UK would be liable to make its contribution to these spending promises. More controversially – and a product of the EU's particular style of accounting – there is a distinction to be drawn between what the EU commits to by way of activities to be funded and what is actually paid for in any given year. In principle the Member States are obliged to fulfil these commitments and year on year the difference between commitments and payments (the *reste à liquider*, or what remains to be paid) is rolled together to produce an estimated €240 billion bill of which the UK would also have its share.[7] Added to these sums are the pensions liabilities for UK officials and MEPs. On the other side of the balance sheet, however, the UK would also have a share of the assets of the EU which one organisation estimated at around €153 billion.[8]

On 4 March 2017, the House of Lords European Union Committee published a report suggesting that the UK might leave the EU without any enforceable legal obligation to pay any debts owed to the EU.[9] While recognising that the political imperatives to negotiate a withdrawal agreement would likely mean some form of negotiated outcome, nonetheless, it believed that were the UK to leave the EU without an agreement, and with the EU treaties and the regulations made under them ceasing to apply to the UK, there would not be a legal basis upon which to enforce payment of any debts.

There are two distinct issue at play. Clearly, with the UK outside of the institutional structures of the EU including the EU courts, enforcement of legal obligations will be difficult. But as to whether those legal obligations exist or not, Article 50 TEU provides no guidance as to what should happen. The idea that those obligations would simply be extinguished appears to run counter to Article 70 of the

[7] For a more detailed account see A Barker, 'The €60 billion Brexit bill: how to disentangle Britain from the EU budget', *Centre for European Reform*, www.cer.org.uk (February 2017).

[8] Z Darvas, K Efstathiou and I Goncalves Raposo, 'The UK's Brexit bill: could EU assets partially offset liabilities?', *Bruegel*, www.bruegel.org (14 February 2017).

[9] House of Lords European Union Committee, 'Brexit and the EU budget', 15th Report (Session 2016–17) HL 125 (4 March 2017).

Vienna Convention on the Law of Treaties which states that unless a treaty provides otherwise, termination of a treaty 'does not affect any right, obligation or legal situation of the parties created through the execution of the treaty prior to its termination'. The fact that, in terms of Article 50, the treaties and regulations made under them relating to the budget will cease to apply to the UK when it withdraws ought not to mean that any obligations created prior to withdrawal cease to exist, any more than an obligation executed under a treaty governed directly by the Vienna Convention would cease to exist if that treaty was terminated. To conclude otherwise would be to render Article 70 devoid of any meaning when applied to obligations incurred prior to the termination of a treaty. By stating that the UK government intends to abide by its international law obligations, the Brexit Secretary, David Davis appeared to accept that there would be potential liabilities without committing to any particular figure as to their likely extent.

The point remains that failure to reach an agreement on the financial issues will make it very difficult for any other issues to be resolved and while the UK might leave the EU without an agreement and unburdened by liabilities, it would also not have any prospect of concluding a future trade deal with the EU.

The other major issue set to feature early in the negotiations would be the situation of EU citizens in the UK and UK citizens in the EU. While the UK government insisted that it was highly likely that a deal could be done swiftly to ensure the protection of the rights of 3 million EU citizens in the UK, it repeatedly made clear that this would only be if equivalent protection was afforded to UK citizens resident in the EU. This led to accusations that citizens were being treated as 'bargaining chips'.

It would be entirely possible for the UK to adopt a unilateral position in which the rights of EU citizens already legally resident in the UK would be protected (although the practicalities of form-filling and establishing legal residence in the UK could create obstacles to the exercise of such an entitlement).[10] Indeed, the protection of rights of those already legally resident was the intention behind amendments proposed to the government's Article 50 bill. After all, the potential loss of rights for individuals lay at the heart of the Article 50 litigation which had resulted in the need for legislation to authorise the triggering of the withdrawal negotiations. On the EU27 side, at a legislative level, Member States (excluding Denmark and Ireland) agreed in 2003 a directive which extended many – but not all – of the benefits of EU citizenship upon third-country nationals who are long-term (more than five years) residents of a Member State.[11] This would apply to many UK nationals who have settled in another EU state. It would also be conceivable to make a legislative amendment to the 2004 'Citizenship Directive'[12]

---

[10] See the proposals made by British Future, 'Report of the inquiry into securing the status of EEA+ nationals in the UK', www.britishfuture.org (December 2016).

[11] Council Directive 2003/109/EC of 25 November 2003 concerning the status of Third Country nationals who are long term residents: [2004] OJ L16/44.

[12] Council Directive 2004/38/EC of the European Parliament and of the Council of 29 April 2004 on the right of citizens of the Union and their

to maintain in the EU27 the rights of those who have already exercised a right of free movement under the directive.

Yet it was sometimes suggested that EU citizens might already have vested or acquired rights which would persist whether or not the UK and EU reached a withdrawal agreement. However, it was a point made more as an assertion than one with strong legal backing. While EU law has a strong ideological commitment to the idea that EU law vests rights in individuals, this has always been in the context of sharing the benefits of EU membership between individuals and states as co-subjects of EU law. It is not one that necessarily applies outside of EU membership. Claims that rights might be acquired as a matter of international law have been doubted,[13] and would, in any event, give rise to significant issues of justiciability and enforcement, particularly in the UK where parliamentary sovereignty typically needs to be exercised to transform international obligations into domestic rights.

Therefore, a resolution of the rights of citizens in the withdrawal agreement itself would seem an appropriate agenda item for early rounds of negotiations. On one view, the imperative is to reach an early agreement on something that is simply workable in order to remove uncertainty.

family members to move and reside freely within the territory of the Member States: [2004] OJ L158/77.

[13] S Douglas-Scott, 'What happens to 'acquired rights' in the event of a Brexit?', UK Constitutional Law Blog, www.ukconstitutionallaw.org (16 May 2016). See also the evidence presented to the House of Lords European Union Committee and its report, 'Brexit: acquired rights', HL82 (14 December 2016).

For others, there may be a more political edge to it, especially those advocating the creation of a form of 'associate citizenship' which might include a capacity to exercise certain rights under EU law in return for a financial charge.[14] The idea has been backed by Guy Verhofstadt but raises not just political issues but also legal ones. Eventual treaty change would likely be necessary to create such a new constitutional category of legal subjects. However, it would be tantamount to accepting the idea that a state could withdraw from the EU but somehow leave its citizens behind in a form of individual membership. Such a bold outcome would seem an unlikely result of the Brexit negotiations, although its adherents suggested it might be on offer even after Brexit.[15]

But even assuming that the UK and the EU27 can come to a resolution both on the financial issues and the rights of citizens, there will be two points of friction. First, the UK will want to play its cards close to its chest while the EU's negotiator has committed to conducting an open and transparent negotiation. Even for those aspects which the EU might seek to keep confidential, the EU's institutions are notoriously leaky. Second, the UK clearly wants to negotiate as much as possible as quickly as possible. But it will take months for the outline of negotiations to be agreed followed by the interruption of French and German elections and

[14] T Barber, 'Brexit briefing: the case for associate EU citizenship', *Financial Times* (28 November 2016).

[15] T Batchelor, 'Britons must be offered "associate EU citizenship" whatever the outcome of May's Brexit negotiations, says MEP', *The Independent* (4 February 2017).

an August European slowdown. All of which will leave little more than twelve months to make substantive progress on withdrawal negotiations before attention will turn to getting any deal through the EP and the UK Parliament. The clock is ticking down. Time is short.

Time for the Future

Choices have consequences. They have consequences for those making the choices. They also have effects on others. In this final chapter, it is appropriate to reflect on what Brexit means for the two states that obtained EEC membership in 1973 alongside the UK, and for the EU itself, not least as the EU engages in a process of reflection on the 'Future of Europe'.

The UK didn't join the EEC on its own in 1973. Denmark and Ireland also chose to join with it.[1] Denmark and Ireland became Member States because the UK had chosen to join the EEC. The balance of interests – political and economic – made Danish and Irish EEC membership together with the UK a logical step. The UK's departure from the EU has consequences for both countries but it is unlikely to lead to either country choosing to leave the EU.

Like the UK, Denmark has, over the years, secured a more differentiated membership in terms of its choices whether to participate in areas of EU co-operation. Following the original rejection of the Maastricht Treaty in a referendum in 1992, Denmark secured three 'opt-outs' concerning monetary union, defence co-operation, justice and

---

[1] P Hansen, 'Denmark and European integration' (1969) 4(1) *Cooperation and Conflict* 13; B Laffan, 'Ireland and the European Union' in WJ Crotty and DE Schmidt (eds), *Ireland on the World Stage* (Longmans, 2002).

home affairs and a clarification that EU citizenship did not replace national citizenship. In a referendum in 2015, Danish voters rejected ending Denmark's justice and home affairs opt-out. These policy-specific referendums have made a 'Dexit' less likely even after Brexit. Voter preferences may be for maintaining control over specific policy domains, rather than for Denmark to quit the EU altogether.[2] Brexit might have been avoided had the UK followed the Danish approach.

The UK's departure from the EU means Denmark has lost one its strongest allies within the EU, and outside the Eurozone. The UK has also been one of Denmark's most important trading partners with the vast majority of exports of pork going to the UK. At the same time, Denmark's trade exposure to the UK is not what it was in the 1970s. The integration of the Single Market now ties Denmark closely to those states remaining in the EU and in the Single Market.

The trade consequences of Brexit for Ireland are also significant, with 17 per cent of Irish exports of goods and services going to the UK. But, like Denmark, Ireland's dependence on the UK for trade has changed since the 1970s when 50 per cent of Irish exports went to the UK. Nonetheless, the economic shock of Brexit will be significant for Ireland and depending on what form Brexit takes – from a trade agreement to no agreement and the application of World Trade Organization (WTO) rules – it is predicted that output in Ireland will fall by between 2.3 and

---

[2] M Eilstrup-Sangiovanni, 'Brexit: the view from Denmark', www.e-ir.info (7 February 2017).

3.8 per cent.[3] Different sectors of the Irish economy will be exposed to the effects of Brexit in different ways, and the potential obstacles to trade will be different across sectors: from the risk of tariffs on agriculture, food and beverages to the non-tariff regulatory barriers in the pharma, chemicals and financial services markets.[4]

The implications of Brexit for Ireland go beyond trade, so much so that Irish politicians were among the few foreign politicians to have been vocal during the 2016 referendum campaign about what the UK's departure from the EU would mean for UK–Irish relations. It was noted that regular meetings of UK and Irish ministers and Prime Ministers in Council and European Council meetings had helped forge the bonds of trust that made the Belfast 'Good Friday' Peace agreement possible and operational. Indeed, the preamble to the agreement is framed as follows:

> Wishing to develop still further the unique relationship between their peoples and the close co-operation between their countries as friendly neighbours and as partners in the European Union

Brexit is a politically destabilising force at a time when the power-sharing arrangements in Northern Ireland are fragile. It is not difficult to see how Brexit can be used as a pretext for suggesting that people in Northern Ireland might have

[3] A Bergin et al, 'Modelling the medium to long term potential macroeconomic impact of Brexit on Ireland', Economics and Social Research Institute, Working Paper No 548 (November 2016).
[4] Department of Finance, 'UK EU exit: an exposure analysis of sectors of the Irish economy', www.budget.gov.ie (October 2016).

a further choice to make between remaining in the UK and outside the EU or remaining in the EU through a united Ireland. As another indication of how important negotiations over Northern Ireland might be, the Irish Taioseach, Enda Kenny, was reported to have had discussions with the European Commission President about the insertion of language into a UK withdrawal agreement that would extend the scope of EU membership to the territory of Northern Ireland in the event of a unification of Ireland.[5] This would parallel the unification of East and West Germany within EU membership without the need for an Article 49 TEU accession process.

When it came to the big decision about the euro, Ireland chose a different path from the UK and Denmark. The UK's decision not to participate in monetary union was not an impediment to Ireland choosing to do so. It was a defining choice for both countries. It now binds Ireland's future more closely to that of the EU and the Eurozone. So much so that the Irish Foreign Minister, Charlie Flanagan, described 'populist' calls for Ireland to follow the UK out of the EU as 'simply madness'.[6]

It is clear, then, that the UK is making its own choice. Indeed, Brexit could be dismissed as the culmination of an 'awkward' membership: the ultimate exceptionalism once all the other opt-outs, derogations and renegotiations had failed to deliver. With no more tools in the bag by which to leverage

[5] A Beesley, 'Enda Kenny calls for united Ireland clause in Brexit deal', *Financial Times* (23 February 2017).
[6] C Flanagan, 'Populist talk about Ireland following Britain out of EU is simply madness', independent.ie (27 March 2017).

further flexibility for the UK within the EU, the only choice was for it to leave. But it would be a mistake to pretend that Brexit doesn't expose difficult questions and choices for the European Union and its future. Or perhaps another way of putting it is that as the EU seeks to define its future, its choices will be shaped, in part, by Brexit.

Following the UK referendum, work started on defining the future of the EU with a meeting of the EU27 leaders in Bratislava in September 2016. The meeting produced a declaration and a 'roadmap' for future discussions.[7] It diagnosed a 'perceived lack of control and fears related to migration and terrorism, and economic and social insecurity'. But in terms of where control – and responsibility – ought to lie, the Bratislava roadmap simply stated the 'need to be clear about what the EU can do, and what is for the Member States to do'. This issue of allocating responsibility was a prominent theme in European Commission President Jean-Claude Juncker's 'State of the Union' speech delivered days before the Bratislava meeting.[8]

The Bratislava 'roadmap' set out more specific objectives for joint action between the EU and its Member States with clear emphases on issues of migration and security (internal, external and economic):

- no uncontrolled flows of migrants, and a reduction in number of irregular migrants

---

[7] Summit of EU 27, 'Bratislava Declaration', www.consilium.europa.eu (16 September 2016).

[8] J-C Juncker, 'State of the Union speech', www.ec.europa.eu (14 September 2016).

- control over external borders, and reinstatement of Schengen
- development of consensus on long-term migration policy
- support of Member States in ensuring security and fighting terrorism
- strengthening EU co-operation on external security and defence
- securing the European economic future and way of life with better opportunities for youth.

In a letter written on 31 January 2017 by the European Council President to the leaders of EU Member States in advance of a meeting in Malta to discuss the future of the EU, Donald Tusk identified different threats to the EU.[9] These included threats emanating from the external geopolitics of the EU: an 'assertive' China, an 'aggressive' Russia, an 'unpredictable' new American administration led by President Trump and an 'anarchic' Middle East unleashing threats from 'radical Islam'. For Tusk while these are external threats, they also create opportunities for the EU to exert itself as a global actor and as an 'equal partner' to other world powers. Indeed, for Tusk, the alternative to EU membership for European states is not sovereignty but dependence upon these external powers. This is consistent with a view which sees the EU's future legitimacy as bound up with its capacities for global economic and political influence.[10]

---

[9] D Tusk, 'United we stand, divided we fall', letter by European Council President to EU27 leaders, www.consilium.europa.eu (31 January 2017).

[10] G de Búrca, 'Europe's *raison d'être*' in D Kochenov and F Amtenbrink (eds), *The European Union's Shaping of the International Legal Order* (Cambridge University Press, 2013).

Whatever the EU may acquire by legitimacy through its external action, the challenge of producing effective and democratic accountable policymaking within the EU remains acute. As Tusk himself acknowledged, the other types of threat to the EU are internal to it. On the one hand, nationalism and populism are directed towards the nation state as the primary location for political expression, while on the other hand, EU leaders and EU institutions appear to struggle to generate an alternative momentum capable of making the EU relevant to the lives of its citizens. The external and internal threats are also clearly connected. The threat of terrorism is both a force that encourages co-operation between EU states, but can equally be co-opted by national politicians to invigorate nationalist discourses about borders, internal security and the protection of the national 'self' from the threat of the external 'other'.

In advance of a gathering of European leaders in Rome to mark the sixtieth anniversary of the Treaty of Rome establishing the EEC, on 1 March 2017, European Commission President Jean Claude-Juncker published the European Commission's White Paper on the *Future of Europe*.[11] Its aim is to encourage a process of reflection on what the EU has achieved, what challenges it faces and what scenarios might shape the evolution of the EU in the period up until 2025. The anniversary, according to the White Paper is an opportunity for a 'united Europe' to 'renew our vows'.

---

[11] European Commission, 'White paper on the future of Europe', COM (2017) 2025.

The White Paper makes one, brief, mention of the fact that a Member State has chosen to leave the EU. This is not, then, a direct response to Brexit. Indeed, it is a White Paper that would not have looked much different had the UK chosen to remain in the EU. Its weakness is its timelessness.

Nonetheless, its repeated references to the values of the Union, to unity and to what binds EU states together is a recognition that for the EU this is a 'critical juncture' that demands a response from the EU and its Member States.[12] The UK's de-membership cannot be a pretext for dismembering the EU itself. Rather, the 'renewal of vows' is a plea to the other EU states to remain faithful just as the EU begins its negotiations on the UK's divorce.

The risks and challenges to the EU27 identified in the White Paper are those which were already present on the EU's agenda, and which were identified in the Bratislava declaration. The risks to the EU's economy are clear and are not just about continuing to manage systemic financial and debt risks in an integrated and interdependent European economy. They are those from a changing world of work and increased automation. There is also the risk of a return to more protectionism and less trade. Meanwhile, the EU's share of global GDP is diminishing as new economic powers like China continue to grow. The demographic challenge – identified more than two decades ago – of an ageing population and its pressures on social protection and healthcare systems is also growing. There are also security challenges from political instability and terrorism. Global security problems fuel

---

[12] Juncker, 'State of the Union speech'.

a migration and refugees crisis that strain the capacity of the EU to co-ordinate responses and distribute responsibilities equitably.

There is some recognition that the EU faces a trust and legitimacy problem. In part, the White Paper presents this as a phenomenon which the EU shares with national authorities. In part, it views the problem as stemming from the 'two-level' game of politics in which political blame is shifted upwards, while political credit is claimed downwards. The difficulty lies in what to do about these problems and what Brexit might tell us about how to approach the task.

At one level, the White Paper is imbued with the themes of the EU's traditional 'mission legitimacy' – the post-war reconstruction of Europe and the maintenance of peace. Wistfully, it acknowledges that time has weakened the force of these achievements as a legitimating resource for the EU, particularly for the generations of European voters born after 1945. Yet, as the post-referendum debate about whether a generation of 'baby boomers' was responsible for quashing the aspirations of a 'millennial' generation of younger voters exposes, views and attitudes towards the EU correlate with a range of factors and not merely age.

Looking more to the future, the White Paper echoes Tusk's vision of the EU as a global leader in combating climate change and promoting 'free and progressive' global trade. But as the UK's EU referendum and the US presidential campaigns dramatised, internationalism, globalisation and the liberalisation of trade is in tension with more nationalistic instincts to protect ways of life and preserve jobs. It is not enough to aspire, as the White Paper does, for international trade that 'benefits all' if by that we simply mean that aggregate welfare is increased. What also matters is how winners and losers are distributed and what efforts are made to protect and compensate those most at risk of losing out.

This matters all the more given that markets are cross-border and global, while democratic decision-making and institutions of social protection are national and local.[13] There is no point in political and economic European elites pursuing their preferences for liberalised trade if it generates negative effects which are felt locally and which are merely left to local political processes and social institutions and services to manage. And so, the added value of the EU has to be seen in terms of a capacity to buffer and manage the process of trade liberalisation and to manage economic interdependence in a way that would be preferable to doing so as twenty-seven individual states. This is the challenge for the EU and it is the challenge to the UK as it seeks to present 'Global Britain' as a champion of trade that 'can work for everyone'. Brexit is a test case for whether going it alone is sovereignty-enhancing or sovereignty-diminishing.

The White Paper stakes out five key scenarios around which it is suggested that the future of the EU will be built:

- carrying on along the same path of integration with incremental change
- focusing solely on the Single Market
- a coalition of the winning in which those who want more co-operation are free to do so while others do not

[13] D Kennedy, 'Law and the political economy of the world' (2013) 26(1) *Leiden Journal of International Law* 7.

- using scarce resources of time and commitment to prioritise areas in need of more effective decision-making while doing less elsewhere
- a step-change to increase collective co-operation and decision-making through the EU.

As intimated earlier, there is a timeless quality to this typology of EU futures. Unsurprisingly, the EU will change in ways that reflect one or more of these scenarios.

The aim of all this reflection is to allow the European Council meeting in December 2017 to set a course for the EU in time to influence the European Parliament elections in June 2019. At the same time as the UK is negotiating its withdrawal, the EU is defining what sort of EU the UK will be withdrawing from.

It is instructive to consider whether it would have made any difference to the outcome of the UK's referendum on membership if David Cameron had not chosen to go for a quick renegotiation and an early referendum but instead had waited till after the UK had held its presidency in the latter half of 2017 when it might also have shaped the direction of the White Paper reflection and steered the orientation of the European Council? Would time and timing have mattered?

The conclusion might be that these kinds of EU reflections simply suffer from a basic problem, namely that they focus on the policy areas where the EU has competence to act, with the debate oriented to whether it should be doing less or more. The issues which tend to be central to voter concerns are those that primarily remain within the powers of the Member States in respect of taxation and public spending on things like education, health, welfare, transport and other public services. The apparent gap between the EU and citizens, therefore, has two manifestations. First, the policy choices exercised through European co-operation either seem remote from the day-to-day immediate concerns of citizens or don't obviously appear to generate benefits on the ground that citizens experience and value. Secondly, there is the anxiety that EU membership undermines the capacities of national governments to do the things that voters do care about.

The 2016 referendum campaign brought these issues to the fore and as previous chapters describe, while they were dramatised in the context of the referendum, they are not unique to the United Kingdom. Tackling these issues requires political leadership. At EU level, that leadership needs to come from the European Council with the European Commission fulfilling a legal mandate under the treaties and a political mandate that comes from the European Council. It is the Prime Minister and Presidents that are the connection between the domestic political arena and that of the EU. Only they have the legitimacy to take control over the future of the EU. It is these leaders and their governments who are also accountable to their national parliaments. It is not just the choices made by EU leaders that will shape the future of the EU. It is also the choice of those leaders. Elections in the Member States take place at a crucial time for the EU and for the Brexit negotiations. More choices in time and of time.

Twenty-seven EU leaders met in Rome on 25 March 2017 not just to commemorate sixty years of the instrument that founded the EEC, but also to proclaim the Rome Declaration and its message of 'unity'. The leaders agreed that:[14]

> Unity is both a necessity and our free choice. Taken individually, we would be side-lined by global dynamics. Standing together is our best chance to influence them, and to defend our common interests and values. We will act together, at different paces and intensity where necessary, while moving in the same direction, as we have done in the past, in line with the Treaties and keeping the door open to those who want to join later. Our Union is undivided and indivisible.

The message is a clear one: membership of the EU is the means by which nation states preserve and protect their interests and values, whereas standing alone puts those interests and values at risk. To underscore the point, in his speech in Rome, European Council President Tusk stated that:

> Only a united Europe can be a sovereign Europe in relation to the rest of the world. And only a sovereign Europe guarantees independence for its nations, guarantees freedom for its citizens.

In other words, whereas a new nationalism and a new internationalism inspires the UK to seek to exercise sovereignty outside of EU membership, for the EU27 it is through EU

---

[14] Declaration of the leaders of twenty-seven member states and of the European Council, the European Parliament and the European Commission (the 'Rome Declaration'), www.consilium.europa.eu (25 March 2017).

membership that sovereignty is maintained and exercised both as between Member States and externally in the EU's relationship to other global actors.

For the EU, as much as for the UK, this is a time of change, a time for change, and a time to change.

Epilogue

On 18 April 2017, the UK Prime Minister Theresa May announced that her government would seek an early general election to be held on 8 June 2017. Despite earlier statements that she would not call a snap election, and despite the Fixed-term Parliaments Act 2011 legislating for a general election on 7 May 2020, the Prime Minister identified divisions over Brexit among the Westminster political parties as her pretext for asking Parliament to permit an early election.

After all, she had become Prime Minister only by virtue of the Conservative Party's leadership contest, following David Cameron's resignation in the wake of his referendum defeat. Her Brexit negotiating objective – to take the UK out not just of the EU but the Single Market as well – also flew in the face of the 2015 Conservative Party manifesto on which a Conservative Government under David Cameron had been elected. With the electoral maths in her favour, Theresa May concluded that this was the time to seek from the electorate a substantive Brexit mandate for her government, as well as a personal mandate for her leadership.

Brexit and time are at the heart of this decision. With substantive withdrawal negotiations unlikely to have made much progress by the time of a June election, the Prime Minister is using the time and the election campaign to build as much political capital as she can before those negotiations get into full swing. Moreover, with the endgame of those negotiations now occurring in the middle of an electoral cycle rather than towards the end as would have been the case with a 2020 election, the Prime Minister is hoping to de-risk the conclusion of those negotiations, not least if she increases the number of Conservative MPs who will vote on the final deal.

If the Prime Minister's political gamble succeeds, we might look back on the eleven months from July 2016 to June 2017 as a time of a transitional Brexit government. It's plausible that some of the prominent Leavers who came into that government might find their positions of power not merely transitional but temporary. But it is a political gamble that also risks the union of the nations of the UK, with Scottish nationalists using the election to seek a mandate for post-Brexit independence.

For those opposed to Brexit, a general election was always going to be the only way to try and either halt Brexit or change its course. But with the decision to hold an early election being taken to secure a Conservative victory in June 2017, the election may well cement and complete a process that began when the Conservatives won a surprise victory in 2015 and legislated for a referendum on the UK's membership of the EU.

Brexit will continue to be shaped in time and through time.

Craig, Paul 44, 243, 250
Cremona, M 131
Cummings, D 2
Curtin, D 111–12
customs unions 127, 144

Dashwood, Alan 198
date for Brexit referendum, setting
    of 58–60
Davis, David 229–30
Delors, Jacques 109
democracy
    EU lack of 98–9, 106–8, 111–12
        European Commission 99–101,
            103, 109–11
    and referendums 45, 46–7
Denmark
    EU membership of 270
        after Brexit 270–1
        after Greenland opt-out 167
        and Faroe Islands 168–9
        and primacy of EU law 116
devolution/devolved parliaments
    and Brexit 186–7, 225–6, 233,
        237–8, 239
    see also Northern Ireland;
        Scotland; Wales
DExEU (Department for Exiting
    the EU) 229–31
direct democracy, attractiveness
    of 45
directives of EU
    incorporation in UK law
        114–15, 184
    see also Working Time Directive
DIT (Department for International
    Trade), creation of 229–30

domestic courts
    EU rights enforcement through
        213–14
    and UK Brexit litigation 4,
        214–28
domestic law, and EU law 115–17,
    220–5
domestic politics
    and EU membership 18–19,
        106–8
    and European integration
        referendums 36
Downes, C 155
Duffy, Gillian 83–4
Duncan-Smith, Iain 56, 78–9

EAGF (European Agricultural
    Guarantee Fund), UK
    receipt of funds from 90
economic governance, 'new
    settlement' deal with EU
    on 31–2
EEA (European Economic Area
    agreement, EU–EFTA)
    access to EU Single Market via
        for Norway 14
    as UK Brexit strategy 143–7,
        175
    and EU law development 188–9
    Scotland's wish to remain party
        to 168–9
    UK withdrawal from 211–12
EEC (European Economic
    Community) see EU
    (European Union)/EEC
    (European Economic
    Community)